Computer Vision

This comprehensive textbook presents a broad review of both traditional (i.e., conventional) and deep learning aspects of object detection in various adversarial real-world conditions in a clear, insightful, and highly comprehensive style. Beginning with the relation of computer vision and object detection, the text covers the various representation of objects, applications of object detection, and real-world challenges faced by the research community for object detection task. The book addresses various real-world degradations and artifacts for the object detection task and also highlights the impacts of artifacts in the object detection problems. The book covers various imaging modalities and benchmark datasets mostly adopted by the research community for solving various aspects of object detection tasks. The book also collects together solutions and perspectives proposed by the preeminent researchers in the field, addressing not only the background of visibility enhancement but also techniques proposed in the literature for visibility enhancement of scenes and detection of objects in various representative real-world challenges.

Computer Vision: Object Detection in Adversarial Vision is unique for its diverse content, clear presentation, and overall completeness. It provides a clear, practical, and detailed introduction and advancement of object detection in various representative challenging real-world conditions.

Topics and Features:

- Offers the first truly comprehensive presentation of aspects of the object detection in degraded and nondegraded environment.
- Includes in-depth discussion of various degradation and artifacts, and impact of those artifacts in the real world on solving the object detection problems.
- Gives detailed visual examples of applications of object detection in the real world.
- Presents a detailed description of popular imaging modalities for object detection adopted by researchers.
- Presents the key characteristics of various benchmark datasets in indoor and outdoor environment for solving object detection tasks.
- Surveys the complete field of visibility enhancement of degraded scenes, including conventional methods designed for enhancing the degraded scenes as well as the deep architectures.
- Discusses techniques for detection of objects in real-world applications.
- Contains various hands-on practical examples and a tutorial for solving object detection problems using Python.
- Motivates readers to build vision-based systems for solving object detection problems in degraded and nondegraded real-world challenges.

The book will be of great interest to a broad audience ranging from researchers and practitioners to graduate and postgraduate students involved in computer vision tasks with respect to object detection in degraded and nondegraded real-world vision problems.

Computer Vision
Object Detection in Adversarial Vision

Mrinal Kanti Bhowmik

CRC Press
Taylor & Francis Group
Boca Raton London New York

CRC Press is an imprint of the
Taylor & Francis Group, an **informa** business

A CHAPMAN & HALL BOOK

Designed cover image: © Mrinal Kanti Bhowmik

First edition published 2024
by CRC Press
2385 NW Executive Center Drive, Suite 320, Boca Raton FL 33431

and by CRC Press
4 Park Square, Milton Park, Abingdon, Oxon, OX14 4RN

CRC Press is an imprint of Taylor & Francis Group, LLC

© 2024 Mrinal Kanti Bhowmik

Library of Congress Cataloging-in-Publication Data
Names: Bhowmik, Mrinal Kanti, author.
Title: Computer vision : object detection in adversarial vision / Mrinal Kanti Bhowmik.
Description: First. | Boca Raton : Taylor and Francis, 2024. | Includes
bibliographical references and index.
Identifiers: LCCN 2023032489 (print) | LCCN 2023032490 (ebook) |
ISBN 9781032551807 (hardback) | ISBN 9781032557496 (paperback) |
ISBN 9781003432036 (ebook)
Subjects: LCSH: Computer vision.
Classification: LCC TA1634 .B4734 2024 (print) |
LCC TA1634 (ebook) | DDC 006.3/7--dc23/eng/20231117
LC record available at https://lccn.loc.gov/2023032489
LC ebook record available at https://lccn.loc.gov/2023032490

ISBN: 978-1-032-55180-7 (hbk)
ISBN: 978-1-032-55749-6 (pbk)
ISBN: 978-1-003-43203-6 (ebk)

DOI: 10.1201/9781003432036

Typeset in Times
by SPi Technologies India Pvt Ltd (Straive)

Dedications

Humble Tribute to my grandfather, the late Sri Nil Krishna Bhowmik (1906–1972), and grandmother, the late Smt. Priyada Sundari Bhowmik, for the memory of spending their initial period of life in the native land of my great-grandfather (the late Sri Arjun Chandra Bhowmik), Dewra, Muradnagar, Tripparah, Comilla in British India;

To my parents, Shri Pijush Kanti Bhowmik and Smt. Kalpana Bhowmik (Shib), who took on the burden of raising our family while also raising me despite the stress and complexity of their own life;

To my wife, Priya, who provided me with numerous sources of inspiration to create and finish this book in its current form;

To my beloved daughter, Sannidhi (Monu);

To my uncle, Sri Pradip Kumar Nath, and my aunt, Prof. (Dr.) Niharika Nath, New Jersey, USA, for their love and extreme support in various issues;

To all of my students across the globe, whose patience allowed me to enhance my teaching techniques; and

To my teachers, who taught me the art of adapting to a changing environment.

Mrinal Kanti Bhowmik
Tripura University
(A Central University)
Agartala, Tripura, India

Contents

Preface

Computer vision is an interesting tool, and its most popular application is surveillance. Computer-based surveillance is important for border security, for security of private and public areas, in crime scene analysis, etc. Real-time surveillance systems should be able to process video frames for detection and recognition of the suspects within a few seconds, and closed-circuit television (CCTV) cameras are mostly used for surveillance. Hence, research is focused on enhancing the video quality of CCTV footage or employing algorithms that can handle the low quality of the CCTV degraded footage. Even though vision-based systems have enjoyed great success in various indoor environments, progress has been slower in outdoor environments. Different factors are responsible for the degradation of the quality of the surveillance video footage, such as sensor noise, lighting conditions, and environmental conditions. The existence of adverse atmospheric/weather conditions is one of the main causes. The types and sizes of the particles present, as well as their concentrations, can determine whether these conditions are static (such as fog, mist, and haze) or dynamic (such as rain and snow). Because of this, images taken in various atmospheric/weather situations lack contrast and color integrity. Hence, vision in degraded videos needs serious attention. This book attempts to fill this gap and to provide a theoretical and mathematical framework for investigation of degraded image/video technologies.

One of the fascinating subfields is object detection problems, such as pedestrian detection and vehicle detection, has begun to show noteworthy improvement in recent years, encouraged by increased demand for surveillance and security monitoring. This book will focus on detailing object detection in various representative challenges of the real world in an indoor/outdoor environment and different lighting levels. It will provide knowledge to the readers related to the fundamentals of object detection, and various applications and challenges of object detection in indoor and outdoor environments. The presence of an object can be detected with proximity sensors. The details of sensors/imaging modalities adopted by various research communities for detection of objects and their key characteristics, advantages, and disadvantages will be described. Also, the book will detail the background of artifacts and impact of different artifacts on object visualization. It will also detail the background of image degradation, its categorization and mechanism, and provide theoretical analysis of the effect of image degradation in outdoor/indoor scenes. Over the years, many vision-based visibility enhancement techniques/algorithms have been proposed in the existing literature that are capable of reducing the negative effects of atmospheric scattering. The most representative strategies of visibility enhancement techniques can be distinguished from each other based on the input information, such as multiple-image approaches and single-image approaches. Based on the study of the relevant works published in the past, the book will detail the methodological review and comparison of various representative methods contributed in each of these strategies. With the advancement of algorithms/methods for object detection, a detailed methodological survey on the existing works, challenges handled by the existing works, benefits of the existing works, and future scopes will be provided. Also, the description of the key characteristics of various public and private benchmark datasets mostly adopted by the research community for object detection will be detailed. Various hands-on practicals for solving the object detection problem in degraded vision using conventional and deep learning approaches based on various implemental platforms will also be covered.

This book begins with the descriptions of fundamentals of object detection in surveillance scenarios, and then proceeds to derive the properties of degradation of the outdoor scenes in the security zones. While presenting the properties of image degradation, mathematical models and algorithms on the degraded video data for a monitoring system are discussed. The book also investigates and analyzes the performance evaluations of object detection systems.

This volume essentially consists of three parts. The first part includes Chapters 1 through 3: fundamentals of object detection, degradation, sensor type. The second part consists of Chapter 4 through 6: real-time benchmark datasets for object detection, background of artifacts and its impact on different object visualization, and visibility enhancement of degraded scenes. The third part has Chapter 7 through Chapter 8: tasks of object detection under various conditions and various hands-on practical problems on object detection in vision-based techniques.

The book discusses three major imaging sensors: visual, CCTV, and infrared. For these three imaging sensors, the study focuses on their basic imaging acquisition protocols under several degraded conditions. A visual digital camera and a standard charge-coupled device (CCD) camera both have the benefit of high resolution, making them more appropriate for usage during the day or at night with the adequate lighting arrangement. Numerous investigations on approaches that identify things with near/far-infrared (NIR/FIR)-based cameras have been undertaken in order to alleviate the shortcomings of vision and CCD cameras at night. NIR cameras are resistant to darkness, but they share a disadvantage with CCD cameras when interference from headlights of moving vehicles occurs. In contrast, FIR cameras are robust in the degraded conditions due to the higher spectrum wavelength. This book is partially based on the lecture notes with problem solving developed for graduates, postgraduates, seniors, and researchers from the field of computer science and applied mathematics, with a strong interest in degraded image and analysis.

Acknowledgements

This book reflects my experience as a researcher and lecturer over the last twelve years. During this period, I have worked closely with many different individuals on research throughout the years, discussing it with them, struggling with it, learning from it, and generally enjoying it. I can only mention few of them here.

At first, I want to acknowledge my research laboratories of Tripura University (A Central University), namely Biometrics Laboratory, EST: January, 2009 (funded by Department of Electronics and Information Technology [DeitY], now Ministry of Electronics and Information Technology [MeitY], Government of India); Bio-Medical Infrared Image Processing Laboratory, EST: March, 2012 (funded by Department of Biotechnology [DBT], Government of India); and Computer Vision Laboratory, EST: June, 2018 (funded by Defence Research and Development Organisation [DRDO], Government of India).

The numerous people who supported me in many ways to complete the book are warmly acknowledged. Before and during the writing of this book, I've had the opportunity to teach most of the material as a postgraduate course entitled "M.Tech in Computer Science and Engineering" in the Computer Science and Engineering Department, Tripura University (A Central University), Tripura, India. I would like to thank my graduate students for attending the course and contributing insightful input.

Next, I would like to thank the former scholars under my supervision for helping in constructing the contents of this book. In this regard, I acknowledge the contribution of Shawli Bardhan, a recipient of PhD degree in 2019; Usha Rani Gogoi, a recipient of PhD degree in 2020; Kakali Das, a recipient of PhD degree in 2021; Tannistha Pal, a recipient of PhD degree in 2021; Anu Singha, a recipient of PhD degree in 2021; Rajib Debnath, a recipient of PhD degree in 2022; and Dipak Hrishi Das, pursuing PhD since 2021.

I also want to express my gratitude to the students I am supervising while they pursue their doctoral degrees. In this regard, I acknowledge the contributions of Sourav Dey Roy (Chapters 1 and 4), Puja Das (Chapter 2), Joydeep Roy (Chapter 3), Saswata Sarkar (Chapter 5), Anindita Mohanta (Chapter 6), Santanu Das (Chapter 7), and Rupak Sharma (Chapter 8).

Among the scholars, I would like to convey heartfelt appreciation and love to Sourav, who helped me in structuring, assembling, and preparation of the book.

I owe a debt of sincere gratitude to Prof. Debotosh Bhattacharjee and Dr. Dipak Kumar Basu, Humboldt Fellow (1989–90) & Retired Professor of the Department of Computer Science and Engineering, Jadavpur University for providing me with both technical and moral support as the PhD supervisors. I am also indebted to Dr. Mita Nasipuri, Retired Professor of the Department of Computer Science and Engineering, Jadavpur University for providing me with the technical as a teacher. I am also indebted to my postdoctoral work supervisor, Prof. Nasir Memon, NYU Center for Cybersecurity (CCS), Department of Computer Science and Engineering, Tandon

School of Engineering, New York University, New York, USA, for his valuable guidance, support as a mentor, and trust over many years.

I also express my sincerest gratitude to Prof. Dipti Prasad Mukherjee, Deputy Director, Electronics and Communication Sciences Unit, Computer and Communication Sciences Division, Indian Statistical Institute, Kolkata, for inspiring me to write a book and spending long hours in valuable discussion during my visit.

I further would like to thank Prof. Ganga Prasad Prasain, Honorable Vice Chancellor, Prof. Badal Kumar Dutta, Dean of Faculty of Science, and Prof. Ranendu Kumar Nath, Department of Chemistry, Tripura University for helping me in various academic and research undertakings at Tripura University.

I would also like to thank Prof. Arunoday Saha, Former Vice-Chancellor, Prof. Sukanta Banik, Former Dean of Faculty of Science and Prof. Barin Kumar De, Retired Professor, Department of Physics, Tripura University; Abhrajit Das, Senior Manager, TSECL; and Dr. Kiran Shankar Chakraborty, Former Regional Director, IGNOU, Agartala Regional Centre, who helped me in many ways throughout my academic journey.

Special thanks go out to Prof. Subhasis Chaudhuri, Director, Indian Institute of Technology Bombay, India, for visiting Tripura University and inspiring me through his expert lectures on computer vision, which later enabled me to write this book.

I would like to thank my friend Dr. Subhadeep Bhattacharjee, Associate Professor, Department of Electrical Engineering, National Institute of Technology (NIT), Agartala for helping me regarding collection of various natural scenes photographs used in this book.

I would like to thank my collaborators: Dr. Gautam Majumder, Associate Professor, Radiotherapy Department, Atal Bihari Vajpayee Regional Cancer Centre, Agartala Government Medical College (AGMC); Prof. (Dr.) Abhijit Datta, Department of Pathology, Agartala Government Medical College (AGMC) and GBP Hospital; Dr. Satyabrata Nath, Associate Professor, Physical Medicine and Rehabilitation (PMR) Department, Agartala Government Medical College (AGMC) and GBP Hospital; Dr. Ranjan Gupta, Additional Professor, Department of Rheumatology, All India Institute of Medical Sciences (AIIMS), New Delhi, Prof. Asim De, Department of Radio-Diagnosis, Agartala Government Medical College (AGMC) and GBP Hospital; Dr. Anjan Dhua, Additional Professor, Department of Paediatric Surgery, All India Institute of Medical Sciences (AIIMS), New Delhi, for their love and support.

I would like to thank editorial board members and staff members at CRC Press for their kind cooperation in connection with writing this book and editorial guidance on this book. I greatly appreciate the constructive and encouraging comments of the reviewers, which have enriched the contents of this book. Several of the diagrams in this book are adapted from the original publications as referred to in the text.

Last but not least, I would like to express my sincere thanks to my family (maternal relatives, especially the late Sri Jadav Chandra Shib Dadu, the late Sri Haradhan Shiv Dadu, late Sri Haripada Shiv Dadu; Sri Dr. Apurba Siva Mama, Sri Debojoti Siva Mama, and late Sri Tapan Siva Mama; and paternal relatives, especially paternal uncles, the late Sri Rupchand Jethu, late Sri Premchand Jethu, Sri Aghore Jethu,

Sri Bijoy Jethu, and Sri Ranjit Kaku, and paternal aunts, Smt. Suniti Pishi, Smt. Minati Pishi, and Smt. Niyati Pishi), PhD students, and friends who have always supported me and helped me through difficult times. I also wish to thank my wife Priya for her tolerance of my seeming indifference to family life during the writing process and her multifaceted assistance in the successful completion of the book.

Mrinal Kanti Bhowmik
Tripura University
(A Central University)
Agartala, Tripura, India

Targeted Readership

Object detection in different vision-based applications has evolved over the years into a thriving, interdisciplinary field of study. This topic attracts researchers and students from a wide range of disciplines, including computer science and information technology, due to the diversity and richness of object detection. The goal of this book is to provide interesting material for courses in these areas. Students in advanced Bachelor's and Master's programmes are the primary audience for this book. Additionally, we anticipate that this textbook will be helpful to scholars who are interested in learning more about object detection in vision-based activities. The chapters are organized in a modular fashion, thus offering lecturers and readers many ways to choose, rearrange, or supplement the material.

Mrinal Kanti Bhowmik
Tripura University
(A Central University)
Agartala, Tripura, India

About the Author

 **Mrinal Kanti Bhowmik** earned a Bachelor of Engineering (BE) degree in Computer Science and Engineering from the Tripura Engineering College, Government of Tripura, in 2004, a Master of Technology (M.Tech) degree in Computer Science and Engineering from Tripura University (A Central University), India, in 2007, and a PhD in Engineering from Jadavpur University, Kolkata, India, in 2014. He has also spent the Fall 2022 session as a DST-SERB International Research Experience (SIRE) Scholar with SIRE Fellowship, sponsored by the Science and Engineering Research Board (SERB), Government of India at the NYU Center for Cybersecurity (CCS), Tandon School of Engineering, New York University, New York City. He has successfully completed two Department of Electronics and Information Technology (DeitY) (Now Ministry of Electronics and Information Technology [MeitY])-funded projects, one Department of Biotechnology (DBT)-Twinning project, one Society for Applied Microwave Electronics Engineering and Research (SAMEER)-funded project, one Indian Council of Medical Research (ICMR) project, and one Defence Research and Development Organisation (DRDO) project as the Principal Investigator. He is currently the Principal Investigator of one Department of Biotechnology (DBT)-funded project and Co–Principal Investigator of one Indian Council of Medical Research (ICMR) project in collaboration with All India Institute of Medical Sciences (AIIMS), New Delhi.

Since July 2010, he has served with the Department of Computer Science and Engineering, Tripura University as an Assistant Professor and from 26th March, 2023 he has been serving with Department of Computer Science and Engineering, Tripura University as an Associate Professor. He was awarded the Short Term Indian Council of Medical Research (ICMR), Department of Health Research (DHR) International Fellowship from 2019 to 2020 as a Senior Indian Biomedical Scientist for bilateral cooperation in cross-disciplinary research area (i.e., biomedical diagnostic and inferencing systems). His research team has also designed two datasets for object detection in degraded vision named Extended Tripura University Video Dataset (E-TUVD) and Tripura University Video Dataset at Night time (TU-VDN) dataset for the research community in the proposed domain of object detection. His current research interests are in the fields of computer vision, security and surveillance, medical imaging, and image and video forensics.

1 Fundamentals of Object Detection

1.1 DEFINING COMPUTER VISION AND OBJECT DETECTION

Computer vision refers to the field of study and technology that enables computers to receive a high-level understanding of visual information from digital images or videos [1]. It involves developing algorithms and techniques to extract meaningful information from visual data and interpret it similarly to how people see and comprehend the visual world. Consequently, these algorithms analyze and process images to identify and locate objects, recognize patterns or features, and make inferences or decisions based on the visual information. The history of computer vision tasks and its evolution year-wise (from 1959 to 2014) is displayed in Figure 1.1. Among various computer vision tasks, object detection is a specific task within various tasks of computer vision that involves locating and identifying objects of interest within an image or video. The general block diagram of computer vision tasks for object detection is shown in Figure 1.2.

Object detection in the domain of computer vision technique comprises identifying and localizing objects within digital images or videos. The aim is to detect and classify objects of interest within the scene and determine their precise location by drawing bounding boxes (or any other forms of representing objects) around them. Consequently, as seen in Figure 1.3, the detection procedure generally entails the two processes of object location and object classification. In the object localization step, the algorithm determines the spatial extent or bounding box coordinates for each detected object within the image. Consequently, in the object classification step, once the objects are localized, the next step is to classify them into different categories. This involves assigning a label or category to each object, such as car, person, or tree.

In real-world situations, the performance of computer vision–based systems (especially object detection tasks) in indoor environments has been observed to provide promising results. However, in the case of the outdoor environment, the proper functioning of vision-based systems is often disrupted due to various adversarial conditions (as shown in Figure 1.4). Such types of adversarial conditions may be unconstrained environments, noise, strong background information, and other effects (details are mentioned in Chapters 2 and 5). Due to such adversarial effects in outdoor environments (or sometimes even in indoor environments), the scenes captured using different imaging modalities (as described in Chapter 3) often suffer from various degradations (as shown in Figure 1.4). Under such degradation conditions, sometimes referred to as adversarial condition effect (ACE), the captured scenes undergo degradation, and certain objects may not be well detected by traditional vision-based

DOI: 10.1201/9781003432036-1

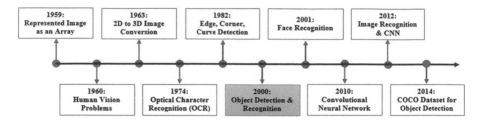

FIGURE 1.1   Milestone for evolution of computer vision task (1959 to 2014).

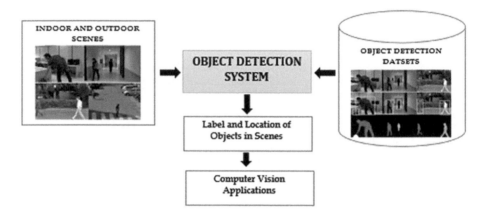

FIGURE 1.2   General block diagram of computer vision task for object detection.

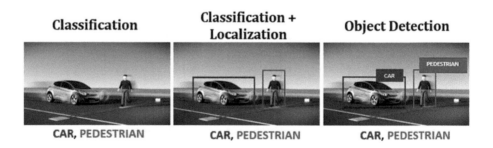

FIGURE 1.3   Object detection in computer vision task.

systems because of the high loss in contrast. Despite the burgeoning research on minimizing the impacts of predefined real-world challenges [2], significant gaps exist in the currently available solutions for detection of objects under adversarial conditions. Therefore, in order to ensure the functional operation of all vision-based devices in any adversarial conditions (as represented in Figure 1.4), a reliable vision-based system is needed to identify the effect pertinent to the scenes for its effective removal.

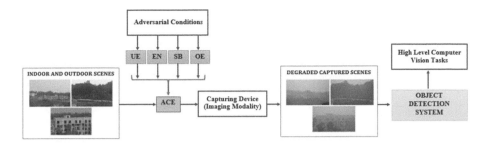

FIGURE 1.4   Jagged diagrammatic representation of object detection in adversarial conditions (UE – Unconstrained Environment; EN – Environment Noise; SB – Strong Background Information; OE – Other Effect; ACE – Adversarial Condition Effect).

1.2   OBJECTS AND APPROACHES OF OBJECT DETECTION

In computer vision, an object refers to a specific entity or item of interest that exists within an image or a video. Consequently, anything that is interesting for more study might be referred to as an object [2]. For instance, a group of items that may be crucial to detect in a particular area or scenario are represented as an object including detecting vehicles, pedestrians, animals in indoor/outdoor surveillance, boats and other aquatic species in sea or river, airplanes or birds in the sky, and detecting guns or other profiles in the surveillance locations. Some of the important scenarios of objects in various scenes are shown in Figure 1.5.

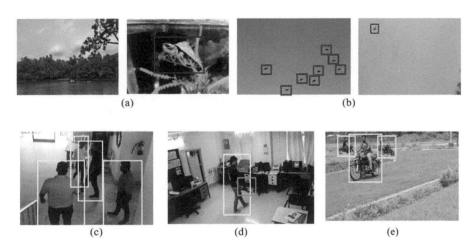

FIGURE 1.5   Scenarios of objects in various scenes: (a) Boat and fishes as objects in sea scenario; (b) Bird and air flights as objects in sky scenario; (c) Pedestrians as objects in indoor scenario; (d) Gun carrying by human as object in indoor scenario; (e) Bikers as objects in outdoor scenario.

In general, static object detection and dynamic object detection are two approaches used in computer vision to recognize and locate objects within an image or a video sequence. Each of these detection approaches are described below:

- **Static Object Detection**: Static object detection refers to the process of detecting and localizing objects in static images, where the objects of interest are relatively stationary and do not change their positions over time. The goal is to identify the presence and location of objects in a given image.
- **Dynamic Object Detection**: Dynamic object detection involves detecting and tracking objects in video sequences, where objects may move and change their positions over time. The goal is not only to identify the objects but also to track their trajectories and understand their motion patterns.

It is important to note that static object detection focuses on images or individual frames of a video and does not consider temporal information or object tracking across multiple frames.

1.3   REPRESENTATION OF OBJECTS

Objects in computer vision tasks are depicted by their shapes and appearances. In this subsection, we will describe various representations of object shape used most frequently for vision-based tasks as displayed in Figure 1.6(a)–(g).

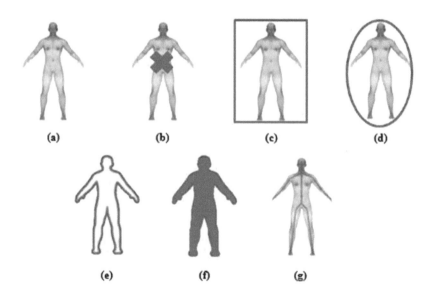

(a)   (b)   (c)   (d)

(e)   (f)   (g)

FIGURE 1.6   Representation of objects in vision based tasks: (a) Object; (b) Point-based representation of object; (c) Rectangular bounding box–based representation of object; (d) Elliptical shape–based representation of object; (e) Contour-based representation of object; (f) Mask-based representation of object; (g) Skeleton-based representation of object.

1.3.1 POINT-BASED REPRESENTATION OF OBJECT

In point-based representation of an object, the centroid of the object or a collection of points are used to represent it as shown in Figure 1.6(b). In general, the point representation works well for monitoring things that only take up a limited amount of space in an image.

1.3.2 RECTANGULAR BOUNDING BOX–BASED REPRESENTATION OF OBJECT

In a bounding box–based representation of an object, a rectangle is used to represent an object's shape as shown in Figure 1.6(c). Although simple rigid things are better represented by primitive geometric shapes, non-rigid objects can also be tracked using these shapes.

1.3.3 ELLIPTICAL SHAPE–BASED REPRESENTATION OF OBJECT

In elliptical shape–based representation of an object, an elliptical shape is used to represent the shape of an object as shown in Figure 1.6(d). This type of representation of an object is also mostly used to represent simple rigid shapes and also sometimes in specific cases used to represent non-rigid objects.

1.3.4 CONTOUR-BASED REPRESENTATION OF OBJECT

In contour-based representation of an object, the boundary of an object is defined by a contour representation as displayed in Figure 1.6(e). This type of representation of objects is mostly suitable for monitoring complicated non-rigid forms of objects.

1.3.5 MASK-BASED REPRESENTATION OF OBJECT

In mask-based representation of an object, region-based masks (i.e., the region inside the contour) are used to represent the shape of an object as shown in Figure 1.6(f). Sometimes these types of representation of objects are also known as a silhouette and are also mostly used for representing complex non-rigid forms of objects.

1.3.6 SKELETON-BASED REPRESENTATION OF OBJECT

In skeleton-based representation of an object, the skeleton of the object obtained from the silhouette of the considered object is used to represent the appearance of the object as displayed in Figure 1.6(g). Applying medial axis transformation [3] to the object silhouette will allow the skeleton to be extracted from the actual objects. Both rigid and non-rigid objects can be modeled using skeleton representation. Additionally, skeleton models of an object, which are specifically employed for recognizing the actions of the considered objects, control the interaction between the parts.

Among these representations of objects, rectangular bounding box–based and mask-based representation of objects are commonly used in object detection algorithms (discussed in Chapter 7 of this book).

1.4   APPLICATIONS OF OBJECT DETECTION

Object detection has a widespread range of applications across various domains. The following are some common applications of object detection.

1.4.1   AUTONOMOUS VEHICLES

Object detection is crucial for autonomous vehicles to perceive and understand the surrounding environment as shown in Figure 1.7. It helps in identifying pedestrians, vehicles, traffic signs, and obstacles on the road, enabling the vehicle to make informed decisions and navigate safely.

1.4.2   SURVEILLANCE AND SECURITY

Object detection plays a significant role in video surveillance and security systems as shown in Figure 1.8. It can detect and track people, suspicious activities, and unauthorized objects in real time, enhancing the overall security measures.

1.4.3   RETAIL AND INVENTORY MANAGEMENT

Object detection is used in retail stores for various purposes, such as tracking products on shelves, analyzing customer behavior, and detecting theft or shoplifting as shown in Figure 1.9. It can also be employed in inventory management systems to automatically count and track stock levels.

FIGURE 1.7   Application of object detection task in autonomous vehicles depicting self-driving cars thereby perceiving the environment while driving.

| (a) | (b) | (c) |

FIGURE 1.8   Application of object detection task in security and surveillance: (a) Detection of objects in degraded conditions; (b) Detection of guns carrying by person for illegal activities; (c) Tracking of objects in outdoor scene.

FIGURE 1.9 Application of object detection task in retail and inventory management.

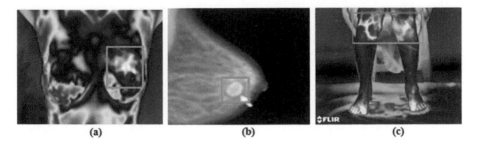

        (a)   (b)   (c)

FIGURE 1.10 Application of object detection task in medical imaging: (a) Breast abnormality detection based on the hot spot regions in the infrared images; (b) Breast cyst detection from mammography images [4]; (c) Inflammation detection in knee region ([a] Our dataset available at http://mkbhowmik.in/dbtTu.aspx; [b] Used by permission; [c] Our dataset available at http://mkbhowmik.in/irD.aspx.).

1.4.4 MEDICAL IMAGING

In medical imaging, object detection algorithms can be used to localize and analyze specific structures or abnormalities in medical scans, such as tumors, organs, or anatomical landmarks as shown in Figure 1.10. It aids in diagnosis, treatment planning, and monitoring of diseases.

1.4.5 INDUSTRIAL AUTOMATION

Object detection is employed in industrial automation scenarios to detect and track objects on assembly lines, inspect products for defects or quality control, and ensure the safety of workers by identifying potential hazards.

1.4.6 AUGMENTED REALITY

Applications for augmented reality employ object detection to find and track real-world objects, enabling interaction between virtual objects and the real world. This technology is used in gaming, visual effects, and virtual try-on applications.

FIGURE 1.11   Robot coordination for apple harvesting [5] Used by permission.

1.4.7   ROBOTICS

Object detection is essential for robots to perceive and interact with the environment. It enables robots to recognize and manipulate objects, navigate in dynamic environments, and perform tasks like pick-and-place operations or object sorting. One example of real-world application, namely robot coordination for apple harvesting, is shown in Figure 1.11.

1.4.8   AGRICULTURE

Object detection can be applied in agriculture for various purposes, such as plant disease detection, fruit and vegetable bruise detection, weed identification, crop monitoring, and yield estimation. It helps farmers optimize their farming practices and improve crop management. Some examples of object detection in agriculture are displayed in Figure 1.12.

1.4.9   HUMAN–COMPUTER INTERACTION

Object detection is utilized in human–computer interaction systems, such as gesture recognition, facial detection, and pose estimation as shown in Figure 1.13. It enables devices to understand and respond to human actions, enhancing user experience and interaction.

1.4.10   WILDLIFE MONITORING AND CONSERVATION

Object detection is used in wildlife monitoring to track and identify endangered species, monitor animal behavior, and detect poaching activities. It aids in conservation efforts and helps protect wildlife populations. Some examples are shown in Figure 1.14.

FIGURE 1.12 Application of object detection task in agriculture: (a) Leaf mold detection; (b) Bruise detection in apples using infrared imaging; (c) Crack detection in the apples; (d) Skin defect detection in apples.

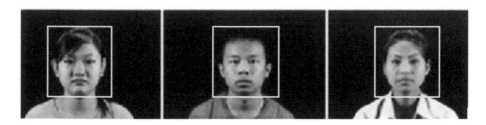

FIGURE 1.13 Application of object detection task in face detection for human–computer interaction (Our dataset available at http://mkbhowmik.in/deityTu.aspx.).

FIGURE 1.14 Application of object detection task in wildlife detection for monitoring and conservation.

1.5 CHALLENGES OF OBJECT DETECTION

Even though there has been substantial advancement in the field of object detection, several challenges still persist that researchers and practitioners strive to overcome in developing an algorithm or model for object detection. As observed from Figure 1.2, the main object detection task is to develop an algorithm or model that can effectively classify and localize the objects present in the scenes by achieving two challenging goals: high quality/accuracy and high efficiency [6]. Table 1.1 summarizes the possible challenges and subchallenges of the general object detection systems in real-world applications. As shown in Table 1.1, high-quality detection requires accurate localization and identification of objects in image or video frames in order to distinguish between the wide variety of object categories present in the real world (high distinctiveness) and to localize and identify object instances belonging to the same category despite intraclass appearance variations (high robustness). Moreover,

TABLE 1.1

Challenges and Subchallenges in Object Detection Systems

Challenges	Subchallenges	Situations
Quality/ Accuracy	Intraclass variation	• Imaging conditions (camera modalities) • Noise (image noise, distortion, compression noise) • Unconstrained environments (poor light/low illumination, occlusion, blur, shadow, object motion, weather conditions, low resolution) • Complex spatial arrangements (crowded objects, small and far distant objects) • Acentric distribution of objects • Strong background information (cluttered background, camouflage) • Diversities in object class (different color, shape, texture, pose, deformation)
	Distinctiveness	• Interclass ambiguities (same class of object with different color, texture, and shape) • Structured and unstructured objects
Efficiency	Time efficiency Memory efficiency Storage efficiency	• Large volume of image/video dataset • Diverse categories of object classes in real world • Requiring localizing and recognizing objects

real-time execution of the full detection procedure with appropriate memory and storage needs is required for high efficiency.

1.5.1 QUALITY/ACCURACY-BASED CHALLENGES

The quality/accuracy-based challenges for object detection mainly occur due to high intra- and interclass variations of objects in the scenes and large number of object classes. It is rather typical in nature for there to be intraclass variance between instances of the same object. These variations could be the result of a number of factors, including occlusion, lighting, position, viewpoint, etc. These unrestricted external factors can significantly alter how an object appears [7]. It is anticipated that the objects may deform non-rigidly, rotate, scale, or become blurred. Some things could be surrounded by unnoticeable elements, making detection tasks challenging. As shown in Table 1.1, imaging conditions represent another subchallenge of the object detection tasks that results from the tremendous effects of capturing sensors/ imaging modalities (such as visual imaging modality, infrared imaging modality, and CCTV modality). Also, an unconstrained environment resulting from the tremendous effects of the poor illumination/low light, atmospheric/weather conditions, occlusion, blur, shadow, and object motion is challenging for the object detection algorithms. Moreover, the presence of objects at different locations of the scenes and complex spatial arrangements of the scenes including crowded objects and small and far distant objects also add a challenge for the object detection problems. Further challenges may be added by artifacts, noise, compression, low imaging resolution, and filtering distortions.

Consequently, existing object detection algorithms or models concentrate mostly on structured object categories, such as the fixed definite number of object classes. It is obvious that the number of object categories taken into account in benchmark datasets is far lower than what people are capable of recognizing. Therefore, in addition to the intraclass variation–based challenges, there are interclass ambiguities, i.e., the appearance of the same class of object with different color, texture, and shape and the presence of structured and unstructured objects in the scenes to be detected that provide a challenge for the object detection task.

1.5.2 Efficiency-Based Challenges

Generally, the designed object detection models require a lot of computing power to produce reliable detection results. Effective object detectors are essential for further advancement in the field of computer vision as mobile and edge devices become more prevalent. The computational complexity increases with the number of object categories (i.e., classes) considered for detection, and with the number of locations and scales of the considered objects in a particular scene. These factors, together with the necessity to localize and recognize objects, contribute to the efficiency challenges. Moreover, scalability of the object detection algorithms presents another challenge where the algorithm or model needs to be capable of handling previously undiscovered objects and unknown environments.

1.6   ORGANIZATION OF THE BOOK

This book has been structured modularly, so that each of the technical chapters (Chapters 2 to 8) can be understood independently of others. The book comprises eight chapters. Chapter 1 provides the background knowledge to the reader that builds the foundation for this book. Chapter 2 gives the introduction to degradation and various types of degradation in indoor and outdoor environments, their brief description, and effects. The information regarding the mechanism of degradation and the effect of degradation on object detection tasks are also provided in this chapter. Chapter 3 describes various imaging modalities/sensors most frequently used by the research community for object detection tasks. The various types of imaging modalities described in this chapter are visual imaging modality, infrared imaging modality, and CCTV surveillance imaging modality for object detection. Chapter 4 presents the description of various public and private datasets utilized by the research community for object detection tasks. Also, the key characteristics and temporal information of the datasets are described in Chapter 4. Chapter 5 discusses the background knowledge of artifacts and also describes various artifacts with respect to object detection tasks in indoor and outdoor degraded vision. Impacts of different artifacts in objects visualization for performing object detection tasks are also described in this chapter. Chapter 6 presents a study on fundamentals of visibility restoration. Various contributions of the researchers for visibility enhancement or restoration in terms of multiple image approaches and single image approaches are described. This chapter also presents various performance evaluation measures used by the researchers for validating the visibility enhancement models. Chapter 7 presents an exhaustive description of the related works in the area of object detection. The description provided in this chapter has been done in two important approaches: background modeling–based approaches for object detection and location-oriented approaches for object detection. Performance evaluation measures used for measuring the effectiveness of the object detection algorithms and comparison of the published results are also described in this chapter. At the end of chapter, the research gaps and problem statements are provided. Chapter 8 offers various hands-on practicals for object detection in degraded and non-degraded vision. Practical approaches and application of these hands-on examples are also discussed in this chapter.

REFERENCES

1. Stockman, G., & Shapiro, L. G. (2001). *Computer vision*. Prentice Hall PTR.
2. Yilmaz, A., Javed, O., & Shah, M. (2006). Object tracking: A survey. *ACM Computing Surveys (CSUR)*, 38(4), 13-es.
3. Lee, D. T. (1982). Medial axis transformation of a planar shape. *IEEE Transactions on Pattern Analysis and Machine Intelligence*, 4, 363–369.
4. Breast Health: Follow-up after an Abnormal Mammogram. [Online]. Available: https://www.cancer.gov/types/breast/breast-changes
5. Davidson, J. R., Hohimer, C. J., Mo, C., & Karkee, M. (2017). Dual robot coordination for apple harvesting. In *2017 ASABE annual international meeting* (p. 1). American Society of Agricultural and Biological Engineers.
6. Liu, L., Ouyang, W., Wang, X., Fieguth, P., Chen, J., Liu, X., & Pietikäinen, M. (2020). Deep learning for generic object detection: A survey. *International Journal of Computer Vision*, 128, 261–318.
7. Zou, Z., Chen, K., Shi, Z., Guo, Y., & Ye, J. (2023). Object detection in 20 years: A survey. *Proceedings of the IEEE*.

2 Background of Degradation

2.1 DEFINING DEGRADATION

Today's digital technologies present functionalities necessary to gather any information needed to recognize images, whether still or moving. This data are most commonly in the form of a visual representation of something, according to the specific needs of a given entity, in the form of photographs or videos. During capturing of visual data, movements of the camera cause degradation of data. Such degradation comes in various forms, such as noise, camera misfocus, motion blur, and insufficient spatial or temporal resolution due to flaws in the measurement instruments.

2.2 CATEGORIZATION OF DEGRADATION

Degradation can be divided generally into three groups. Figure 2.1 represents the types of degradation.

2.2.1 Noise

Noise causes fluctuations in the pixel values that causes disturbance in the images and videos. Noise patterns are categorized based on distribution, correlation, nature, and source [1].

2.2.1.1 Distribution
The fluctuation of the pixel values is the characterization of uncertain variables. An uncertain variable's probability distribution is a mathematical relation between the values of statistical results and their probability of occurrence. Degradation of images and videos based on probability distribution of the fluctuation of the pixel values is classified as Gaussian noise, impulse or salt-and-pepper noise, Poisson noise, exponential noise, gamma noise, Rayleigh noise, and uniform noise [1].

2.2.1.2 Correlation
The dependency parameter of the pixels and its neighbor pixels is known as correlation. Colored noise is more challenging because its origin is unknown. The correlated pixel finding of colored noise is difficult, as the components involved in its origins are uncertain. These noises are white noise and pink noise, also known as flicker noise [1].

2.2.1.3 Nature
Based on the nature of the presence of the pixel fluctuations, degradation can be classified as additive noise or multiplicative noise. Additive noise is a linear problem whereas multiplicative noises are speckle noise and periodic noise [1].

DOI: 10.1201/9781003432036-2

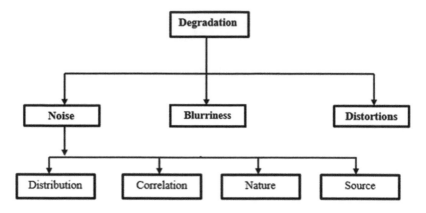

FIGURE 2.1 Categorization of image degradation.

2.2.1.4 Source

Quantization noise and photon noise are classified based on source in degraded vision. The difference between the actual and allotted values causes this type of noise. Photon noise generates degraded vision and the statistical nature of electro-magnetic waves [1].

2.2.2 BLUR

An inaccurately focused lens, the camera's movement in relation to the scene, or atmospheric turbulence can all cause blur. It can be classified as Gaussian blur, out-of-focus blur, and motion blur. Long-term exposure to the atmosphere results in Gaussian blur. A defocused optical system causes out-of-focus blur. Relative movement between the recording device and the scene causes motion blur. A motion-blurred picture is also created when a moving subject or the camera is exposed to light [1].

2.2.3 DISTORTIONS

Extreme intensity or color changes known as distortions or artifacts render an image useless. The image has a misleading error or any other type of systematic error as a result of a poor image capture method or as an undesirable consequence of the attributes of the image object [1].

2.3 MECHANISM OF DEGRADATION

Image degradation is the loss of image quality for a variety of reasons. When there is image deterioration, the quality of the image is greatly diminished and becomes hazy. The general mathematical model describing image degradation, i.e., how it is observed, is represented as Equation (2.1).

$$g(x,y) = f(x,y)*h(x,y) + e(x,y) \qquad (2.1)$$

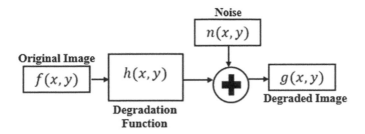

FIGURE 2.2   Basic background model used for image degradation.

where convolution is denoted by '*', noiseless image is $f(x, y)$, the degradation function is $h(x, y)$ (considered to be linear), and each pixel value's noisy perturbations is $e(x, y)$. A fairly accurate depiction of noisiness in an image is provided by the degradation model as shown in Figure 2.2.

2.3.1   GAUSSIAN NOISE

The Gaussian distribution is followed everywhere by Gaussian noise, which is additive in nature. In a noisy image this means that each manipulated pixel is made up of the aggregation of the original pixel value and a random Gaussian distributed noise quantity. The intensity of the pixel value has no bearing on the noise at any given position. Both the frequency and the spatial domains are tractable mathematically (Figure 2.3). The expression for the probability density function of a Gaussian random variable is:

$$P_G\left(z\right) = \frac{1}{\sigma\sqrt{2\pi}}\, e^{-\frac{\left(z-\bar{z}\right)^2}{2\sigma^2}} \tag{2.2}$$

where z = Intensity, $\bar{z}$ = Mean, σ = standard Deviation, and σ^2 = variance of z.

Figure 2.3(b) shows the image of a bird with the impact of Gaussian noise on the original image represented by Figure 2.3(a).

FIGURE 2.3   (a) Original image; (b) Gaussian noise–imposed image; and (c) scientific diagram of Gaussian noise.

(a)   (b)   (c)

FIGURE 2.4   (a) Original image; (b) Rayleigh noise–imposed image; (c) scientific diagram of Rayleigh noise.

2.3.2   RAYLEIGH NOISE

In the case of positive values for random variables, the Rayleigh distribution is a continuous probability distribution. This commonly occurs when a vector's magnitude and directional components are related. Rayleigh noise is frequently seen in radar and velocity images. Rayleigh noise is usually utilized to characterize noise phenomena in range imaging. The effect of this kind of noise on an object is presented by Figure 2.4.

$$p(z) = \frac{2}{b}(z-a)e^{\frac{-(z-a)^2}{b}} \text{ for } z \geq a, \text{ otherwise } p(z) = 0 \tag{2.3}$$

where Mean (m) $_{= a/b}$, $\sigma^2 = \dfrac{b(4-\pi)}{4}$ is the variance, and a and b are the positive integers.

2.3.3   ERLANG (OR GAMMA) NOISE

Gamma noise occurs mostly due to illumination problems. It follows gamma distribution, or continuous probability distribution, to describe continuous variables (noises) with skewed distributions that are always positive. Gamma noise density finds application in laser imaging. The impact of gamma noise on image creation is shown in Figure 2.5(b).

(a)   (b)   (c)

FIGURE 2.5   (a) Original image; (b) Erlang (or gamma)-imposed image; (c) scientific diagram of Erlang (or gamma) noise.

$$p(z) = \begin{cases} \dfrac{a^b x^{b-1}}{(b-1)!} e^{-az} & \text{for } z \geq 0 \\ 0 & \text{for } z \leq 0 \end{cases} \tag{2.4}$$

where $a > 0$ (i.e., 'a' is a positive integer), 'b' is also a positive integer, and factorial is denoted by '!'. The expressions for mean and variance are given below:

$$\text{Mean } m = \frac{a}{b} \quad \text{and} \quad \text{variance } \sigma^2 = \frac{b}{a^2}$$

2.3.4 EXPONENTIAL NOISE

Gamma or Erlang noise is a specific example of exponential noise, when the b parameters are equal to 1. If we look at the formula for the input parameter b and the gamma noise probability distribution function, then we can see the changes of the value of b.

Gamma noise probability distribution function is shown below:

$$p(z) = \begin{cases} \dfrac{a^b z^{b-1}}{(b-1)!} e^{-az} & \text{for } z \geq 0 \\ 0 & \text{for } z < 0 \end{cases} \tag{2.5}$$

In essence, the formula for the exponential noise probability distribution is made considerably simpler by removing the influence of parameter b. However, it reduces our ability to adjust the distribution curve's form, as there is now just one parameter remaining.

$$p(z) = \begin{cases} ae^{-az} & \text{for } z \geq 0 \\ 0 & \text{for } z < 0 \end{cases} \tag{2.6}$$

Let's define what the other formula parameters stand for. First, the intensity value is represented by the z variable. Second, a parameter is a factor that allows us to modify the exponential function curve's form. Finally, e is the Eulers constant, which is 2.71828. Figure 2.6(b) represents the exponential noise effect on the object.

(a)   (b)   (c)

FIGURE 2.6 (a) Original image; (b) exponential noise imposed image; (c) scientific diagram of exponential noise.

2.3.5   Uniform Noise

One other type of noise that can be used to imitate data corruption is uniform noise. This type of noise is consistently dispersed across a band of intensities, contrary to what its name might imply. A probability distribution function that distributes the values of the noise pixel intensities. Since it distributes among chosen intensities equally, the formula is pretty straightforward. Quantization noise is another name for this noise used by certain writers. Uniform noise function is shown below:

$$p(z) = \begin{cases} \dfrac{1}{b-a} & \text{if } a \leq z \leq b \\ 0 & \text{otherwise} \end{cases} \tag{2.7}$$

The mean and variance of this noise are expressed in the following terms:

$$m = \frac{a+b}{2} \quad \sigma^2 = \frac{(b-a)^2}{12}$$

where parameters a and b are essentially the intensity boundaries between which we distribute uniform probability distribution function. In addition, let's address the following probability distribution graph that this function makes, as displayed in Figure 2.7(c). The distortion effect of uniform noise is shown in Figure 2.7(b).

2.3.6   Impulse (Salt and Pepper) Noise

Salt and pepper noise is also known as impulse noise. It is the most straightforward noise model we can apply to an image. But we should only apply it to grayscale images, where the black and white values are represented by the minimal and maximal color values. This is among the simplest noise models, as was already indicated. Because of the probability distribution function, each impulse's possibilities of randomly appearing throughout the image are all that exists. Figure 2.8(b) displays

(a)   (b)   (c)

FIGURE 2.7   (a) Original image; (b) uniform noise–imposed image; (c) scientific diagram of uniform noise.

(a) (b) (c)

FIGURE 2.8 (a) Original image; (b) salt and pepper noise–imposed image; (c) scientific diagram of salt and pepper (impulse) noise.

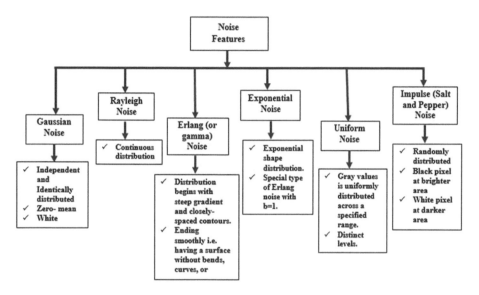

FIGURE 2.9 Noises of many forms and their characteristics.

the salt and pepper noise imposed in an image. We could, for instance, adjust it so that there are twice as many black as white pixels. Impulse noise function is represented as:

$$p(z) = \begin{cases} P_a & \text{for } z = a \\ P_b & \text{for } z = b \\ 0 & \text{otherwise} \end{cases} \tag{2.8}$$

The distribution of each value is shown in the graph in Figure 2.8(c). As we can see, there are only two intensity numbers where there are spikes. Different types of noise's effects on the image and their corresponding characteristics are presented in Figure 2.9.

2.4   EFFECT OF IMAGE DEGRADATION IN OBJECT DETECTION

In computer vision, digital images are important aspects for localization, classification, and detection of objects. In real-world applications like autonomous driving, video surveillance, medical imaging, etc., required images are imperceptible. They have a variety of types of degradation. For instance, images shot in cloudy conditions, images taken while moving, and images taken underwater often include different levels of blur. Fish-eye camera images typically have spatial abnormalities. Low resolution, salt and pepper, and Gaussian-blurred images can be produced by security and surveillance cameras as well as medical imaging facilities. As discussed in Section 2.2, various degradations are categorized. These types of challenges present in degraded content may create problems in object detection, which are present as information in images. Some of them are discussed below.

2.4.1   Target Object Information Loss in Object Detection Task

Due to image degradation, the consequence of different noise imposed on the image, the target object in the image loses its original information [2]. Thus, with such degradation, precisely detecting the target object is very challenging, as shown in Figure 2.10.

2.4.2   Inaccurate Localization of Far Distant and Small Objects in Detection Task

When the targeted object is captured as a far object, the information of that object is contained by the smaller number of pixels. Image degradation destroys the original pixel information with imposed noise at the time of image creation. Thus, objects captured from far away are not precisely detectable, as shown in Figure 2.11. Similarly, in case of small objects, the information is contained within a smaller number of pixels throughout the entire image.

2.4.3   Atmospheric Turbulence in Object Detection Task

In this condition objects in images and video frames have a low enough quality to show little to no detail, just appearing as blobs or blurry silhouettes [3]. Each

(a)   **(b)**

FIGURE 2.10   (a) Target object without noise; (b) target object with noise.

(a)   **(b)**

FIGURE 2.11   (a) The captured image with small and far object vessel; (b) small and far object vessel.

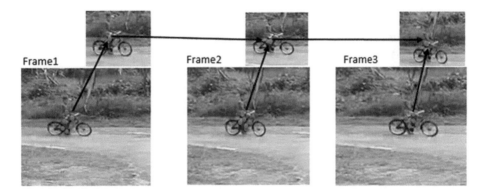

FIGURE 2.12   Visualization of the effect of turbulence distortion in object detection.

pixel's phase is randomly changed, but the amplitude of high frequency is often reduced as a result of signal mixing, creating blur. Because of this, images seem to be waves in time, because the pixels randomly move relative to their original places (Figure 2.12).

With all of these above-discussed effects, there are many more effects of image degradation in object detection. Overlapping objects are hard to detect with the effect of image degradation.

HOMEWORK PROBLEMS

1. Explain the concept of image degradation with the help of suitable real-world examples.
2. What are the categories of degradation in outdoor and indoor scenes?
3. Explain the mechanism behind the degradation process.
4. Explain each type of noise for which degradation occurs.
5. Explain in detail how object detection faces big problems due to image degradation.

REFERENCES

1. Jayaraman, S., Esakkirajan, S., & Veerakumar, T. (2009). *Digital image processing* (Vol. 7014). New Delhi: Tata McGraw Hill Education.
2. Fiaz, M., Mahmood, A., & Jung, S. K. (2018). Tracking noisy targets: A review of recent object tracking approaches. arXiv preprint arXiv:1802.03098.
3. Hu, D., & Anantrasirichai, N. (2022). Object recognition in atmospheric turbulence scenes. arXiv preprint arXiv:2210.14318.

3 Imaging Modalities for Object Detection

3.1 VISUAL IMAGING MODALITY

In object detection, the visual image refers to the image which will be typically a 2D grid of pixels, and each pixel will represent a specific color or intensity value in the RGB (red, green, and blue) format. Each pixel of the visual image is represented by three color channels from which objects will be detected and localized. For this purpose, different sensors are required in the cameras with different modalities to detect the existence of objects or colors within their field of view and transform this information into a visual image for display. Visual imaging modality plays a vital role in processing of the image with different processes, which will be discussed later in the chapter, for the purpose of object detection as shown in Figure 3.1.

Visual imaging modality captures images or video frames of the environment, providing a visual representation of the scene. These images contain valuable information about objects, their shapes, colors, textures, and spatial relationships [1]. Also, these images consist of various activities that are then processed by the visual image sensors for the purpose of object detection. Some of them are:

- **Object Localization**: Visual sensors help determine the precise location of objects within the scene. By analyzing the captured images, object detection algorithms can estimate objects' position, size, and orientation relative to the sensor's coordinate system [3].
- **Object Recognition**: Visual sensors enable object recognition by analyzing the visual features and patterns present in the captured images. Object detection algorithms can compare these features against predefined models or learned patterns to identify specific objects or object classes [2].
- **Object Tracking**: Visual sensors facilitate object tracking by continuously capturing images and monitoring the movement of objects over time. By comparing consecutive frames, object detection algorithms can estimate object trajectories and track their positions and movements in real time.
- **Scene Understanding**: Visual sensors provide rich contextual information about the scene. By analyzing the captured images, object detection algorithms can infer the relationships between objects, understand the scene layout, and make higher-level interpretations about the environment.
- **Depth Perception**: Some visual sensors, such as depth cameras or stereo vision systems, provide depth information in addition to visual images. The depth data enable 3D perception and help in estimating the distance of objects from the sensor, which is essential for accurate object detection and scene understanding [3].

DOI: 10.1201/9781003432036-3

| Sensor used in | Visual | Visual image produced by Visual |
| visual camera | Camera | Camera |

FIGURE 3.1   Example of visual imaging modality.

FIGURE 3.2   Sample images for various high-level object detection tasks using visual imaging modality: (a) Object Localization; (b) Object Recognition; (c) Scene Understanding with respect to weather condition; (d) Object Tracking; (e) Depth Perception and construction [4]. Used by permission.

Some example images representing visual images for various high-level object detection tasks are displayed in Figure 3.2.

Moreover, sensors play a crucial role in visual imaging modalities in terms of capturing and converting light into electronic signals that can be processed and interpreted to create images. In visual imaging, sensors play the role of detecting and measuring the intensity of light across different wavelengths and spatial locations. Here are the critical roles of sensors in visual imaging modality:

- **Light Detection**: Sensors, typically in the form of charge-coupled devices (CCDs) or complementary metal-oxide-semiconductor (CMOS) sensors, are used to detect photons (light particles). These sensors have an array of photosensitive elements called pixels that absorb photons and generate an electrical charge proportional to the intensity of the light [5].
- **Signal Conversion**: When photons strike the pixels of the sensor, the energy is converted into electrical charges. The sensor's circuitry then converts these charges into digital signals or analog voltages that represent the captured light intensity. This conversion enables further processing and analysis of the captured image.

- **Spatial Resolution**: Sensors consist of an array of pixels, each capable of measuring the intensity of light at a specific location in the image. The total number of pixels determines the spatial resolution of the sensor. Higher-resolution sensors capture more detail and enable sharper and more precise images.
- **Spectral Sensitivity**: Sensors are intended to be sensitive to specific wavelengths of light or cover a broad spectrum. This spectral sensitivity allows for imaging in different parts of the electromagnetic spectrum, such as visible light, infrared, or ultraviolet. By selecting appropriate sensors, visual imaging modalities can be tailored for specific applications or to capture specific phenomena.
- **Image Processing**: Sensors capture raw image data, which often undergoes preprocessing and correction to account for various factors such as noise, distortion, and artifacts. This preprocessing may involve such techniques as noise reduction, color calibration, and image enhancement. Sensors with higher dynamic range and low noise characteristics contribute to better image quality.
- **Image Reconstruction**: The data captured by sensors are processed and reconstructed to form a visual representation of the scene being imaged. This reconstruction involves mapping the pixel values to corresponding locations in the image and generating a final image output. The accuracy and fidelity of the sensor's measurements have a direct impact on how well the picture is reconstructed.

In summary, sensors in visual imaging modalities are responsible for detecting light, converting it into electrical signals, providing spatial resolution, enabling imaging in specific wavelengths, and contributing to the overall image quality through signal processing and reconstruction.

3.2 INFRARED IMAGING MODALITY

Infrared imaging modality is a technology used to capture and visualize infrared radiations emitted by objects. Infrared sensors are used to detect infrared radiation emitted by objects as they are commonly used in proximity sensors, motion detection, and heat detection applications [6]. According to Figure 3.3, the image sensors in the cameras are sensitive to wavelengths in the infrared regions of the electromagnetic spectrum. Various types of sensors are used in the infrared imaging modality, which is used for object detection with the help of infrared radiation (heat radiation), which may change over time and space emitted by the objects [7]. The primary sensors used in infrared imaging are used to convert the infrared radiation into an electrical signal, which is then further processed to create an image (Figure 3.4).

Several types of sensors are used in infrared imaging modalities for the purpose of object detection in different fields such as night vision, thermal imaging, digital forensics, and medical diagnostics. Some of them are as follows:

- **Infrared Photodiodes**: Infrared photodiodes are semiconductor devices that generate a current when exposed to light, including infrared radiation. Infrared photodiodes are used to detect and measure the reflected or emitted

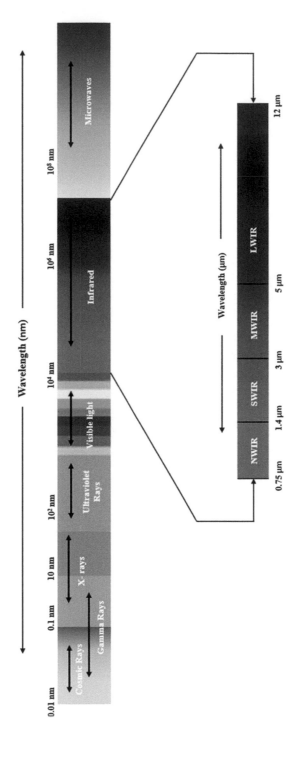

FIGURE 3.3 Infrared imaging wavelength range.

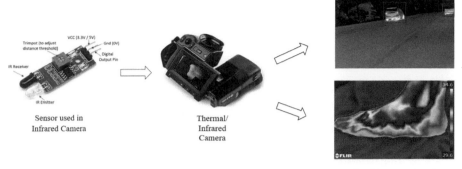

Sensor used in Infrared Camera

Thermal/ Infrared Camera

Infrared images produced by Thermal or Infrared Camera

FIGURE 3.4 Example of infrared imaging modality.

infrared light. These photodiodes are sensitive to specific wavelengths of infrared light and can convert the received light into an electrical signal. They are used in a range of applications, including infrared imaging.

- **Infrared Filters**: Infrared filters are used to selectively transmit or block specific ranges of infrared wavelengths. They help enhance image quality by reducing unwanted light and improving contrast.
- **Infrared (IR) Light-Emitting Diodes (LEDs)**: Active infrared object detection systems often use IR LEDs to emit infrared light. These LEDs emit light at wavelengths that are invisible to the human eye but can be detected by specialized sensors. The emitted infrared light is then reflected off objects in the detection area.
- **Infrared Proximity Sensors**: Infrared proximity sensors utilize a combination of IR LEDs and photodiodes to detect the presence of objects. The IR LED emits infrared light, and the photodiode measures the intensity of the reflected light. By analyzing the received light intensity, these sensors can determine the proximity of objects and detect their presence.
- **Passive Infrared (PIR) Sensors**: PIR sensors are commonly used for motion detection based on changes in infrared radiation emitted by objects. These sensors consist of multiple segments that detect variations in the infrared energy within their field of view. When an object moves within the detection area, it creates a change in the detected infrared energy, triggering the sensor.

Thermal imaging cameras, also known as infrared cameras, utilize arrays of infra-red detectors to capture the heat emitted by objects. These cameras can detect temperature differences and create an image based on the infrared radiation emitted by objects. They are often used in applications of object detection such as security systems, surveillance, and search-and-rescue operations. These are some of the commonly used sensors in infrared imaging modalities. It is important to note that the specific sensor or combination of sensors used for object detection in infrared imaging can vary depending on the application requirements, detection range, ambient conditions, and desired level of accuracy. There are different infrared cameras with different detectors based on their thermal bands that are used in infrared imaging and act with different sensors used for the various purposes of object detection as mentioned below [8, 9]:

- **Shortwave Infrared Cameras (SWIR)**: The photon-converting detector in these cameras is built of indium gallium arsenide (InGaAs). These cameras can be either cryogenically cooled for high-end scientific-grade cameras, non-cooled, or thermoelectrically cooled (single, double, or triple stage). These detectors have a 0.9 m to 1.7 m range of sensitivity. Even at greater surface temperatures, these cameras still detect significant quantities of reflected light, and only then do they begin to detect actual thermal effects. FLIR A6260sc camera is a prime example of this type of camera [8].
- **Midwave Infrared Cameras (MWIR)**: These types of cameras use a detector that is made from indium antimonide (InSb). These are exclusively cryogenically cooled. Therefore, Stirling coolers are now incorporated into the bodies of modern cameras, eliminating the need for external cooling gas. These cameras are employed to take adequate and precise thermal measurements. Since their detector is photon-based, integration times of microsecond can be achieved. These detectors have the capability of detecting temperature changes within the range of 0.018 mK. Some of the applications of this type of camera used in the field of object detection are optical gas imaging, precision imaging, high-speed temperature measurements, military applications, automated thermal imaging, plastic film inspection, microscopy, etc. The FLIR A8300sc series is a prime example of a camera [8].
- **Longwave Infrared Cameras (LWIR)**: Cameras in this category used to be equipped with HgCdTe or mercury cadmium telluride detector. These detectors are also exceedingly nonlinear, which makes it challenging to calibrate and use these cameras. These kinds of cameras are useful when the application is interested in the longwave infrared region yet needs a faster integration time and higher sensitivity. The FLIR A6750SLS camera is a good illustration.

Furthermore, for detecting objects, both a visual digital camera and a typical charge-coupled device (CCD) camera, as mentioned in Section 3.1, have the advantage of high resolution, which renders them more suitable for daytime or nighttime use with a proper lighting setup. However, they are ineffective in environments with poor illumination or visibility due to atmospheric conditions because the appearance of objects in the captured images is not as clear as in images captured under normal atmospheric conditions. Several related works have been conducted in such environments. To address the limitations of visual and CCD cameras at nighttime, many studies have been conducted on methods that detect objects with near/far infrared (NIR/FIR)-based cameras. NIR cameras are robust against darkness, but they have

TABLE 3.1
Key Characteristics of Different Infrared Imaging Modalities

Types of Camera	Wavelength Range	Sensors Used	Commonly Used Camera Model
Shortwave Infrared Cameras (SWIR)	0.9–1.7 μm	Indium Gallium Arsenide (InGaAs)	FLIR A6260, SWIR 640 P-Series
Midwave Infrared Cameras (MWIR)	3–5 μm	Indium Antimonide (InSb)	FLIR GFX 320, FLIR A8300sc, FLIR G300-A(Drone Camera)
Longwave Infrared Cameras (LWIR)	7–12 μm	Mercury Cadmium Telluride (HgCdTe), Microbolometer	FLIR PathFindIR, FLIR A6750SLS, FLIR XT2(Drone Camera)

a similar drawback to that in CCD cameras when the interferences are produced by vehicle headlights. In addition, the attenuation of visual, CCD, and NIR radiation that is produced through atmospheric aerosols is mostly due to their short wavelengths. In contrast, FIR cameras enable robust object detection regardless of the atmospheric conditions because as the spectrum wavelength increases, the effect of bad atmospheric conditions decreases (Table 3.1).

Infrared imaging plays a crucial role in object detection across various applications. Here are some notable applications where infrared imaging is used for object detection:

- **Security and Surveillance**: Infrared imaging is extensively used in security and surveillance systems for object detection. Infrared cameras can detect and visualize objects based on their heat signatures, allowing for enhanced surveillance in low-light conditions or complete darkness. They can detect intruders, monitor perimeters, and identify potential threats, providing an added layer of security [10].
- **Automotive Safety**: Infrared imaging is utilized in automotive safety systems for object detection. For instance, some vehicles are equipped with infrared sensors or cameras to detect pedestrians, cyclists, or animals in low-visibility conditions, helping prevent collisions. Infrared imaging can also be used for driver-monitoring systems, detecting drowsiness or distraction.
- **Industrial Automation**: Infrared imaging is employed in industrial automation for object detection and monitoring. In manufacturing environments, infrared sensors can detect the presence or absence of objects on conveyor belts, facilitating automated sorting, packaging, and quality control processes. Infrared cameras can also monitor equipment and machinery for abnormalities in temperature, helping prevent failures or malfunctions.
- **Robotics**: Infrared imaging is used in robotics for object detection and localization. Robots equipped with infrared sensors or cameras can detect objects in their surroundings, enabling them to navigate and interact with their environment. Infrared sensors can also be utilized for obstacle avoidance, allowing robots to safely maneuver in dynamic environments.

FIGURE 3.5   Sample images for various high-level object detection tasks using infrared imaging modality: (a) Security and surveillance; (b) Abnormality detection in medical imaging; (c) Automotive safety by surrounding salient object detection (vehicle, pedestrians, and animals); (d) Victim detection.

- **Firefighting and Search and Rescue**: Infrared imaging is employed in firefighting and search-and-rescue operations. Infrared cameras can detect heat signatures emitted by humans or objects, even in smoke, darkness, or debris. This enables firefighters and rescuers to locate individuals who may be trapped or in need of assistance.
- **Medical Diagnostics**: Infrared imaging finds application in medical diagnostics, particularly in thermography. It can be used to detect abnormalities in body temperature distribution, aiding in the identification of conditions such as inflammation, circulatory disorders, or certain types of cancers. Infrared imaging can also assist in non-contact temperature measurement, monitoring patient vital signs, and identifying fever symptoms [10].

These are just a few examples highlighting the diverse applications of infrared imaging in object detection. The technology's ability to detect and visualize objects based on their thermal characteristics makes it invaluable in numerous fields where conventional visual imaging may be limited or ineffective and some of the applications are displayed in Figure 3.5.

3.3   CCTV SURVEILLANCE IMAGING MODALITY

Closed-circuit television (CCTV) is the most popular form of video surveillance that helps in monitoring the activities, and behaviors with different scenes are visible through the surveillance cameras for the purpose of object detection as shown in Figure 3.6. This imaging modality may also be utilized to manage, direct, or automatically detect security issues [11]. For the purpose of object detection, CCTV cameras are employed in a variety of settings, including banks, airports, and military applications. These cameras record activity in their area of operation and then transmit the video stream to displays in the monitoring station or control room [11].

| Sensor used in CCTV | CCTV surveillance | Visual image produced by CCTV surveillance |

FIGURE 3.6 Example of CCTV surveillance imaging modality.

There are various sensors used in CCTV surveillance cameras, as they play a vital role in the potential of a surveillance system for the purpose of object detection. Here are some:

- **Charge-Coupled Device (CCD) Sensors**: CCD sensors are widely employed in CCTV cameras for video capture. These sensors convert light into electrical signals, which are then processed to generate a video image. It is made up of optical detector integrated circuits that use semiconductors. The sensors used by the CCD receive light focused by the camera lens, thus photodiodes sense the image areas of the bright and dark parts in the picture, which results in an electric charge in proportion to the level of light. A higher charge will be produced by a brighter region. The photodiodes, also known as image cells or pixels, are arranged in a matrix of rows and columns [12]. The charged diodes are then processed. CCD sensors offer good image quality, high sensitivity, and low noise, making them suitable for capturing detailed surveillance footage [5].
- **Complementary Metal-Oxide-Semiconductor (CMOS) Sensors**: CMOS sensors are an alternative to CCD sensors and have gained popularity in CCTV cameras. CMOS sensors use an array of pixels to capture light and convert it into electrical signals [5]. CMOS sensors used in CCTV cameras come in various sizes, ranging from small sensors suitable for compact cameras to larger sensors for high-end surveillance cameras. The size of the sensor affects the resolution and the amount of light the sensor can capture, which impacts image quality. They are known for their low power consumption, fast readout speeds, and cost effectiveness [5].
- **Infrared (IR) Sensors**: Infrared sensors are used in CCTV cameras for capturing video footage in low-light or nighttime conditions. Infrared sensors can detect infrared light, which is invisible to the human eye, allowing cameras to capture images in the absence of visible light. IR sensors can be either active, such as IR LEDs that emit infrared light, or passive, such as IR photodiodes that detect infrared radiation.
- **Wide Dynamic Range (WDR) Sensors**: WDR sensors are designed to capture scenes with a wide range of lighting conditions, including areas with both bright and dark areas. These sensors have the ability to balance the exposure across the image, ensuring that details in both bright and

shadowed areas are captured effectively. WDR sensors are beneficial in surveillance scenarios where there are challenging lighting conditions.

- **Thermal Imaging Sensors**: Thermal imaging sensors are used in specialized CCTV surveillance cameras for capturing thermal information. These sensors detect the heat emitted by objects and generate images based on temperature differences. Thermal cameras are particularly useful for surveillance in low-light conditions, detecting human or animal presence, and monitoring areas where traditional cameras may struggle, such as through smoke or foliage [5] [12].
- **Motion Detection Sensors**: Motion detection sensors, such as passive infrared (PIR) sensors or video analytics algorithms, are utilized in CCTV surveillance systems to detect movement within the camera's field of view. PIR sensors can sense changes in infrared radiation caused by moving objects, while video analytics algorithms analyze video frames to identify and track moving objects.

The specific sensors used in CCTV surveillance imaging depend on factors such as the desired image quality, lighting conditions, surveillance environment, and specific requirements of the application. CCTV systems often incorporate a combination of these sensors to enhance surveillance capabilities and improve the accuracy of object detection and monitoring. It has a broad range of applications based on object detection. Here are some key areas where CCTV imaging modality is applied for object detection:

- **Security and Surveillance**: CCTV systems are extensively used for object detection in security and surveillance applications. Cameras are strategically placed to monitor areas such as public spaces, airports, banks, retail stores, and parking lots. Object detection algorithms, combined with video analytics, can identify and track suspicious activities, intruders, or unauthorized objects, enhancing security measures.
- **Traffic Monitoring and Management**: CCTV cameras are employed for object detection and tracking in traffic monitoring and management systems. They can detect and analyze vehicles, pedestrians, and other objects within the traffic flow. This information is used for traffic monitoring, congestion management, incident detection, and enforcement of traffic rules.
- **Retail Analytics**: In retail environments, CCTV imaging modality is utilized for object detection to analyze customer behavior, optimize store layouts, and improve sales strategies. Object detection algorithms can track customer movements, count people entering or exiting the store, and identify popular product areas. This information helps retailers make data-driven decisions to enhance the shopping experience and optimize operations.
- **Industrial Automation and Manufacturing**: CCTV imaging modality is used in industrial automation and manufacturing settings for object detection and process monitoring. Cameras are employed to detect and track

objects on assembly lines, inspect product quality, monitor equipment operation, and ensure safety compliance. Object detection algorithms can identify defects, count products, and trigger automated processes.

- **Crowd Management and Public Safety**: CCTV cameras with object detection capabilities are utilized in crowded areas such as stadiums, concert venues, and public gatherings for crowd management and public safety. Object detection algorithms can monitor crowd density, detect overcrowding or unusual behavior, and identify potential safety hazards.
- **Perimeter Protection**: CCTV systems are used for object detection along the perimeter of secured areas such as residential complexes, industrial sites, or sensitive facilities. Cameras equipped with object detection algorithms can detect and track intrusions, unauthorized access, or objects crossing predefined boundaries, triggering alerts or activating security measures.
- **Transportation Security**: CCTV imaging modality is applied in transportation systems, such as airports and train stations, for object detection and security screening. Cameras with object detection algorithms can identify suspicious objects or baggage left unattended, enabling timely responses and enhancing security protocols.

These are examples illustrating the application of CCTV imaging modality in object detection as shown in Figure 3.7. The combination of cameras, video analytics, and object detection algorithms allows for improved situational awareness, threat identification, and proactive decision-making across various domains.

FIGURE 3.7 Sample images for various high-level object detection task using CCTV imaging modality: (a) Security and surveillance; (b) Traffic monitoring; (c) Retail analysis for identification of misplaced products in shopping mall; (d) Crowd management and public safety.

3.4   UNMANNED AERIAL VEHICLE (UAV) IMAGING MODALITY

Unmanned aerial vehicles (UAVs), also known as drones, are a new form of aircraft or aerial vehicle that does not carry a human pilot in it and uses the aerodynamics principle to lift it up. They either are controlled through a ground-based control station or operate autonomously using preprogrammed flight plans and onboard sensors that are used for the purpose of aerial photography and videography [13]. UAVs have gained significant popularity and have been adopted in various industries and fields due to their versatility, maneuverability, and ability to access hard-to-reach or hazardous areas. UAVs play a vital role in object detection applications and come in various sizes, shapes, designs, and multiple capabilities. With the advancement in computer vision and onboard sensor technologies, UAVs can be equipped with various sensors and cameras to detect and identify objects in real time. UAVs can capture both visual and infrared images based on their camera models and sensors used for capturing the images or videos [13]. Basically, UAVs are equipped with five sensors:

- **RGB sensors or camera**: UAVs can be equipped with various sensors depending on the imaging modality that will be required for the object detection. RGB cameras are one of the most important sensors used for object detection. RGB cameras are the standard sensors used in UAVs for capturing visible light imagery [13]. The quality of the charged couple device (CCD) and complementary metal oxide semiconductor (chips), as well as the focus point of the camera, all affect the range of RGB cameras that will give the best resolution while taking aerial images and videos [14].
- **Multispectral sensor or camera**: Multispectral sensors capture imagery in multiple or narrow spectral bands beyond the visible range. These types of sensors are lightweight and the most widely used sensors in addition to RGB sensors. These sensors enable UAVs to collect data in specific wavelengths, allowing for analysis in applications such as agriculture, environmental monitoring, and mineral exploration [14]. The data that can be accessed by the UAV-based multispectral sensors have a significantly greater resolution: better than 30 cm ground sampling distance (GSD).
- **Hyperspectral sensor**: Hyperspectral sensors are advanced imaging systems that capture imagery in hundreds or even thousands of narrow and contiguous spectral bands. They provide a high spectral resolution, allowing for detailed analysis of the electromagnetic spectrum. When integrated into UAVs, hyperspectral sensors enable a range of applications requiring precise spectral information. Hyperspectral sensors divide the electromagnetic spectrum into numerous narrow bands, typically ranging from the visible to the shortwave infrared (SWIR) region [14]. Each band captures data at a specific wavelength, creating a hyperspectral image cube. This cube contains spectral information for each pixel in the image, resulting in detailed spectral signatures of objects. Hyperspectral sensors can capture high volumes of information that can be further used for various applications [14].

- **Thermal infrared sensor**: Thermal infrared sensors are mid-range passive sensors that have a wavelength that spans from 3μm to 35μm. They are mostly used for estimating thermal outflows and the measurement of the temperature that then helps in object detection. Thermal infrared sensors detect and measure the infrared radiation emitted by objects in the form of heat. Unlike visible light cameras, thermal sensors operate in the long-wave infrared (LWIR) or mid-wave infrared (MWIR) spectral ranges [14]. They capture the temperature variations of objects and convert them into gray-scale or false-color images based on the detected thermal radiation.
- **Light Detection and Ranging (LiDAR)**: Light detection and ranging sensors are one of the most popular processes to get geometric information. UAVs frequently employ LiDAR sensors to collect accurate three-dimensional (3D) data about the surroundings. When LiDAR-emitted laser pulses reflect off objects, the system tracks the amount of time it takes for the pulses to come back [14]. By calculating the time of flight, the sensor can determine the distance to objects in its field of view. This technology enables UAVs to create detailed 3D point clouds and perform accurate mapping, surveying, and object detection. LiDAR systems in UAVs provide geometrical extraction and spectral detection in addition to helping with planning and understanding for managing urban infrastructure [14].

When equipped with imaging sensors, UAVs can be used for object detection in various applications. Here are some of the applications of UAV imaging modality in object detection:

- **Agriculture**: UAVs equipped with imaging sensors can be used for crop monitoring and management. They can detect diseases, pests, nutrient deficiencies, and other anomalies in crops by capturing high-resolution images of agricultural fields. Object detection algorithms can then be applied to these images to identify specific objects of interest, such as diseased plants or weeds.
- **Environmental Monitoring**: UAVs can be used for environmental monitoring and conservation efforts. They can detect and track wildlife, monitor deforestation activities, and identify changes in ecosystems. Object detection techniques can be applied to UAV-captured images to identify and track specific animals or detect illegal activities, such as poaching.
- **Search and Rescue**: In search-and-rescue operations, UAVs equipped with imaging sensors can help detect and locate missing persons or objects. By capturing aerial images of large areas, object detection algorithms can be used to identify individuals or specific objects, such as life jackets or wreckage, in a faster and more efficient manner than traditional ground-based search methods.
- **Infrastructure Inspection**: UAVs can be used for inspecting critical infrastructure, such as bridges, power lines, and pipelines. By capturing high-resolution images of these structures, object detection algorithms can

identify potential structural defects or anomalies, such as cracks or corrosion, allowing for timely maintenance and repair.

- **Urban Planning and Surveillance**: UAVs can aid in urban planning and surveillance by capturing aerial images of cities and towns. Object detection algorithms can then be used to detect and analyze various objects, such as vehicles, buildings, and infrastructure, to assess traffic patterns, urban development, or detect unauthorized constructions or suspicious activities.
- **Disaster Management**: During natural disasters, UAVs equipped with imaging sensors can assist in assessing the extent of damage and identifying areas that require immediate attention. Object detection techniques can be used to locate and identify damaged buildings, blocked roads, or trapped individuals, enabling rescue and relief teams to respond effectively.
- **Border Security**: UAVs can play a vital role in border security by monitoring and detecting illegal activities, such as smuggling or unauthorized border crossings. Imaging sensors on UAVs can capture images and videos of border regions, and object detection algorithms can be used to identify suspicious objects, vehicles, or individuals for further investigation.

These are just a few examples of how UAV imaging modality can be applied to object detection in various fields as shown in Figure 3.8. The combination of UAVs and object detection techniques enables efficient and accurate analysis of aerial imagery, providing valuable insights and aiding decision-making processes. The various key characteristics of imaging modalities and sensors for object detection are summarized in Table 3.2.

FIGURE 3.8 Sample images for various high level object detection task using unmanned aerial vehicle (UAV) imaging modality: (a) Monitoring vehicles and peoples [15]; (b) Traffic monitoring in security zones [15]; (c) Rescue of peoples in various disasters (e.g., flood) [15]. ([a–c] Used by permission.)

TABLE 3.2

Key Characteristics of Imaging Modalities and Sensors for Object Detection

Type of Sensor	Imaging Modality	Application	Merit	Demerit
Charge-Coupled Device (CCD)	CCTV/ visual camera	Surveillance and monitoring	• High performance in light conditions • High wide range view • Less susceptible to vibration effect • High sensitivity • High definition	• High power consumption • Low frame rate • Expensive
Complementary Metal-Oxide-Semiconductor (CMOS)	CCTV/ Visual Camera	Surveillance and monitoring	• High resolution • Excellent color • High-speed imaging capability • Power efficient • Cost-effective	• High noise • Moderate sensitivity
Microbolometer	Thermal camera/ infrared camera	Thermography, security and surveillance in night vision or poor illumination	• Does not require cooling • Operated at room temperature • Light weight • Less power consumption • Expensive	• Lower sensitivity • Response time is longer • Cannot be used for multi-spectral applications
Indium Gallium Arsenide (InGaAs)	Thermal camera/ infrared camera	Thermography, security and surveillance in night vision or poor illumination	• Extended wavelength • High sensitivity • Fast response time	• Limited spectral range • Low resolution • Higher cost
Indium Antimonide (InSb)	Thermal camera/ infrared camera	Thermography, security and surveillance in night vision or poor illumination	• High sensitivity • Wide spectral range • High quantum efficiency	• Fragility • Sensitivity to temperature changes • Reduced resolution • Higher cost
Mercury Cadmium Telluride (HgCdTe)	Thermal camera/ infrared camera	Thermography, security and surveillance in night vision or poor illumination	• High sensitivity and low noise • High frame rate • High temperature operation	• Fragility • Sensitivity to temperature changes • Dark current and stability
Light Detection and Ranging (LIDAR)	UAVs/ visual camera/ infrared camera	Aerial inspection, rescue and relief	• High-resolution mapping • Good view of remote areas • Accurate distance measurement	• High cost • Sensitive to environmental factors (heavy rains) • Prone to damage • Inaccurate data in water depth and turbulent waves

REFERENCES

1. Zhao, Z. Q., Zheng, P., Xu, S. T., & Wu, X. (2019). Object detection with deep learning: A review. *IEEE Transactions on Neural Networks and Learning Systems*, 30(11), 3212–3232.
2. Kaur, J., & Singh, W. (2022). Tools, techniques, datasets and application areas for object detection in an image: A review. *Multimedia Tools and Applications*, 81(27), 38297–38351.
3. Depth Estimation: Basics and Intuition. [Online] Available: https://towardsdatascience.com/depth-estimation-1-basics-and-intuition-86f2c9538cd1
4. NYU Depth Dataset V2. [Online]. Available. https://cs.nyu.edu/~silberman/datasets/nyu_depth_v2.html
5. Sukhavasi, S. B., Sukhavasi, S. B., Elleithy, K., Abuzneid, S., & Elleithy, A. (2021). CMOS image sensors in surveillance system applications. *Sensors*, 21(2), 488.
6. What is IR sensor [Online] Available: https://www.fierceelectronics.com/sensors/what-ir-sensor
7. IR Sensor [Online] Available: https://www.infratec.in/sensor-division/service-support/glossary/infrared-sensor/
8. Thermal Infrared Imaging in IR Camera – Explained. [Online]. Available: https://movitherm.com/knowledgebase/thermalinfraredimagingexplained/#:~:text=The%20majority%20of%20all%20thermal,resistance%20in20their%20detector%20elements.
9. Kwan, C., et al. (2019). Target tracking and classification using compressive measurements of MWIR and LWIR coded aperture cameras. *Journal of Signal and Information Processing*, 10(3), 73–95.
10. IR-sensor-working. [Online]. Available: https://robocraze.com/blogs/post/ir-sensor-working
11. Bhusal, S. (2015). Object detection and tracking in wide area surveillance using thermal imagery.
12. CCTV Camera Explained. [Online]. Available: https://www.techcube.co.uk/blog/cctv-cameras-explained/#:~:text=At%20the%20core%20of%20a,integrated%20circuits%20that%20use%20semiconductors
13. Jumani, A. K., Laghari, R. A., & Nawaz, H. (2022). Unmanned aerial vehicles: A review. *Cognitive Robotics*.
14. Yao, H., Qin, R., & Chen, X. (2019). Unmanned aerial vehicle for remote sensing applications—A review. *Remote Sensing*, 11(12), 1443.
15. Mishra, B., Garg, D., Narang, P., & Mishra, V. (2020). Drone-surveillance for search and rescue in natural disaster. *Computer Communications*, 156, 1–10.

4   Real-Time Benchmark Datasets for Object Detection

4.1   INDOOR DATASETS AND THEIR KEY CHARACTERISTICS

The benchmark datasets that are readily available and offer a balanced coverage of the challenges like those encountered in the actual world are the root cause of the rapid development of complex object detection algorithms. Furthermore, the availability of such a dataset makes it easier to compare state-of-the-art techniques fairly. As a result, establishing large-scale datasets gives moving object detection a strong basis and regularly directs the field's advancement. Large indoor datasets have been developed during the last several decades to accommodate the growing need for developing and assessing novel object detection models. These datasets are all extensive in terms of both complexity and quantity. Descriptions and distinguishing features of the most popular indoor datasets are given below.

4.1.1   VSSN 2006 (Video Surveillance & Sensor Networks 2006) Dataset

VSSN 2006 dataset [7] contains nine synthetic videos consisting of real background and artificial moving objects. In total, the dataset contains 1000 frames where pixel-based labeling of moving objects in each frame are annotated and provided with the dataset. The spatial resolution of the frames is 400 × 400 pixels. The representative challenges of this dataset include animated background, bootstrapping, illumination changes, and shadows. The VSSN 2006 dataset is available for the research community at [8].

4.1.2   CAVIAR (Context Aware Vision Using Image-based Active Recognition) Dataset

CAVIAR dataset [12] contains 80 indoor video clips (overall 152,000 frames), each of which represents some form of group activity. These include people walking and interacting with others, shopping, fighting, and dropping/leaving a package/items in a public place. The resolution of the frames are 384 × 288 pixels. Similar to work of PETS 2009, bounding boxes are annotated with each moving object. The CAVIAR dataset is available for the research community at [47].

DOI: 10.1201/9781003432036-4   **39**

4.1.3   I-LIDS (Imagery Library for Intelligent Detection Systems) Dataset

A video library specifically created for action recognition, the i-LIDS dataset [23] includes videos of parked cars, abandoned objects, individuals walking through doorways, and persons in restricted areas. The dataset includes a total of 14 videos that were recorded by a multi-camera CCTV network in an airport arrivals hall. The spatial resolution of the dataset is 64 × 128. Due to the large size of the videos (i.e., 24 hours of surveillance footage) and computation burden, manual annotation or labeling of dataset are not provided. The i-LIDS dataset is available for the research community at [48].

4.1.4   SBM-RGBD Dataset

A Microsoft Kinect sensor recorded 33 RGBD videos totaling 15,033 video frames in an indoor setting for the SBM-RGBD dataset [32]. A few videos were chosen from five open datasets, while others were self-captured in 2017 by the organizers. Seven categories representing various difficulties with background modeling were created from the videos: illumination changes (4 videos with 2,579 video frames), color and depth camouflage (4 videos with 1,707 and 1,953 frames, respectively), intermittent motion (6 videos with 1,854 and 1,854 frames), out of sensor range (5 videos with 4,610 and 1,301 frames, respectively), shadows (5 videos with 1,301 and 1,029 frames), and bootstrapping (5 videos with 1,029 and 1,029 frames). The SBM-RGBD dataset is available for the research community at [49].

4.1.5   ADE20K (ADE20K-Scene Parsing) Dataset

ADE20K [41] is a dataset specifically designed for scene parsing, but it includes object bounding box annotations. It consists of 20,210 images with pixel-level annotations for 150 object categories, including a variety of indoor objects. The ADE20K dataset is available for the research community at [50].

4.1.6   RGB-D Scene Understanding (Sun RGB-D) Dataset

The Sun RGB-D dataset [42] focuses on indoor scenes and contains RGB-D images (color images with depth information) along with semantic and instance-level annotations for 37 object categories. It includes over 10,000 images captured in various indoor environments. The Sun RGB-D dataset is available for the research community at [51].

4.1.7   NYU Depth V2 Dataset

NYU Depth V2 [44] is another dataset that provides RGB-D images and dense annotations for various indoor scenes. It contains 1,449 RGB-D images with 894 labeled instances across 40 object categories. Some samples of the NYU Depth V2 dataset are displayed in Figure 4.1. The NYU Depth V2 dataset is available for the research community at [52].

FIGURE 4.1 Sample images of NYU depth V2 dataset [44]. Used by permission.

4.1.8 STANFORD 2D-3D-SEMANTICS DATASET

Stanford 2D-3D-Semantics dataset [45] includes RGB images with 2D and 3D annotations for object instances in indoor scenes. It consists of 450 different scenes with more than 30 object categories. The Stanford 2D-3D-Semantics dataset is available for the research community at [53].

4.2 OUTDOOR DATASETS AND THEIR KEY CHARACTERISTICS

The progress of designing object detection datasets with predefined real-world challenges in an outdoor environment has been ongoing in the research community. Large datasets have been designed in outdoor settings during the last few decades to accommodate the rising need for developing and accessing new object identification models. The most popular outdoor datasets are described below.

4.2.1 CD.NET 2014 (CHANGE DETECTION. NET) DATASET

CD.Net 2012 [1] is a pioneering video dataset consisting of 53 videos nearing 159,279 frames (each video has from 1,000 to 1,800 frames) depicting indoor and outdoor scenes of cars, boats, and pedestrians. They are grouped into six categories, i.e., baseline, camera jitter, dynamic background, shadows, intermittent motion of object, and thermal. The spatial resolution of the videos varies from 320×240 to 720×480. Also, to validate the complex algorithms, the ground truth images of 97,334 frames are provided along with the dataset in the form of object masks (i.e., pixel-based labeling). Some sample images of the Fish4Knowledge dataset are displayed in Figure 4.2. The CD.Net 2014 dataset is available for the research community at [54].

4.2.2 BMC 2012 (BACKGROUND MODELS CHALLENGE 2012) DATASET

BMC 2012 dataset [2] is mainly designed for complex backgrounds of crowded scenes including shadows and illumination/climatic conditions. It comprises 20 videos, some of which are synthetic, and each has a 640×480 resolution. Although only a small subset of the images have been labeled—out of 29,980 total frames, pixel-based manual labeling of moving objects in 15,980 frames are supplied with the dataset—ground truth is also accessible for both actual and synthetic images. The BMC 2012 dataset is available for the research community at [55].

FIGURE 4.2   Sample images of CD.Net 2014 datasets [1]. Used by permission.

4.2.3   PETS 2009 (PERFORMANCE EVALUATION OF TRACKING AND SURVEILLANCE 2009) DATASET

PETS 2009 [3] is a well-known dataset designed with the motivation for evaluating the visual tracking and surveillance algorithms. The dataset consists of eight videos with shadow and illumination variations of crowded and occluded objects in an outdoor environment. The resolution of the dataset varies from 720×576 to 768×576. In order to assess the effectiveness of tracking algorithms, the dataset has been manually labeled as bounding boxes. The PETS 2009 dataset is available for the research community at [56].

4.2.4   I2R (INSTITUTE FOR INFOCOM RESEARCH) DATASET

I2R dataset [4] contains nine videos of vehicles and pedestrians, each of which represents major challenges of motion segmentation like dynamic background, bootstrapping, and illumination change. The entire dataset has a total of 37,958 frames (each video has 1,054 to 3,658 frames), and ground truth of moving objects in each frame is provided in the form of object masks.

4.2.5   ETISEO (EVALUATION OF THE TREATMENT AND INTERPRETATION OF VIDEO SEQUENCES) DATASET

ETISEO dataset [5] is mainly designed to foster performance improvement of video surveillance algorithms. The dataset contains 85 videos covering predefined scenarios of visible and IR clips with graduate difficulties like illumination variations, crowded, occlusion, and shadow. The ground truth consists of high-level information like bounding box, class of an object and event type of 153,243 frames, and is more appropriate for tracking and classification than object detection. The ETISEO dataset is available for the research community at [57].

4.2.6   DAVIS (DENSELY ANNOTATED VIDEO SEGMENTATION) DATASET

The DAVIS [9] dataset was created especially for the task of segmenting video objects. The dataset consists of 50 sequences in total, 3,455 annotated frames, all of which were recorded at 24 frames per second. Pixel-oriented hand segmentation was provided in the form of a binary mask. Instances like quick motion, occlusion, and crowded backgrounds that frequently provide challenges for video segmentation algorithms are represented by the collection of video characteristics. The DAVIS dataset is available for the research community at [58].

4.2.7 WALLFLOWER DATASET

The Wallflower [10] dataset contains realistic background scenes with dynamic events including moving objects, the time of day, light switches, waving trees, camouflage, and foreground aperture. The dataset contains seven indoor and outdoor video sequences at a spatial resolution of 160 × 120. The dataset contains a total of 9,917 frames and varies from 293 to 3,054 frames per scene. For each video sequence, only one frame is manually annotated based on pixel labeling. The Wallflower dataset is available for the research community at [59].

4.2.8 ViSal (VIDEO-BASED SALIENCY) DATASET

The ViSal [11] dataset contains 17 indoor and outdoor videos of animals, vehicles, humans, etc. Each video contains 3 to 100 frames, and out of 803 total frames, salient objects of 193 frames are annotated in the form of object masks. Major challenges of this dataset include cluttered background, camera motion, complex color distributions, and rapid change in object topology. The ViSal dataset is available for the research community at [11].

4.2.9 SEGTRACK (SEGMENTS TRACK) DATASET

One of the widely used datasets for assessing the segmentation accuracy in video tracking is SegTrack [13]. It contains six outdoor videos depicting humans and animals with predefined challenges such as occlusion, change in shapes, and interframe motion. In total there are 244 frames, and the spatial resolution varies from 320 × 240 to 414 × 352. Only one foreground object is annotated per frame. The SegTrack dataset is available for the research community at [60].

4.2.10 SEGTRACK V2 (SEGMENTS TRACK VERSION 2) DATASET

SegTrack V2 [15] is an enhanced version of the SegTrack dataset [13] in which eight new videos are included to cover some additional representative challenges of segmentation algorithms such as motion blur, appearance change, complex deformation, slow motion, and multiple objects. The resolution of the image sequences varies from 259 × 327 to 640 × 360. The dataset contains a total of 11 new objects and 732 pixel-level annotated frames, which amounts to a grand total of 14 sequences with 24 objects over 976 annotated frames. The SegTrack V2 dataset is available for the research community at [61].

4.2.11 FBMS (FREIBURG-BERKLEY MOTION SEGMENTATION) DATASET

The FBMS dataset [16] is designed for motion segmentation with typical challenges like multiple objects, little occlusion, non-translation motions, and illumination variations. It was first proposed with 26 videos and further was extended with another 33 videos. The resolution of the dataset is 960 × 540. In total, the dataset contains 59 videos with 720 pixel label ground truth annotated frames. Every 20th frame includes the ground truth annotation, which is consistent across time. The FBMS dataset is available for the research community at [62].

4.2.12   VOS (Video-based Salient Object Detection) Dataset

The VOS dataset [18] consists of two categories, VOS-E and VOS-N, based on the complexity of the dataset. The first subset (i.e., VOS-E) contains 97 videos including foreground objects usually captured with many slow-motion cameras. Each video has 83 to 962 frames (i.e., 49,206 frames in total), and the spatial resolution of the video sequences is 800 × 800. The second subset (i.e., VOS-N) contains 103 videos including highly complex foreground objects with dynamic or cluttered background regions. Each video has 710 to 2,249 frames (i.e., 66,897 frames in total). In particular, the VOS dataset contains 200 indoor and outdoor videos that include 64 minutes in total, i.e., 116,103 frames at 30fps. In pixel label ground truth generation procedure, only 1 key frame out of every 15 frames is uniformly sampled and manually annotated, for a total of 7,467 key frames in the dataset.

4.2.13   Fish4Knowledge Dataset

A well-known benchmark dataset for background modelling that contains 14 films divided into 7 separate challenging problems is Fish4Knowledge [19]. This dataset's typical challenges include hazy, complicated backgrounds, congested areas, variations in luminance, foreground objects that are camouflaged, and a mix of all of the above. Image sequences have a spatial resolution of 320 × 240. About 250 sequences were annotated for each video and presented as binary masks. Some sample images of the Fish4Knowledge dataset are displayed in Figure 4.3.

4.2.14   ViSOR (Video Surveillance Online Repository) Dataset

The ViSOR dataset [20] is a web archive for collection and annotation of surveillance videos. The archive presently has more than 623 indoor and outdoor videos (often under 10 seconds each) with a spatial resolution of 704 × 576 that are all bounding

FIGURE 4.3   Sample images of Fish4Knowledge dataset [63]. Used by permission.

box annotations. These videos frequently feature staged human interactions and activities in situations using shadow, occlusion, and changing lighting. The ViSOR dataset is available for the research community at [64].

4.2.15   BEHAVE Dataset

BEHAVE [21] video dataset contains four video clips totaling 76,800 individual frames. The dataset has 640 × 480 spatial resolution with video images captured at 25 frames per second using a professional camcorder set on a tripod. These videos include challenges of object detection like groups interacting, intermittent object motion, multiple objects, and occlusion. There are 83,545 bounding boxes in total for the 125 instances of persons that interacted. Each interacting person has a bounding box. Some sample images of the BEHAVE dataset are displayed in Figure 4.4.

4.2.16   MarDCT (Maritime Detection, Classification and Tracking) Dataset

The MarDCT dataset [22] contains 27 videos that represent one of the most challenging scenarios for background subtraction due to the complexity of the monitored scene, i.e., waves on the water surface, boat wakes, and haze. The spatial resolution varies from 352 × 288 to 1676 × 576 pixels. Due to the complexity of the dataset, manual annotation of moving objects on the created dataset is not provided. The MarDCT dataset is available for the research community at [65].

4.2.17   LASIESTA (Labeled and Annotated Sequences for Integral Evaluation of Segmentation Algorithms) Dataset

The segmentation and detection dataset LASIESTA [25] consists of 48 actual indoor and outdoor sequences arranged into categories, each of which addresses a particular difficulty in moving object identification algorithms such as camouflage, occlusions, illumination changes, bootstrapping, camera motion, camera jitter, and

FIGURE 4.4   Sample images of BEHAVE dataset [21]. Used by permission.

weather (sunshine; snow; rain; clouds). The resolution of the dataset is 352 × 288. The LASIESTA dataset is available for the research community at [66].

4.2.18 REMOTE SCENE IR Dataset

The REMOTE SCENE IR dataset [21] consists of 1,263 frames across 12 video sequences. Pixel-wise foreground was manually added to each frameEach video sequence's frames are provided in .bmp format and have a resolution of 480 × 320. These IR video sequences show a variety of background subtraction problems, such as a moving foreground and background, ghosts, camera jitter, camouflage, noise, and dynamic backgrounds.

4.2.19 CAMO-UOW Dataset

For the purpose of detecting camouflaged foregrounds (background removal), the CAMO-UOW dataset [28] is employed. It includes 10 high-definition videos that were shot in actual outdoor and indoor situations. In each film, one or two people enter the frame wearing attire that matches the background color. The resolution of the dataset varies from 1600 × 1200 to 1920 × 1080.

4.2.20 Grayscale-Thermal Foreground Detection (GTFD) Dataset

A comprehensive grayscale thermal video benchmark for moving object recognition is the GTFD dataset [30]. It is a collection of 25 videos totaling 1,067 frames that show both rigid and flexible objects. The videos were shot both indoors and outdoors to capture a variety of difficult situations. Seven significant problems are included in the dataset: thermal crossover, sporadic motion, inclement weather, low illumination, intense shadow, dynamic scene, and extreme motion.

4.2.21 Extended Tripura University Video Dataset (E-TUVD)

The E-TUVD dataset [33] is a pioneering ground truth annotated video dataset for moving object detection in degraded atmospheric/weather conditions (i.e., fog, haze, dust, rain, and poor illumination). Other than these weather-degraded conditions, E-TUVD also contains video clips of clear days where horizontal sunlight casts long shadows and gives subjects a warm glow with high-contrast scenes. The current dataset consists of 147 video sequences (approximately 793,800 frames) that were captured under various atmospheric/weather conditions. Each frame of the E-TUVD contains multiple types of moving objects; in addition, the scenes were captured mostly in urban areas, which are subjected to larger surface variations because of the presence of objects such as trees, houses, warehouses, office buildings, streets, and residents. All the features of E-TUVD reflect its significance in the domain of moving object detection and high-level vision tasks from outdoor scenes comprising various weather-degraded challenges of real-world scenarios. Some sample frames of the E-TUVD dataset are shown in Figure 4.5.

FIGURE 4.5 Sample images of E-TUVD dataset [33].

4.2.22 OSU-T (OSU THERMAL PEDESTRIAN) DATASET

The OSU-T dataset [34] is a part of OTCBVS benchmark dataset collection used to assess cutting-edge computer vision algorithms. It exclusively discusses the detection of people in outdoor settings when it is overcast, rainy, or hazy. Only 284 frames from 10 daytime video sequences were recorded in this database. Bounding boxes are used to annotate the people who are present in a frame. The OSU-T dataset is available for the research community at [67].

4.2.23 BU-TIV (THERMAL INFRARED VIDEO) DATASET

The BU-TIV dataset [35] is the only dataset that addresses several visual analysis tasks such as single- or multi-view object tracking, counting, group motion, etc. There are 16 video clips totaling 63,782 frames in it, and they feature a runner, a car, a bike, a motorbike, and a bat. Annotation using bounding boxes has been successful. The BU-TIV dataset is available for the research community at [68].

4.2.24 ASL-TID DATASET

The ASL-TID dataset [37] is intended for object detection rather than object tracking with significant challenges such as moving cameras, crowded backgrounds, and occlusion. It has 4,381 frames divided into eight sequences concerning people, cats, and horses that use bounding box–based ground truth that has been manually annotated. The ASL-TID dataset is available for the research community at [69].

4.2.25 TRIPURA UNIVERSITY VIDEO DATASET AT NIGHTTIME (TU-VDN)

The TU-VDN dataset [38] provides a realistic diverse set of outdoor night videos. The dataset consists of 60 video sequences that were captured under various atmospheric conditions such as dusty, rainy, and foggy with key challenges like flat cluttered background and dynamic background under static camera. Each video clip is 2 minutes in duration and was recorded with an FLIR camera. In contrast, for a motion background, the video is captured by mounting the camera on a moving vehicle (20~30 km/h) such that the objects, camera, and background are moving simultaneously. Samples of the TU-VDN dataset are shown in Figure 4.6.

FIGURE 4.6   Sample images of TU-VDN dataset [38].

4.2.26   COCO (COMMON OBJECTS IN CONTEXT) DATASET

While not exclusively focused on indoor scenes, COCO [39] is one of the most widely used datasets for object detection. It contains a large collection of images with bounding box annotations for 80 object categories, including many common indoor objects. The COCO dataset is available for the research community at [70].

4.2.27   PASCAL VOC (VISUAL OBJECT CLASSES) DATASET

Similar to COCO, PASCAL VOC [40] is a popular dataset for object detection. It includes a subset of images with bounding box annotations for 20 object categories, some of which are relevant to indoor scenes. The PASCAL VOC dataset is available for the research community at [71].

4.2.28   KITTI DATASET

The KITTI dataset [46] focuses on object detection and tracking for autonomous driving. It includes various challenges such as detecting cars, pedestrians, and cyclists. KITTI provides high-resolution images and accurate annotations for these objects, making it a valuable resource for researchers in the field of autonomous vehicles. Some samples of the KITTI dataset are shown in Figure 4.7.

FIGURE 4.7   Sample images of Stanford 2D-3D-Semantics dataset [46]. Used by permission.

REFERENCES

1. Goyette, N., Jodoin, P. M., Porikli, F., Konrad, J., & Ishwar, P. (2014). A novel video dataset for change detection benchmarking. *IEEE Transactions on Image Processing*, 23(11), 4663–4679.
2. Vacavant, A., Chateau, T., Wilhelm, A., & Lequievre, L. (2013). A benchmark dataset for outdoor foreground/background extraction. In *Computer Vision-ACCV 2012 Workshops: ACCV 2012 International Workshops*, Daejeon, Korea, November 5–6, 2012, Revised Selected Papers, Part I 11 (pp. 291–300). Springer Berlin Heidelberg.
3. Ferryman, J., & Shahrokni, A. (2009, December). Pets2009: Dataset and challenge. In *2009 Twelfth IEEE International Workshop on Performance Evaluation of Tracking and Surveillance* (pp. 1–6). IEEE.
4. Li, L., Huang, W., Gu, I. Y. H., & Tian, Q. (2004). Statistical modeling of complex backgrounds for foreground object detection. *IEEE Transactions on Image Processing*, 13(11), 1459–1472.
5. Nghiem, A. T., Bremond, F., Thonnat, M., & Valentin, V. (2007, September). ETISEO, performance evaluation for video surveillance systems. In *2007 IEEE Conference on Advanced Video and Signal based Surveillance* (pp. 476–481). IEEE.
6. Chaquet, J. M., Carmona, E. J., & Fernández-Caballero, A. (2013). A survey of video datasets for human action and activity recognition. *Computer Vision and Image Understanding*, 117(6), 633–659.
7. VSSN 2006 Test Images Sequences. [Online]. Available: http://mmc36.informatik.uni-augsburg.de/VSSN06_OSAC/
8. Evan Dong University of Missouri–logo University of Missouri–Columbia. [Online]. Available: http://vigir.missouri.edu/~evan/BG.htm
9. Perazzi, F., Pont-Tuset, J., McWilliams, B., Van Gool, L., Gross, M., & Sorkine-Hornung, A. (2016). A benchmark dataset and evaluation methodology for video object segmentation. In *Proceedings of the IEEE Conference on Computer Vision and Pattern Recognition* (pp. 724–732).
10. Toyama, K., Krumm, J., Brumitt, B., & Meyers, B. (1999, September). Wallflower: Principles and practice of background maintenance. In *Proceedings of the Seventh IEEE International Conference on Computer Vision* (Vol. 1, pp. 255–261). IEEE.
11. CAVIAR Test Case Scenarios [Online]. Available: http://groups.inf.ed.ac.uk/vision/CAVIAR/CAVIARDATA1/
12. Wang, W., Shen, J., & Shao, L. (2015). Consistent video saliency using local gradient flow optimization and global refinement. *IEEE Transactions on Image Processing*, 24(11), 4185–4196.
13. Tsai, D., Flagg, M., Nakazawa, A., & Rehg, J. M. (2012). Motion coherent tracking using multi-label MRF optimization. *International Journal of Computer Vision*, 100, 190–202.
14. Motion Coherent Tracking with Multi-label MRF optimization. [Online]. Available: https://www.cc.gatech.edu/cpl/projects/SegTrack/
15. Li, F., Kim, T., Humayun, A., Tsai, D., & Rehg, J. M. (2013). Video segmentation by tracking many figure-ground segments. In *Proceedings of the IEEE International Conference on Computer Vision* (pp. 2192–2199).
16. Ochs, P., Malik, J., & Brox, T. (2013). Segmentation of moving objects by long term video analysis. *IEEE Transactions on Pattern Analysis and Machine Intelligence*, 36(6), 1187–1200.
17. Freiburg-Berkeley Motion Segmentation Dataset (FBMS-59). [Online]. Available: https://lmb.informatik.uni-freiburg.de/resources/datasets/moseg.en.html

18. Li, J., Xia, C., & Chen, X. (2017). A benchmark dataset and saliency-guided stacked autoencoders for video-based salient object detection. *IEEE Transactions on Image Processing*, 27(1), 349–364.
19. Boom, B. J., He, J., Palazzo, S., Huang, P. X., Beyan, C., Chou, H. M., ... Fisher, R. B. (2014). A research tool for long-term and continuous analysis of fish assemblage in coral-reefs using underwater camera footage. *Ecological Informatics*, *23*, 83–97.
20. Vezzani, R., & Cucchiara, R. (2010). Video surveillance online repository (visor): An integrated framework. *Multimedia Tools and Applications*, 50, 359–380.
21. Blunsden, S., & Fisher, R. B. (2010). The BEHAVE video dataset: Ground truthed video for multi-person behavior classification. *Annals of the BMVA*, 4(1–12), 21.
22. Bloisi, D., Iocchi, L., Fiorini, M., & Graziano, G. (2012, July). Camera based target recognition for maritime awareness. In *2012 15th International Conference on Information Fusion* (pp. 1982–1987). IEEE.
23. Branch, H. O. S. D. (2006, June). Imagery library for intelligent detection systems (i-lids). In *2006 IET Conference on Crime and Security* (pp. 445–448). IET.
24. Kim, J., Kang, B., Wang, H., & Kim, D. (2012, September). Abnormal object detection using feedforward model and sequential filters. In *2012 IEEE Ninth International Conference on Advanced Video and Signal-Based Surveillance* (pp. 70–75). IEEE.
25. Cuevas, C., Yáñez, E. M., & García, N. (2016). Labeled dataset for integral evaluation of moving object detection algorithms: LASIESTA. *Computer Vision and Image Understanding*, 152, 103–117.
26. Fadl, S., Han, Q., & Li, Q. (2019). Surveillance video authentication using universal image quality index of temporal average. In *Digital Forensics and Watermarking: 17th International Workshop, IWDW 2018*, Jeju Island, Korea, October 22–24, 2018, Proceedings 17 (pp. 337–350). Springer International Publishing.
27. Yao, G., Lei, T., Zhong, J., Jiang, P., & Jia, W. (2017). Comparative evaluation of background subtraction algorithms in remote scene videos captured by MWIR sensors. *Sensors*, 17(9), 1945.
28. Li, S., Florencio, D., Zhao, Y., Cook, C., & Li, W. (2017, September). Foreground detection in camouflaged scenes. In *2017 IEEE International Conference on Image Processing (ICIP)* (pp. 4247–4251). IEEE.
29. Ha, S. V. U., Chung, N. M., Phan, H. N., & Nguyen, C. T. (2020). TensorMoG: A tensor-driven Gaussian mixture model with dynamic scene adaptation for background modelling. *Sensors*, 20(23), 6973.
30. Li, C., Wang, X., Zhang, L., Tang, J., Wu, H., & Lin, L. (2016). Weighted low-rank decomposition for robust grayscale-thermal foreground detection. *IEEE Transactions on Circuits and Systems for Video Technology*, 27(4), 725–738.
31. Kalsotra, R., & Arora, S. (2019). A comprehensive survey of video datasets for background subtraction. *IEEE Access*, 7, 59143–59171.
32. Camplani, M., Maddalena, L., Moyá Alcover, G., Petrosino, A., & Salgado, L. (2017). A benchmarking framework for background subtraction in RGBD videos. In *New Trends in Image Analysis and Processing–ICIAP 2017: ICIAP International Workshops, WBICV, SSPandBE, 3AS, RGBD, NIVAR, IWBAAS, and MADiMa 2017*, Catania, Italy, September 11–15, 2017, Revised Selected Papers 19 (pp. 219–229). Springer International Publishing.
33. Roy, S. D., & Bhowmik, M. K. (2020). Annotation and benchmarking of a video dataset under degraded complex atmospheric conditions and its visibility enhancement analysis for moving object detection. *IEEE Transactions on Circuits and Systems for Video Technology*, 31(3), 844–862.
34. Davis, J., & Keck, M. (2005). A two-stage approach to person detection in thermal imagery. In *Proceeding of Workshop on Applications of Computer Vision (WACV)*.

35. Wu, Z., Fuller, N., Theriault, D., & Betke, M. (2014). A thermal infrared video benchmark for visual analysis. In *Proceedings of the IEEE Conference on Computer Vision and Pattern Recognition Workshops* (pp. 201–208).

36. Rizvi, S. Z., Farooq, M. U., & Raza, R. H. (2021, December). Performance comparison of deep residual networks-based super resolution algorithms using thermal images: case study of crowd counting. In *Conference on Multimedia, Interaction, Design and Innovation* (pp. 75–87). Cham: Springer International Publishing.

37. Portmann, J., Lynen, S., Chli, M., & Siegwart, R. (2014, May). People detection and tracking from aerial thermal views. In *2014 IEEE International Conference on Robotics and Automation (ICRA)* (pp. 1794–1800). IEEE.

38. Singha, A., & Bhowmik, M. K. (2019, September). TU-VDN: Tripura University video dataset at night time in degraded atmospheric outdoor conditions for moving object detection. In *2019 IEEE International Conference on Image Processing (ICIP)* (pp. 2936–2940). IEEE.

39. Lin, T. Y., Maire, M., Belongie, S., Hays, J., Perona, P., Ramanan, D., ... Zitnick, C. L. (2014). Microsoft coco: Common objects in context. In *Computer Vision–ECCV 2014: 13th European Conference*, Zurich, Switzerland, September 6-12, 2014, Proceedings, Part V 13 (pp. 740–755). Springer International Publishing.

40. Shetty, S. (2016). Application of convolutional neural network for image classification on Pascal VOC challenge 2012 dataset. arXiv preprint arXiv:1607.03785.

41. Zhou, B., Zhao, H., Puig, X., Fidler, S., Barriuso, A., & Torralba, A. (2017). Scene parsing through ade20k dataset. In *Proceedings of the IEEE Conference on Computer Vision and Pattern Recognition* (pp. 633–641).

42. Song, S., Lichtenberg, S. P., & Xiao, J. (2015). Sun RGB-D: A RGB-D scene understanding benchmark suite. In *Proceedings of the IEEE Conference on Computer Vision and Pattern Recognition* (pp. 567–576).

43. Huang, S., Qi, S., Zhu, Y., Xiao, Y., Xu, Y., & Zhu, S. C. (2018). Holistic 3d scene parsing and reconstruction from a single rgb image. In *Proceedings of the European Conference on Computer Vision (ECCV)* (pp. 187–203).

44. Ma, F., & Karaman, S. (2018, May). Sparse-to-dense: Depth prediction from sparse depth samples and a single image. In *2018 IEEE International Conference on Robotics and Automation (ICRA)* (pp. 4796–4803). IEEE.

45. Dourado, A., Kim, H., de Campos, T. E., & Hilton, A. (2020, February). Semantic Scene Completion from a Single 360-Degree Image and Depth Map. In *VISIGRAPP (5: VISAPP)* (pp. 36–46).

46. Geiger, A., Lenz, P., Stiller, C., & Urtasun, R. (2013). Vision meets robotics: The KITTI dataset. *The International Journal of Robotics Research*, 32(11), 1231–1237.

47. CAVIAR. [Online]. Available: https://homepages.inf.ed.ac.uk/rbf/CAVIARDATA1/

48. Imagery Library for Intelligent Detection Systems. [Online]. Available: https://www.gov.uk/guidance/imagery-library-for-intelligent-detection-systems#i-lids-datasets

49. SBM-RGBD dataset. [Online]. Available: https://rgbd2017.na.icar.cnr.it/SBM-RGBD dataset.html

50. ADE20K. [Online]. Available: https://groups.csail.mit.edu/vision/datasets/ADE20K/

51. SUN RGB-D: A RGB-D Scene Understanding Benchmark Suite. [Online]. Available: https://rgbd.cs.princeton.edu/

52. NYU Depth Dataset V2. [Online]. Available: https://cs.nyu.edu/~silberman/datasets/nyu_depth_v2.html

53. Stanford 2D-3D-Semantics Dataset (2D-3D-S). [Online]. Available: http://buildingparser.stanford.edu/dataset.html

54. ChangeDetection.Net (CDNET). [Online]. Available: http://changedetection.net/

55. BMC. [Online]. Available: http://backgroundmodelschallenge.eu/

56. PETS 2009. [Online]. Available: http://www.cvg.rdg.ac.uk/PETS2009/a.html

57. ETISEO: Video understanding Evaluation. [Online]. Available: https://www-sop.inria.fr/orion/ETISEO/download.htm

58. DAVIS: Densely Annotated VIdeo Segmentation. [Online]. Available: https://davischallenge.org/

59. [Online]. Available: https://www.microsoft.com/en-us/download/details.aspx?id=54651

60. Motion Coherent Tracking with Multi-label MRF optimization. [Online]. Available: https://www.cc.gatech.edu/cpl/projects/SegTrack/

61. SegTrack v2 Dataset. [Online]. Available: https://web.engr.oregonstate.edu/~lif/SegTrack2/dataset.html

62. [Online]. Available: https://lmb.informatik.uni-freiburg.de/resources/datasets/

63. Fish4Knowledge Ground-Truth datasets. [Online]. Available: https://homepages.inf.ed.ac.uk/rbf/Fish4Knowledge/GROUNDTRUTH/

64. ViSOR: Video Surveillance Online Repository. [Online]. Available: https://aimagelab.ing.unimore.it/visor/

65. MarDCT: Maritime Detection, Classification and Tracking data set. [Online]. Available: http://www.diag.uniroma1.it/~labrococo/MAR/

66. LASIESTA (Labeled and Annotated Sequences for Integral Evaluation of SegmenTation Algorithms). [Online]. Available: http://www.gti.ssr.upm.es/data/LASIESTA

67. OTCBVS Benchmark Dataset Collection. [Online]. Available: https://vcipl-okstate.org/pbvs/bench/

68. BU-TIV (Thermal Infrared Video) Benchmark. [Online]. Available: http://csr.bu.edu/BU-TIV/BUTIV.html

69. ASL Datasets. [Online]. Available: https://projects.asl.ethz.ch/datasets/doku.php?id=ir:iricra2014

70. COCO: Common Objects in Context. [Online]. Available: https://cocodataset.org/#home

71. The PASCAL Visual Object Classes Homepage. [Online]. Available: http://host.robots.ox.ac.uk/pascal/VOC/

5 Artifacts Impact on Different Object Visualization

5.1 BACKGROUND OF ARTIFACTS

When visual information is captured, processed, and delivered to the final recipient, the displayed image may differ from the original. Any observable variations that are the direct product of a technological constraint at any point in the communication process are called artifacts. Based on their place of origin, image and video artifacts may be roughly divided into four categories. They must be processed through capture and display [1]. In the capturing phase, artifacts might include obvious interlaced scanning effects, aliasing (both temporal and spatial), or perspective distortion. Processing is done before delivery over the communication channel. This processing is necessary to adhere the restrictions like the medium's bandwidth restrictions and to offer insulation against medium noise. In the time of transmission through a medium, some data may be distorted or lost and may produce multiple data with reflection. The reason behind display artifacts may be due to low contrast range, poor ability to reproduce color, display device persistence, resolution limitations, and many more.

- When the radiance of the target object is reduced by absorption or obstruction.
- The intermediate layer added some radiance to the image sensor by scattering light or reflecting the light from the layer surface.

Here, Figure 5.1 represents the image construction with light incident relation between the target object and the camera lens. Here, occluders create a difference with the actual light reflection process for image formation, which is known as artifacts. In an outdoor environment, occluders can be aerosol particles that interfere with the smooth reflection of the light incident on the object's body. The multiplier effect of the present occluder depending on the layer depth was donated by 'a' as shown in Figure 5.1. When the depth of the occluder is high, the light gets scattered by the reflection of the occluder before reaching the camera lens. In some cases, the occluder absorbs a few portions of the light before reaching the camera sensor. Thus the created image is not containing accurate information about the object due to such scenarios.

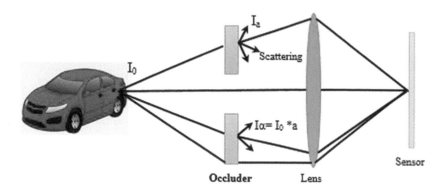

FIGURE 5.1   Image formation model due to occluder [2], where I_0 represents the initial incident ray, 'a' acts as the attenuation pattern of the intermediate layer, i.e., the fraction of light transmitted (0 = completely blocked), and I_α represent the scattering ray due to occluder with respect to attenuation 'a'.

5.2   ARTIFACTS WITH RESPECT TO OBJECT DETECTION IN DEGRADED VISION

Human visual systems can very easily detect and identify the present object in the captured image and video. Likewise, to develop a computer-aided system that can automatically detect and identify an object from image and video using the advancement of computer vision techniques needs meaningful information. Due to the appearance of different artifacts in the image and video sequence, developing a computer-aided system precisely is a great challenge as show in Figure 5.2. Most of the time artifacts cover up the meaningful information about the object which we are looking into which can lead to misidentification of the objects.

- **Degraded Vision**: When vision is not clear during capturing, the resulting image and video frames get affected by the degraded factors. Those degraded factors' reflections are imposed in captured images and video frames. These factors are dust, rain, fog, and light intensity, in outdoor scenarios. Dirty camera lenses also cause artifacts in the image and video frames.
- **Affects**: Due to the presence of dust, rain, and fog in the medium of capturing and lack of light can make the resultant images contain darkness, blurriness, etc. This can lead to meaningful information loss, cover-up, mixed information, etc.

5.2.1   ARTIFACTS IN CAPTURED IMAGES AND VIDEOS

Images and videos can be captured in outdoor as well as indoor environments with respect to the target task that differentiates the occurring artifacts, categorized as shown in Figure 5.3 with respect to the environment.

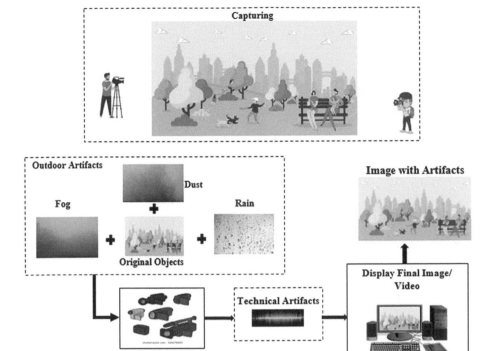

FIGURE 5.2   Image and video processing steps in degraded vision.

5.2.1.1   Indoor Environment

Object detection in indoor environments is affected by poor lighting, background clutter, etc. Due to poor visibility, target object maps in images and video frames do not contain all the original meaningful information, or additional unwanted information was mapped in it. Figure 5.4 represents some indoor artifacts that make object detection challenging, as in (a) we can see for poor lighting objects are not properly visible, and (b) shows background clutter, i.e., the texture of the background wall is similar to the texture of the object table. In an indoor environment, artifacts can be taken under control with more ease compared to the outdoor environment.

5.2.1.2   Outdoor Environment

The light transmitted from the target in outdoor settings is scattered in the atmosphere by the presence of aerosol and other associated particles. As a result, the collected images typically have poor contrast, pale color, and decreased visibility, which reduces the effectiveness of complex computer vision tasks [3]. Figure 5.5 presents some situations in an outdoor environment, which is a very complex phase for computer vision–related object detection tasks. Fog, rain, dust, and poor illumination, among other factors, are the main artifacts affecting automatic object detection in outdoor conditions in captured images and videos. With these aspects, image-related complex tasks become more complex in the case of video-related tasks, as the video

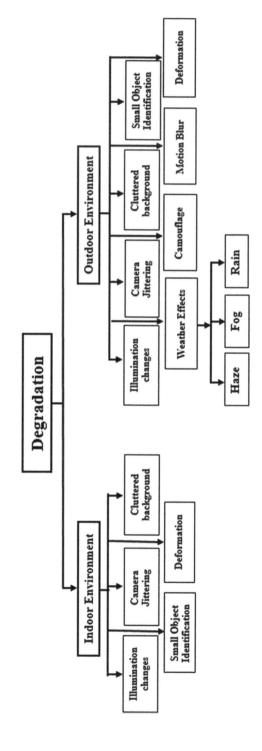

FIGURE 5.3   Taxonomy of artifacts in images and videos for object detection task.

FIGURE 5.4 Some indoor images in (a) poor lighting conditions; (b) background clutter conditions for detecting the objects of interests (i.e., water bottles).

FIGURE 5.5 Images of different views of outdoor scene with degraded conditions: (a) Foggy conditions; (b) Haze conditions; (c) Dust conditions; (d) Rain conditions; (e) Poor illumination conditions; (f) Clear day.

may contain frame sequences with detailed effects of the artifacts, and if the target object is in motion, then object detection tasks get more difficult due to motion blur.

5.3 IMPACT OF DIFFERENT ARTIFACTS IN OBJECTS VISUALIZATION

The visibility in the images is affected by the weather. The captured images suffer greatly when there is haze, rain, or fog. The image's feature is warped as a result, and the image-processing method cannot achieve the desired precision [4]. From Figure 5.5

it is observed that fog, haze, dust, rain, and poor illumination can affect the image clarity, which does not occur in the clear day condition.

5.3.1 POOR ILLUMINATION/LIGHTING

Presence of less lightning or too much lightning in the video and image acquired in the indoor environment causes poor lighting conditions as shown in Figure 5.4(a). It can map the objects of the targeted scenario in the image and video frames that have less meaningful information. In computer vision, object detection tasks are challenging due to a lack of original or covered information.

5.3.2 WEATHER CONDITION

Color information is the main contributor to the atmospheric or weather effect where fog, dust, rain, and other elements interfere with vision and rob images of their contrast. Due to scattering by air particles, these circumstances essentially change the fundamental properties of sunlight, including its intensity, color, polarization, and coherence [5]. Also, images taken in such conditions frequently contain undesired artifacts such as weak contrast, lack of color, or color cast. The elements for which the visual degradation occurs in terms of weather conditions are explained below:

- **Fog**: Fine liquid water droplets or ice crystals with diameters less than 100 μm suspended in the air or close to the earth's surface make up fog. It is admitted in theory that fog typically forms when dew point temperature is less than 2.5°C below air temperature and relative humidity exceeds the saturation threshold (i.e., close to 100%). The World Meteorological Organization (WMO) states that when fog is prevalent, water droplets in the air keep visibility below 1 kilometer (km).
- **Haze**: Visibility in a fog can range from the appearance of haze to virtually zero visibility, depending on the concentration of the water droplets in the air. Aerosol, a dispersed system of microscopic particles floating in gas, is the primary component of the meteorological phenomena known as haze. Unlike fog, in the case of haze, the particles are too small (usually having diameters between 0.1 and 1 μm) to be seen or felt individually, but they reduce visibility. The term "haze" is often used in meteorological literature to refer to visibility-reducing wet aerosols with relative humidity levels above 80% and ranges between 1 and 2 km.
- **Dust**: Dust is a meteorological phenomenon and the single largest component of the aerosols in Earth's atmosphere that arise when wind blows loose sand and dirt from a dry surface. In other instances, dust is a suspension of small solid particles with a size range from 0.2 to 10 μm. Thus, the strong scatter of sunlight by the dust particles and high concentrations of them reduces visibility. According to the WMO's definition, during the dust conditions caused by strong dust-raising winds, surface visibility is below 1 km.
- **Rain**: Rain is a collection of water drops that arc dispersed randomly, have a wide range of sizes and shapes, and are moving quickly. The visual appearance of rain is highly complex. Generally, raindrop sizes range from

0.1 mm to 3.5 mm, and depending on the size of the water drops, visibility is maintained between 1 and 2 km. Raindrops are relatively big and visible to the naked human eye, in contrast to the air particles that generate other meteorological conditions such as haze and fog. Each of these water drops refracts and reflects environmental illumination toward an observer and produces spatial and temporal intensity fluctuations in the captured scenes.

The physical characteristics of these atmospheric circumstances, such as the kinds and sizes of the particles involved and their concentrations in space, have been measured in great detail. Table 5.1 provides a summary of these atmospheric conditions' main features. Some of the sample images of outdoor scenes and their effect in degraded weather conditions are displayed in Figure 5.6.

TABLE 5.1

Brief Summary of Visibility Range, Associated Particles, Radius, and Concentration of Different Atmospheric/Weather Conditions

Atmospheric Condition (s)		Range of Visibility	Associated Particles	Radius (μm)	Density (cm^{-3})
Fog	(F)	Less than 1 km	Water droplet	1–10	100–10
Haze	(H)	Between 2 and 5 km	Aerosol	10^{-2}–1	10^3–10
Dust	(D)	Less than 1 km	Dust particles	0.2–10	100–10
Rain	(R)	Between 1 and 2 km	Water droplet	10^2–10^4	10^{-2}–10^{-5}

(a)   (b)   (c)

(d)   (e)

FIGURE 5.6 Images of visual degradation occurring due to weather-degraded elements. (a) Objects like people riding a bicycle are not clearly visible due to heavy rain; (b) Pedestrians are not visible due to haze; (c) Object (i.e., street sign board) is not visible due to snow [5]. (Used by permission); (d) Pedestrian is not clearly visible due to dust particles; (e) Building is not clearly visible due to fog.

(a)   (b)

FIGURE 5.7   Poor illumination: (a) Indoor scene; (b) Outdoor scene.

FIGURE 5.8   Camera jitter in the scenes due to which objects (surrounded by red bounding boxes) are not clearly visible [5]. Used by permission.

5.3.3 POOR ILLUMINATION

Outdoors, the lighting effect generally comes on by changes in sunlight intensity during the day [6]. In low-illumination environments, due to weak light or insufficient exposure, the dim image will have low brightness, low contrast, and noise as shown in Figure 5.7. Due to the uneven distribution of brightness, it is difficult to detect an object's features even with additional light sources. Existing literature on object detection in degraded vision research suggests working with image quality enhancement techniques before employing any traditional and deep-based techniques.

5.3.4 CAMERA JITTER

When synchronization signals are corrupted or electromagnetic interference affects video transmission, it results in video or image jitter. This could also happen as a result of a camera vibration or a photographer's shaky hand [7]. The efficiency of object recognition and tracking is significantly diminished by jitter, which produces vibration or distortion of the video and results in the position deviation of precalibrated ROIs. Jitter is the term used in optics to describe motion with a high temporal frequency in comparison to the integration/exposure time as shown in Figure 5.8. This could occur as a result of a camera shake or an assembly vibrating.

5.3.5 MOTION BLUR

When the subject or the camera moves during the exposure time, motion blur develops [8]. Motion blur is getting tougher to overlook as more and more pictures are

FIGURE 5.9 Motion blur effect in outdoor scene.

(a)   (b)

FIGURE 5.10 Object overlapping or occlusion. (a) A person is occluded by another person in indoor environment; (b) A car is partially occluded by biker in outdoor environment.

taken while moving [9]. Camera handling while capturing also causes motion blur, and in the case of video and moving objects, motion blur is mostly occurring artifacts as shown in Figure 5.9.

5.3.6 Object Overlapping or Occlusion

Occlusion occurs when one object hides some part of another object or combines with another as shown in Figure 5.10. One of the most frequent occurrences that reduce the amount of visual information that is available is occlusion [10]. Occlusion is one of the primary reasons for which many tasks in image processing and computer vision are still highly challenging to complete, since a great deal of visual information is hidden and cannot be recorded.

5.3.7 Camouflage Effect

The goal of camouflage is to blend the texture of a foreground object into the backdrop of an image [11]. A critical field in machine vision applications is identifying camouflaged items in images for military and civilian requirements. A camouflage image is one in which the objects in the foreground are mixed in with the background as shown in Figure 5.11.

FIGURE 5.11   Camouflage effect. The appearance of the animal (i.e., dog) gets mixed with the background.

5.3.8   SMALL OBJECT IDENTIFICATION

Small object identification faced a problem in the degraded image. Autonomous detection modules in computer vision applications failed in localizing and detecting small objects in degraded images. For example, small object identification such as satellite imagery creates problems for the identification of buildings, and small objects like a jar also face problems in identifying this type of object, as shown in Figure 5.12.

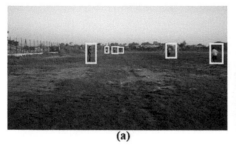

(a)   (b)

FIGURE 5.12   Small object identification: (a) pedestrians (surrounded by yellow bounding boxes) in playing ground appears smaller; (b) small object (i.e., ear pod surrounded by red bounding box) in the desk.

(a) **(b)**

FIGURE 5.13 Deformation of object in (a) indoor scene (the cloth gets deformed due to some uneven air blown up) and (b) outdoor scene (the bark of the tree gets deformed).

5.3.9 DEFORMATION

Deformation is the term used to describe a change in an object's size or shape [12] as shown in Figure 5.13 in the case of both indoor and outdoor environments. Displacements are the whole shift in an object's location at a certain point. It is built on the concept of encasing an object inside a cube or another hull, then having that object change when the hull deforms. This type of challenge occurs frequently during object detection.

5.3.10 BACKGROUND CLUTTER

In image processing, a large agglomeration of objects in a small space, otherwise known as clutter, makes it difficult to distinguish particular elements or characteristics [2]. In computer vision, automatic detection of the objects is very challenging with this artifact. In most of cases this artifact appears in indoor capturing as shown in Figure 5.14.

From the aforementioned artifacts it can be observed that poor lighting conditions, such as low light, shadows, or glare, can affect object detection. Insufficient lighting may result in reduced visibility and make it challenging for object detection algorithms to accurately detect objects. Similarly, harsh lighting conditions, such as direct sunlight from reflective surfaces, can create overexposed or washed-out images, affecting object detection performance. Consequently, rain and fog can significantly reduce visibility and make it difficult for object detection systems to detect and recognize objects accurately. Raindrops on the camera lens or fog in the scene can cause blurring or distortions, obscuring objects and reducing the effectiveness of object detection algorithms. Also, strong winds can cause objects to move or sway, which may lead motion blur in images. Rapid movement of objects can make it challenging to detect and track them accurately, especially for real-time object

(a)   (b)

FIGURE 5.14 (a) Background cluttered effect in indoor scene. (b) Background cluttered effect in outdoor scene.

detection systems. Moreover, adverse weather conditions, such as heavy rain, snowfall, or fog, can lead to occlusions, where objects are partially or completely hidden from view. Occlusions can make it difficult for object detection systems to perceive the entire object, leading to incomplete or inaccurate detection results. Considering a real-world example as shown in Figure 5.15, it can be noted that the detection of salient objects after applying certain visibility restoration suppresses all the false detections, and the shapes of the extracted moving objects appear clearer in the restored frames compared to the weather-degraded frames [13]. In Figure 5.15 (e1) it is much easier to note that the moving objects detected are two walking human beings, one scooter rider, and one rickshaw puller after visibility enhancement,

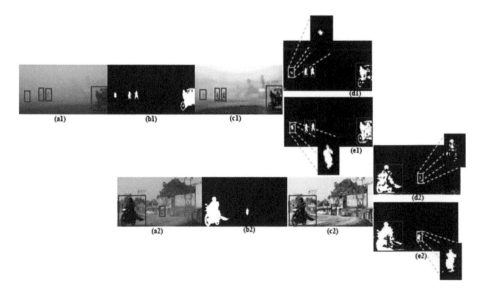

FIGURE 5.15 Impact of artifacts (such as weather conditions) in outdoor scenes for detection of moving/static objects.

compared to Figure 5.15 (d1) where the scooter rider (far distance object) is not well detected due to the presence of fog. Similarly, in Figure 5.15 (e2) it can be seen that the moving objects detected are two bike riders, whereas in the corresponding degraded frame due to dust in Figure 5.15 (d2) it is very hard to make such a determination. This emphasizes the benefit of visibility restoration as a basic tool for high-level target acquisition (such as recognition) for both the human visual system and computerized applications.

HOMEWORK PROBLEMS

1 Explain the concept of image degradation due to artifacts.
2 Explain the impact of artifacts on object visualization.
3 Explain how artifacts create problems during object detection.
4 How does disturbance due to artifacts occur during capturing?

REFERENCES

1. Punchihewa, A., & Bailey, D. G. (2002, December). Artefacts in image and video systems; classification and mitigation. In *Proceedings of Image and Vision Computing New Zealand* (pp. 197–202).
2. Shahbaz, A., & Jo, K. H. (2017, October). Optimal background modeling for cluttered scenes. In *IECON 2017-43rd Annual Conference of the IEEE Industrial Electronics Society* (pp. 5240–5244). IEEE.
3. Roy, S. D., Pal, T., & Bhowmik, M. K. (2021, September). Benchmarking of Natural Scene Image Dataset In Degraded Conditions For Visibility Enhancement. In *2021 IEEE International Conference on Image Processing (ICIP)* (pp. 1999–2003). IEEE.
4. Roy, S. D., & Bhowmik, M. K. (2020). Annotation and benchmarking of a video dataset under degraded complex atmospheric conditions and its visibility enhancement analysis for moving object detection. *IEEE Transactions on Circuits and Systems for Video Technology*, 31(3), 844–862.
5. Goyette, N., Jodoin, P. M., Porikli, F., Konrad, J., & Ishwar, P. (2014). A novel video dataset for change detection benchmarking. *IEEE Transactions on Image Processing*, 23(11), 4663–4679.
6. Roy, S. D., & Bhowmik, M. K. (2022). AWDMC-Net: Classification of Adversarial Weather Degraded Multiclass scenes using a Convolution Neural Network. *Computer Vision and Image Understanding*, 222, 103498.
7. Ben-Ezra, Moshe, Assaf Zomet, and Shree K. Nayar. (2004). Jitter camera: High resolution video from a low resolution detector. *Proceedings of the 2004 IEEE Computer Society Conference on Computer Vision and Pattern Recognition*, 2004. CVPR 2004. Vol. 2. IEEE.
8. Kurimo, E., Lepistö, L., Nikkanen, J., Grén, J., Kunttu, I., & Laaksonen, J. (2009). The effect of motion blur and signal noise on image quality in low light imaging. In *Image Analysis: 16th Scandinavian Conference, SCIA 2009*, Oslo, Norway, June 15–18, 2009. Proceedings 16 (pp. 81–90). Berlin, Heidelberg: Springer.
9. Dimou, A., Medentzidou, P., Garcia, F. A., & Daras, P. (2016, September). Multi-target detection in CCTV footage for tracking applications using deep learning techniques. In *2016 IEEE International Conference on Image Processing (ICIP)* (pp. 928–932). IEEE.
10. Chen, X., Li, Q., Zhao, D., & Zhao, Q. (2013). Occlusion cues for image scene layering. *Computer Vision and Image Understanding*, 117(1), 42–55.

11. Pulla Rao, C., Guruva Reddy, A., & Rama Rao, C. B. (2020). Camouflaged object detection for machine vision applications. *International Journal of Speech Technology*, 23, 327–335.
12. Chung, H. V., & Lee, I. K. (2005). Image-based deformation of objects in real scenes. In *Advances in Visual Computing: First International Symposium, ISVC 2005*, Lake Tahoe, NV, December 5–7, 2005. Proceedings 1 (pp. 159–166). Berlin, Heidelberg: Springer.
13. Roy, S. D., & Bhowmik, M. K. (2020). Annotation and benchmarking of a video dataset under degraded complex atmospheric conditions and its visibility enhancement analysis for moving object detection. *IEEE Transactions on Circuits and Systems for Video Technology*, 31(3), 844–862.

6 Visibility Enhancement of Images in Degraded Vision

6.1 FUNDAMENTAL OF VISIBILITY RESTORATION

Visibility restoration refers to the process of improving the visual quality of images or videos that have poor visibility due to degraded or bad atmospheric conditions such as fog, rain, haze, or snow (Figure 6.1). Visibility restoration aims to enhance the perceptual quality of the image or video, making it more visually appealing and easier to interpret. Visibility in the atmosphere is reduced by bad or degraded weather conditions. Images taken by the camera in unfavorable weather (e.g. rain, fog, snow, dust) conditions typically have low contrast and poor visibility [1]. Poor visibility reduces the effectiveness of computer vision algorithms for object tracking, object detection, navigation, and surveillance, as well as the quality of perceptual images [2]. To create reliable computer vision algorithms for images in degraded atmospheric conditions, it is crucial to make visibility restoration of such images [3]. For object detection and recognition applications, processing images taken under degraded atmospheric conditions requires image preprocessing for visibility improvement and restoration. For many image processing and computer vision applications, recovering images in poor weather conditions might be crucial [4, 5]. For example, the visibility of the vehicle's visual system should be improved in poor lighting or other adverse weather conditions in order to prevent accidents. It seems more satisfying to do visibility restoration and enhancement on the image preprocessing than to analyze poor visibility images for object detection and recognition tasks. Furthermore, visibility restoration is one of the most crucial and difficult image enhancement techniques used in image processing for many computer vision applications. The goal of visibility restoration is to increase an image's appearance and quality without losing any useful information, and to provide a more accurate representation of the image for computer vision tasks. The overall visibility restoration framework for poor visibility enhancement is shown in Figure 6.2. There are two types of weather conditions: (1) static weather conditions such as haze, fog, etc.; and (2) dynamic weather conditions such as snow, rain, hail, etc. In static weather, separate droplets are too small (1–10 μm) to be captured by a camera, and pixel intensity is caused by the combined effect of several droplets inside the pixel's solid angle (Figure 6.1(a)–(c)). As a result, volumetric scattering models like airtight, and attenuation [6] can be applied to effectively characterize the impacts of static weather. Conversely, dynamic weather droplets are larger (0.1–10 mm) and are

DOI: 10.1201/9781003432036-6

FIGURE 6.1 Sample images of different weather degradation conditions [3]: (a) Foggy conditions; (b) Haze conditions; (c) Dust conditions; (d) Rain conditions; (e) Poor illumination conditions; (f) Clear day.

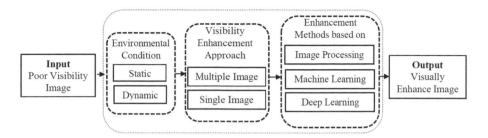

FIGURE 6.2 Overview of visibility restoration framework for poor visibility enhancement.

visible to a camera (Figure 6.1(d)) [7, 8]. Hence, visibility restoration models used for static weather conditions are not applicable for dynamic weather conditions. It was necessary to create stochastic models to capture the spatial and temporal effects of numerous particles moving rapidly (as in rain) and maybe with complex trajectories (as in snow) in order to restore visibility based on dynamic weather conditions.

Many visibility restoration or enhancing algorithms for images are developed for static and dynamic weather conditions. The main techniques for visibility restoration involve image-processing algorithms that seek to reduce or eliminate the impact of atmospheric degradation on the visual quality of images. These algorithms can be broadly divided into two groups (Figure 6.3): (1) multiple-image approaches for

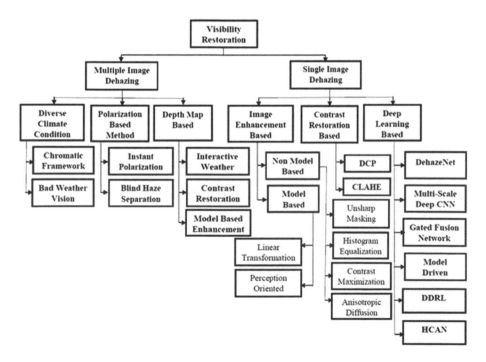

FIGURE 6.3 Types of visibility restoration methods.

visibility enhancement (discussed in Section 6.2) and (2) single-image approaches for visibility enhancement (discussed in Section 6.3).

6.2   BACKGROUND OF VISIBILITY RESTORATION

Poor visibility is caused by the attenuation of light as it travels through the atmosphere via absorption and scattering, which only allows a portion of the light to be reflected to reach the observer as shown in Figure 6.4 [9].

For poor visibility enhancement or restoration, Koschmieder law has been widely adopted during the past century. According to Koschmieder's law, visibility is inversely proportional to the extinction coefficient of air. Based on the Koschmieder's law, only a portion of the reflected light reaches the viewer due to the poor visibility in degraded scenes [10, 11]. By using the Koschmieder law researchers are trying to recover poorly visible images by analyzing the extinction coefficient of air. According to the Koschmieder's law, light intensity I for each pixel (x,y) that reaches the observer is described by two additive components (i.e., airlight $A(x,y)$ and direct attenuation $I_{att}(x,y)$) and is mathematically represented as [10–12]:

$$I(x, y) = I_{att}(x, y) + A(x, y) \tag{6.1}$$

The first component in Equation (6.1), i.e., direct attenuation $I_{att}(x,y)$, represents how the scene radiance is attenuated due to medium and is expressed as:

$$I_{att}(x, y) = I_0(x, y) e^{-\beta d(x,y)} \tag{6.2}$$

where $I_0(x, y)$ is the haze-free image, β is the attenuation coefficient due to scattering, and $d(x, y)$ is the distance between the surface and the viewer.

The second component in Equation (6.1), i.e., airlight $A(x,y)$, is the main cause of the color shifting in the scene and is expressed as:

$$A(x, y) = I_\infty \left(1 - e^{-\beta d(x,y)}\right) \tag{6.3}$$

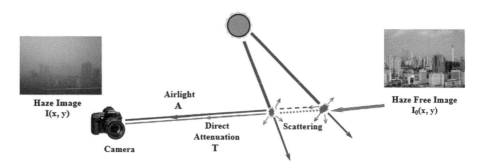

FIGURE 6.4   Diagrammatic representation of optical model applied to a natural scenario with haze.

where I_∞ is the global atmospheric constant. By using Equations (6.2) and (6.3) in Equation (6.1), Koschmieder's law may be mathematically represented as:

$$I(x,y) = I_0(x,y)e^{-\beta d(x,y)} + I_\infty\left(1 - e^{-\beta d(x,y)}\right) \tag{6.4}$$

The proposed task of enhancement technique is to recover the intrinsic appearance $I_0(x, y)$ from its poorly visible or low-contrast image representation $I(x, y)$ in degraded weather conditions.

6.3 MULTIPLE IMAGE APPROACHES FOR VISIBILITY ENHANCEMENT

To improve visibility using multiple image approaches, at least two images of a scene under different atmospheric conditions are required [2, 13–15]. These approaches typically work with known parameters while avoiding unknowns. In degraded atmospheric conditions, it is acceptable for fog, snow, haze, rain, etc. to form, which is a function of depth, in order to improve visibility in a foggy, hazy, or rainy image. In multiple image approaches for improving visibility a number of assumptions are made while estimating the depth information. Typically, two images are needed for depth estimation. It is possible to obtain the depth information using an air-light map, a transmission map, or a depth map [6.16]. A generic framework for visibility enhancement using multiple image approaches is shown in Figure 6.5. The depth information has been estimated by some visibility improvement techniques using scene properties. Shading functions and contrast-based cost functions are some examples of these scene properties [16]. Once depth is calculated, it is easier to enhance visibility of an image.

The image's contrast and color properties are significantly diminished in poor atmospheric circumstances. Images taken during a clear day have more contrast than those taken during a foggy, hazy, or rainy day. Therefore, a fog, haze, or rain removal method should improve the contrast of a foggy, hazy, or rainy image. The effort in recovering brightness and chrominance while keeping color accuracy makes it difficult to improve the visibility of an image. Overly enhanced visibility in foggy, hazy, or rainy images causes pixel values to become saturated. To avoid image saturation and maintain proper color accuracy, enhancement should be constrained by certain procedures. The different types of multiple image approaches for visibility enhancement are discussed next.

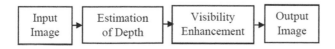

FIGURE 6.5 Framework for visibility enhancement.

6.3.1   DIVERSE CLIMATE CONDITION (DCC)-BASED METHODS

In DCC-based approaches, several images from various climatic situations are used [2, 13, 17]. In this method, two or more images are taken into consideration. These methods improve visibility but hold off until medium belongings change. For these methods, it is challenging to deliver good outcomes in unusual settings. Additionally, these techniques do not perform well in dynamic scenes [2]. The DCC-based method can be categorized into two types as follows.

6.3.1.1   Chromatic Framework–Based DCC

In the chromatic framework–based DCC method [2], the scene point direct transmission ratio (T_2/T_1) under two dissimilar atmospheric conditions is calculated by:

$$\frac{T_2}{T_1} = \frac{I_2}{I_1} e^{(B_2 - B_1)d} \tag{6.5}$$

where $(B_2 - B_1)d$ is the scale depth or depth map of a scene, d is the depth of a scene, I_1, I_2 are the brightness values, and B_1, B_2 are the scattering coefficients.

By applying logarithms in Equation (6.5), we get

$$\left(B_2 - B_1\right)d = \ln\left(\frac{I_2}{I_1}\right) - \ln\left(\frac{T_2}{T_1}\right) \tag{6.6}$$

Thus, we estimate the depth map $((B_2 - B_1)d)$ of a scene.

6.3.1.2   Bad Weather Vision–Based DCC

The bad weather vision–based DCC method [13] locates depth discontinuities from two bad weather images. Consider the pixel values E_1 and E_2 of the same scene point under two atmospheric conditions (B_1, I_1) and (B_2, I_2) where B and I are the scattering coefficient and brightness, respectively. The brightness of this scene point-shifts from the first atmospheric condition to the second as:

$$
\begin{aligned}
E_1 &= I_1 P e^{-B_1 d} + I_1 \left(1 - e^{-B_1 d}\right) \\
E_2 &= I_2 P e^{-B_2 d} + I_2 \left(1 - e^{-B_2 d}\right)
\end{aligned}
\tag{6.7}
$$

where d is the depth of scene and P is the normalized radiance. By eliminating P from Equation (6.7) we get

$$E_2 = \left[\frac{I_2}{I_1} e^{(B_2 - B_1)d}\right] E_1 + \left[I_2 \left(1 - e^{-(B_2 - B_1)d}\right)\right] \tag{6.8}$$

We may get the scaled depth $((B_2 - B_1)d)$ of each scene point by substituting the values of I_1 and I_2 in Equation (6.8):

$$\left(B_2 - B_1\right)d = -\ln\frac{I_2 - E_2}{I_1 - E_1} - \ln\frac{I_1}{I_2} \tag{6.9}$$

Thus, using two images captured in various weather circumstances we estimated the depth map $((B_2 - B_1)d)$ of a scene.

6.3.2 POLARIZATION-BASED METHODS

These techniques reverse the degradation process in order to restore the true image using polarization filters [14, 18, 19]. Except under specific circumstances, polarization filters could not be used to clear haze on their own. By taking into account the polarization effects of atmospheric scattering, the image generation process is examined. The technique can be applied by using a polarizer to take two input images with various orientations. Using this technique, scene contrast and color correction are significantly enhanced [18]. The blind-haze separation-based polarization method [19] is blindly recovering the parameter needed for air-light separation. For instant polarization method, after air-light $\bar{A}$ estimation [18], the attenuation of image $\left(\widehat{e^{-\beta z}}\right)$ is calculated by Equation (6.10) to obtain a dehazed image:

$$\widehat{e^{-\beta z}} = 1 - \frac{\bar{A}}{A_\infty} \tag{6.10}$$

where A_∞ is the air-light radiance and $\bar{A}$ is the air-light. This equation estimates the scene radiance of the image, and as a result, it yields a dehazed image using $\bar{A}$.

6.3.3 DEPTH AND TRANSMISSION MAP-BASED METHODS

These techniques make use of the depth information and image degradation process for dehazing and relighting images [13, 20–22]. These methods rely on 3D geometrical scene models that are provided by a few databases. After the image and the model have been added to the framework, a bunch of information becomes easily accessible to the framework. This collection of data consists of dehazing, relighting, and overlaying with geographic information [13]. Let I_n and I_r be the regular shades of two sky arches. Then the shading state exchange coefficient (Y_g) is (I_n/I_r). The resultant image is calculated by using color temperament coefficient (Y) as:

$$Y = Y_g.Y_s.\left(Y_a + Y_d.\left(n.I\right)\right) \tag{6.11}$$

where Y_s, Y_a, and Y_d are the shadow coefficient, ambient coefficient, and diffusion coefficient, respectively. I and n are the sun direction and point normal, respectively. Dehazed or restored image is obtained by multiplying input image by Y.

6.4 SINGLE-IMAGE APPROACHES FOR VISIBILITY ENHANCEMENT

Single-image approaches require only a single image as input [10]. These techniques rely on recovering images using some statistical assumptions and prior knowledge. Nowadays, single-image approaches for visibility enhancement are becoming more interesting for researchers. The most-used single-image approaches for visibility enhancement are described below.

6.4.1 IMAGE ENHANCEMENT–BASED MODEL

Different image restoration methods are used to improve the contrast of an image for visibility enhancement. Contrast-based image enhancement can be categorized as non-model-based and model-based approaches.

6.4.1.1 Non-Model-Based Visibility Restoration

Non-model-based techniques are used without any additional data collection or prior knowledge of the image. Most commonly used methods for contrast enhancement are:

- **Unsharp Masking**: The fundamental idea behind this approach is to emphasize boundaries. This model has the ability to recognize boundaries and modify the brightness level on each side of an edge. This imitates an overshoot and undershoot of the brightness curve of the edge pixels, respectively. High-frequency components that would improve the image's sharpness are amplified by an unsharp mask.
- **Histogram Equalization**: Histogram equalization (HE) [23] achieves a more improved resultant image with a visibility-prominent local contrast by regulating the intensities of the pixels. HE makes distinct adjustments to the image's foreground and background values before fusing them into a new frame.
- **Contrast Maximization**: The contrast maximization [10] depends on two basic interpretations. First, the smoothness of air-light variation should rely on the object's distance from the viewers or camera. Second, the contrast of visible images is high as compared to degraded images. Any kind of geographic information about the images is not necessary for this method to work. Due to uncertain halo sections apparent in images, scene depth continuities are unknown.
- **Anisotropic Diffusion**: Anisotropic diffusion (AD) [25] is used to remove fog or haze without affecting other sections of images. AD achieves intra-zone leveling, and edges remain constant for quite a while [24]. When air-light factor A is estimated, color component $I_0(x, y)$ of the output image can be restored as:

$$I_0\left(x, y, z\right) = \frac{I\left(x, y, z\right) - A\left(x, y\right)}{1 - \dfrac{\left(A\left(s, y\right)\right)}{I_\infty\left(z\right)}} \qquad (6.12)$$

where $A(x,y)$ denotes the air-light and $I(x,y,z)$ denotes normalized foggy or hazy image with color component, $I_0(x,y,z)$ is the final restored image, whereas $z \in (r, g, b)$.

6.4.1.2   Model-Based Visibility Enhancement

These methods estimate the pattern of vision deprivation using physical degradation models. They require additional data and prior knowledge of the imaging atmosphere, unlike non-model-based methods. These types of methods are very useful for offline systems.

- **Linear Transformation**: In these types of techniques, the additional channel method is employed [26] to accurately approximate the atmospheric light. When retrieving foggy images using an atmospheric light model, assessment criteria are used that take into account regions with average gray and gradient levels. This technique successfully recovers depth-field images, particularly in areas where specific edge modifications take place. Additionally, it runs faster and requires fewer computer resources. In linear transformation scene images can be restored using:

$$I\left(x\right) = \frac{I_0\left(x\right) - z_0}{\max\left(T\left(x\right),\ T_0\right)} + z_0 \tag{6.13}$$

where T_0 is the lower bound that is used for restricting transmission map. Z_0 is the atmospheric air-light and $T(x)$ is the transmission. $I_0(x)$ and $I(x)$ denoted the original hazy image and resultant dehazed image, respectively.

- **Perception-Oriented-Based Method**: Quantization artifacts affect the most of the visibility enhancement techniques in regions of densely hazy images with the hazy sky. This model has the ability to passively control local contrast gain by eliminating haze [28]. This approach has two steps. The first step is to determine the level of condensed scattering in each pixel using a scattering-aware Bayesian framework. Following that, prominence threshold estimation can be implemented using the perception function. Perception-oriented-based methods can be implemented through:

$$I\left(x\right) = \begin{cases} x_0 1 - \left(\dfrac{k}{127}\right)^{0.5} + 3k < 127; \\ y\left(k - 127\right) + 3; \ \textit{otherwise} \end{cases} \tag{6.14}$$

Where, k represents background luminance in the range 0 to 255. X_0 denotes pixel transmission. X_0 and y depends on view distance between object and viewer, which are set based on the subjective experiments.

6.4.2   Contrast Restoration–Based Model

Images with poor visibility caused by fog, haze, or other atmospheric conditions can be made more visible using contrast restoration–based models [27]. In order to uncover hidden details and enhance visual clarity, these models are made to eliminate the impacts of certain atmospheric conditions from the image. In papers [29, 30] for the contrast restoration process, Koshmieder's law is applied, while [13] used the inverse of Koshmieder's law. Some methods additionally include tone mapping and gamma correction before the restoration process to preserve the quality of the resultant image. Some other contrast restoration procedures are discussed below.

6.4.2.1 Dark Channel Prior (DCP)

The DCP technique is dependent on outdoor haze-free image measures [31]. Using DCP [31, 32] high-quality haze-free images are improved by assessing haze thickness. In the majority of local areas of outdoor haze-free images, one of the three color channels has a very low intensity. Estimates of haze transmission are provided by the dark pixels. This approach could be improved by combining DCP with a foggy imaging model. Although, the DCP method is more effective in dense haze regions. It refined transmission maps before visibility restoration. Cost function $g(l)$ is minimized by rewriting transmission maps into the vector form as given in:

$$g(l) = l^T L l + \lambda (l - \tilde{l})^T (l - \tilde{l}) \tag{6.15}$$

where $g(l)$ is the cost function, L is Laplacian matrix for soft matting, λ represents regularization parameter, ($l^T L l$) is smoothen term, $\left((l - \tilde{l})^T (l - \tilde{l})\right)$ is the data term, and $l(x), \tilde{l}(x)$ are well-refined transmission maps.

6.4.2.2 CLAHE (Contrast-Limited Adaptive Histogram Equalization)

CLAHE is a visibility restoration technique used to improve an image's contrast. It is a variant of the adaptive histogram equalization, which redistributes the pixel values in an image to create a more consistent histogram. Fog-damaged images frequently exhibit deficient contrast [33]. CLAHE does not need any prior knowledge, such as forecasted climate data for the process image. Histogram equalization works by calculating the cumulative distribution function of the image's pixel intensities and then mapping each pixel to its corresponding value in the equalized histogram. Although this method can be useful for enhancing low-contrast image's contrast, it can also result in an image that appears overcontrasted or unnatural. CLAHE addresses this problem by limiting the contrast enhancement applied to each local region of the image rather than to the image as a whole.

6.4.3 Deep Learning–Based Model

Different deep neural network models are used for image dehazing and restoration using deep learning models to investigate the causes of image degradation. The most commonly used deep learning–based models for image restoration are discussed below.

6.4.3.1 DehazeNet

DehazeNet [34] is a trainable end-to-end model for transmission estimation. DehazeNet adopts a CNN and its layers present prior information in image visibility restoration. A nonlinear dimension reduction function called Maxout is used for haze-relevant features extraction. An activation function called Bilateral-ReLU (BReLU) is used to enhance the quality of restored image, which is inspired by ReLU and Sigmoid activation function. The BReLU function has a better convergence rate as compared to Sigmoid and ReLU. Figure 6.6 shows the architecture of DehazeNet method.

The DehazeNet [34] consists of four modules that are connected sequentially. First one is the feature extraction module that is constructed by three convolution layers for feature extraction. The second module is multiscale mapping that is constructed by a max-pooling function. The third and fourth modules are local extremum and nonlinear regression that are constructed by a Maxout operation and BReLU activation function, respectively.

6.4.3.2 Multiscale Deep CNN (MSCNN)

A MSCNN for single-image visibility restoration is presented by [35]. This model, which is based on coarse-scale networks, predicts a transmission map that uses all comprehensive images. The transmission maps that follow degraded images have been learned by MSCNN. Figure 6.7 shows the architecture of the MSCNN method. In Figure 6.7(a), we generate synthesize hazy images and corresponding transmission maps using a depth image dataset to train the multi-scale network. The trained model is used to estimate the transmission map of the input hazy image during the test phase. The estimated atmospheric light and computed transmission map are then used to produce the dehazed image. In Figure 6.7(b), the coarse-scale network predicts an overall transmission map from a hazy image and feeds that prediction to the fine-scale network, which creates a refined transmission map.

6.4.3.3 Gated Fusion Network (GFN)

To restore the visibility of a hazy image, the GFN [36] model includes an encoder and a decoder. The decoder estimates how much each input image contributed to the final dehazed image, whereas the encoder is used to capture the context of the input images. Figure 6.8 shows the GFN model. In Figure 6.8, dilation convolution (DC) is used to increase the receptive field in the convolutional layers of the encoder block in order to extract additional contextual information. The convolutional feature maps and the de-convolutional feature maps are coupled via skip shortcuts. The initial hazy image is transformed into three improved variants. These three inputs are then assigned a weight based on one of the three confidence maps that the network has learned.

6.4.3.4 Model-Driven Deep Visibility Restoration Approach

Model-driven deep dehazing [37] combines the benefits of data-driven deep learning and conventional prior-based techniques. In order to dehaze a single image, an energy

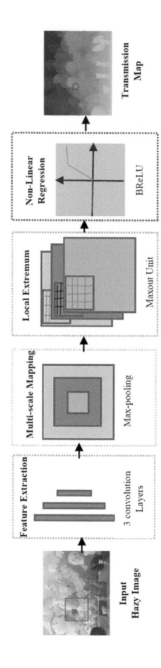

FIGURE 6.6 The architecture of DehazeNet.

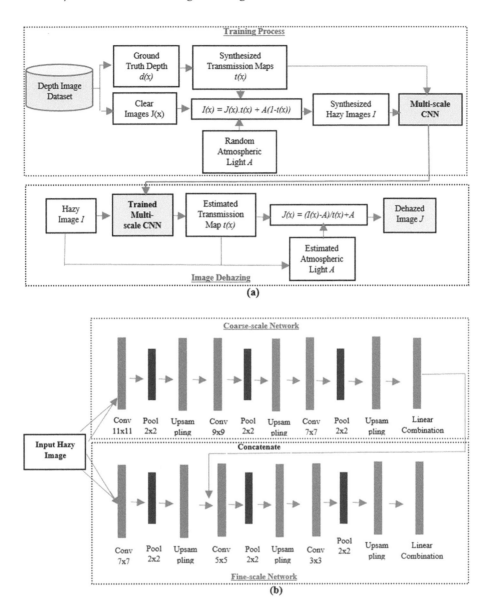

FIGURE 6.7 (a) Overall workflow of the restoration model; (b) MSCNN architecture.

model is first constructed with physical constraints in both the color image space and degradation-related feature space. Then, based on the half-quadratic splitting technique, an iterative optimization algorithm is created for visibility restoration. In Figure 6.9, consider using residual encoder-decoder (RED) as the fundamental architecture for the subnetworks in this approach. For up-sampling, two-stride transposed

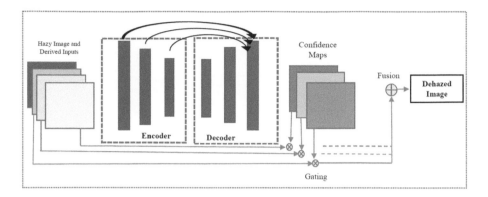

FIGURE 6.8   Gated fusion network (GFN) model architecture.

convolution is used, whereas two-stride convolution is used for down-sampling. Blocks of stacked residuals are the RED's bottleneck.

6.4.3.5   Dehazing Using Reinforcement Learning System (DDRL)

The haze is less dense close to the camera and gets denser as the image goes away from the camera, which is exploited by DDRL [38]. The DDRL is composed of a regression network and a policy network. The dehazing network will use the policy network's estimation of the current depth. Additionally, a new regularization term is suggested for the policy network to construct the sequence that follows the near-to-far order. In Figure 6.10, section-A is the agent element and section-B is the environment element in the reinforcement learning system. To create depth slices at the present stage, the agent uses the policy network. The present dehazed image in the environment is produced by the haze-model equation and the dehazing network. The depth slice produced by the policy network was used to dehaze the part of the image that is currently less hazy.

6.4.3.6   Haze Concentration Adaptive Network (HCAN)

HCAN [39] is an end-to-end haze concentration adaptive network that combines a pyramid feature extractor (PFE), a feature enhancement module (FEM), and a multiscale feature attention module (MSFAM) for visibility restoration. For clear image prediction, PFE based on the feature pyramid structure uses complementary features that are introduced. The network is then instructed to interpret images adaptively under various haze situations by FEM fusing four different types of images with different haze densities. The output of FEM are features containing different types of hazy images, which is the input of the MSFAM. MSFAM is used to reduce the difficulty of training by using attention mechanisms. Figure 6.11 shows the HCAN model architecture.

The overall summary of visibility restoration methods in the literature is presented in Table 6.1.

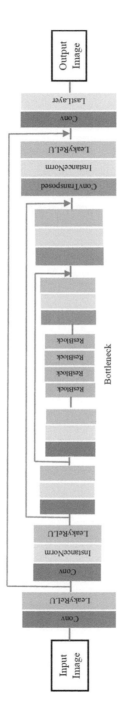

FIGURE 6.9 Model-driven deep visibility restoration model.

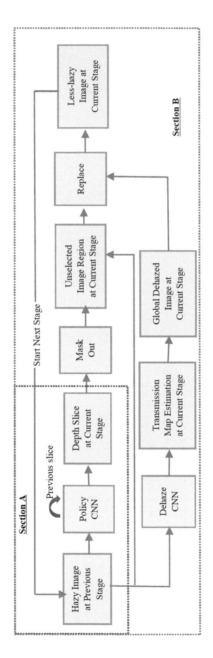

FIGURE 6.10 DDRL model architecture.

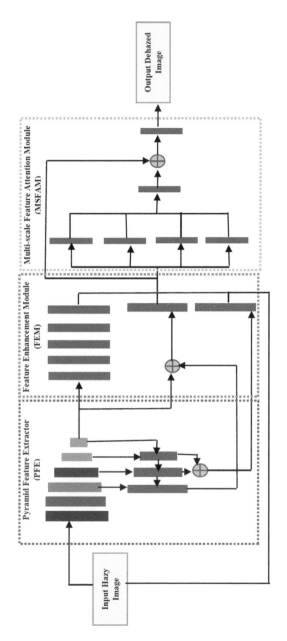

FIGURE 6.11 HCAN model architecture.

TABLE 6.1

Summary of Visibility Restoration Techniques in the Literature

Approach	Technique	Method	Pros and Cons
Multiple image dehazing	Diverse climate condition	Chromatic framework [2] Bad weather vision [13]	**Pros**: High restoration quality and efficiency **Cons**: High algorithmic complexity
	Polarization-based method	Instant polarization [18] Blind haze separation [19]	**Pros**: High restoration quality **Cons**: The experimental setup is complicated.
	Depth map based	Interactive weather [20] Contrast restoration [21] [13] Model-based enhancement [22]	**Pros**: High restoration quality and efficiency **Cons**: Completely depend on depth map calculation, if depth map is not calculated correctly then produce blur or less clear output.
Single image dehazing	Image enhancement based (non-model based)	Unsharp masking Histogram equalization [23] Contrast maximization Anisotropic diffusion [25]	**Pros**: Simplicity and quick processing **Cons**: Noise amplification
	Image enhancement based (model based)	Linear transformation [26]	**Pros**: Simple, fast, and less computational complexity **Cons**: Increased dehazing level may cause the color of the output image to become darker, although several image-processing methods can be employed to fix this.
		Perception oriented [28]	**Pros**: Robust for atmospheric light estimation **Cons**: High algorithmic complexity
	Contrast restoration based	Dark channel prior (DCP) [31] [32]	**Pros**: High restoration quality and efficiency **Cons**: Failures in sky regions
		CLAHE [33]	**Pros**: Improved local contrast **Cons**: Ring artifacts at strong edges and noise amplification in flat regions.
	Deep learning based	DehazeNet [34] Multiscale deep CNN [35] Gated fusion network [36] Model-driven deep dehazing [37] Dehazing using reinforcement learning system (DDRL) [38] Haze concentration adaptive network (HCAN) [39]	**Pros**: High restoration quality and spatial invariance **Cons**: Ineffective performance under different lighting conditions as well as domain-shifting problem

6.5 PERFORMANCE EVALUATION METRICS

The effectiveness of the visibility restoration techniques is measured using different evaluation metrics. Depending on whether or not the ground truth image is available, these measures are divided into two groups as discussed below.

6.5.1 FULL REFERENCE MATRIX

Within this group, the ground truth image, which serves as a reference image, is already available. It is necessary when attempting to test the dehazing technique on a typical dataset of degraded images. Several researchers who have contributed to the literature have taken into account several evaluation metrics to measure the performance of the visibility restoration method. Some of the most commonly used full reference–based performance evaluation matrices are:

6.5.1.1 Peak Signal to Noise Ratio (PSNR)

In order to determine the actual pixels ratio (maximum value) to the error being evaluated, PSNR uses the mean square error (MSE). The quality of the resultant image is better when PSNR is higher. PSNR value is calculated using [40]:

$$PSNR = 10 \log_{10} \left(\frac{R^2}{MSE} \right) \qquad (6.16)$$

where R is the maximum possible pixel value of the image.

6.5.1.2 Mean Square Error (MSE)

The accuracy between the restored image (R) and the ground truth image (J) must be predicted using a well-known performance measurement matrix. It is described as the mean squared difference between the original image and the degraded image. MSE's value ranges from 0 to ∞. To reduce error, it should be close to 0. Equation (6.17) can be used to calculate MSE [40]:

$$MSE = \frac{1}{MN} \sum_{i=1}^{M} \sum_{j=1}^{N} \left(J(i,j) - R(i,j) \right)^2 \qquad (6.17)$$

where i and j are the pixel coordinates; $J(i, j)$ and $R(i, j)$ represent the pixel intensities of a haze-free image and restored images, respectively; and M and N define the number of rows and columns, respectively. R can have a maximum value of 255 in an RGB image.

6.5.1.3 Structural Similarity Index (SSI)

The structural similarity of edges between the restored images and the ground truth images, which was discarded during the calculation of PSNR, is evaluated using the quality reconstruction metric known as structural similarity index (SSI). SSI is usually a number between 0 and 1. A value that is close to 1 denotes a restored image with better structural edge quality. The SSI is calculated using [40]:

$$SSI\,(i,j) = \left(\frac{2\mu_i\mu_j + c_1}{\mu_i^2 + \mu_j^2 + c_1} \right)\left(\frac{2\mu_{ij} + c_2}{\sigma_i^2 + \sigma_j^2 + c_2} \right) \tag{6.18}$$

where i and j are the pixel coordinates, μ_i and μ_j represent the sample means, and σ_i^2 and σ_j^2 are the sample variances. μ_{ij} represents the sample cross-covariance between i and j. A finite value is represented by the constants c_1 and c_2.

6.5.1.4 Mean Absolute Error (MAE)

Mean absolute error compares haze-free and hazy images and measures the difference in terms of absolute value. For an 8-bit image, its value can be any nonnegative integer between 0 and 255. Image quality is better when the value is close to 0. The MAE is calculated [40]:

$$MAE = \frac{1}{MN} \sum_{i=1}^{M}\sum_{j=1}^{N} \left| J\left(i,j\right) - R\left(i,j\right) \right| \tag{6.19}$$

where $J(i, j)$ and $R(i, j)$ are the actual output and predicted output value, respectively. $M \times N$ is the image dimension.

6.5.2 No-Reference Matrix

In most cases, real-time ground truth images are not available for the applications. As a result, determining the effectiveness of the particular visibility restoration method is challenging. When compared to a haze-free image, the hazy image has less contrast. Therefore, the effective parameters taken into account to assess the effectiveness of the dehazing method are:

6.5.2.1 Saturated Pixel Percentage (ρ)

The pixels of the haze-free image get saturated if the contrast gain value is set too high. As a result, it is important to determine the percentage of saturated pixels, which can be stated mathematically as [41], [34]:

$$\rho = \frac{S_p}{MN} \tag{6.20}$$

where S_p is the amount of saturated pixels that are either black or white that are absent from the hazy image. $M \times N$ is the image dimension. For the best haze reduction method, ρ must be a small value [42].

6.5.2.2 Perceptual Haze Density

By taking into account the Mahalanobis-like distance (D) in relation to the restoration level (L_f) of a hazy test image, the perceptual haze density can be determined [43]. The equation used for haze density calculation is:

$$D_h = \frac{D}{1 + L_f} \tag{6.21}$$

The Mahalanobis-like distance is calculated by:

$$D = \sqrt{(m_1 - m_2)^t \left(\frac{c_1 + c_2}{2} \right)^{-1} (v_1 - v_2)} \tag{6.22}$$

where m_1 and m_2 are the mean vectors and c_1 and c_2 are the covariance matrices for the restored and test images of the multivariate Gaussian (MVG) model [42, 44].

6.5.2.3 Contrast Gain (CG)

The mean contrast (MC) difference between the ground truth image (MC_{hfi}) and the hazy image (MC_{hi}) is referred to as contrast gain (CG). Highest possible CG is required for best visibility restoration [42, 44]. The equation used for CG calculation is:

$$CG = MC_{hfi} - MC_{hi} \tag{6.23}$$

The mean contrast different is calculated as:

$$MC = \frac{1}{MN} \sum_{i=1}^{M} \sum_{j=1}^{N} C_t(i, j) \tag{6.24}$$

where C_t is the image contrast and $M \times N$ is the image dimension.

6.5.2.4 Visible Edges Ratio

Visibility edges ratio is another measure that calculates two values, i.e., the average gradient (r) and the new visible edges (e).

- **Average Gradient (r):** In order to show the degree of edges restoration and texture details, r calculates the gradient of visible edges in a dehazed image. The value of r should be maximum for better result and is calculated by [44]:

$$r = e^{\left[\frac{1}{n_k} \sum_{i \in \varnothing_k} \log r_i \right]} \tag{6.25}$$

where r_i denotes the number of visible edges of the resultant image and n_k represents the essential number of visible edges of the resultant image.

- **New Visible Edge (e):** New visible edge (e) is the enhanced visible edge rate after applying visibility restoration method. The value of e should be maximum for better results and is calculated by [45]:

$$e = \frac{n_k - n_i}{n_i} \tag{6.26}$$

where n_i and n_k represent the essential number of visible edges in the input image (I) and the resultant image (J).

6.5.2.5 Blind/Referenceless Image Spatial Quality Evaluator (BRISQUE)

BRISQUE extracts the point-wise statistics of local normalized luminance signals and measures image's naturalness based on measured deviations from a natural image model [46, 47]. The value of BRISQUE should be maximum for better results. BRISQUE uses local normalized luminance signals (I') and is calculated by [46, 47]:

$$I'(i,j) = \frac{I(i,j) - \mu(i,j)}{\sigma(i,j) + 1} \tag{6.27}$$

where I is the intensity image, μ is the mean, and σ is the standard deviation.

6.5.2.6 Natural Image Quality Evaluator (NIQE)

NIQE is used to measure the image's quality based on quality-aware collection of statistical features created on a successful and simple space domain natural scene statistic model [48]. The value of NIQE should be maximum for better results. The quality of the distorted image is measured as [48]:

$$D(v_1, v_2, \Sigma_1, \Sigma_2) = \sqrt{\left((v_1 - v_2)^T \left(\frac{\Sigma_1 + \Sigma_2}{2} \right)^{-1} (v_1 - v_2) \right)} \tag{6.28}$$

where v_1, v_2 are the mean vectors and Σ_1, Σ_2 are the covariance matrix of natural and distorted image's multivariate Gaussian (MVG) model.

6.5.2.7 Perception-Based Image Quality Evaluator (PIQUE)

PIQUE is used for image quality score prediction for blind image quality measurement [49]. It attempts to quantify distortion without any ground truth. The value of PIQUE should be maximum for better results and is calculated by [49]:

$$PIQUE = \frac{\left(\sum_{k=1}^{N_{SA}} D_{sk} \right) + C_1}{N_{SA} + C_1} \tag{6.29}$$

where N_{SA} is the number of spatially active blocks of an image, C_1 is a positive constant, and D_{sk} is the distortion assignment procedure for a given block.

HOMEWORK PROBLEMS

1. What are the different types of filters used for visibility restoration?
2. Write the types of problems that occur during the visibility restoration process.
3. Write the problem statement of visibility restoration.
4. Which is the best visibility restoration method and why?
5. What is the purpose of visibility restoration?
6. What are the differences between image denoising and visibility restoration?
7. What is the difference between image restoration and image reconstruction?
8. What are the performance metrics used in image restoration?
9. What is mean squared error? How do you calculate it?
10. What does mean squared error tell us?
11. What metrics are used to quantify image quality?
12. What is PSNR and SSIM? How are PSNR and SSIM values calculated?
13. What is the ideal PSNR value that signifies high-quality image?
14. Why is SSIM better than MSE?
15. What are the limitations of visibility restoration?
16. Let the original image be $I(x, y) = \begin{bmatrix} 74 & 2 & 60 \\ 23 & 54 & 86 \\ 64 & 88 & 9 \end{bmatrix}$ and the restored image

    be $\hat{I}(x, y) = \begin{bmatrix} 74 & 5 & 63 \\ 22 & 54 & 86 \\ 64 & 87 & 9 \end{bmatrix}$. Find the values of MSE, SNR, and PSNR for the image.

17. Consider the following image:

    $$\begin{bmatrix} 6 & 1 & 8 \\ 3 & 4 & 5 \\ 7 & 5 & 2 \end{bmatrix}$$

    Apply histogram equalization to this image.

REFERENCES

1. Ackar, H., Abd Almisreb, A., & Saleh, M. A. (2019). A review on image enhancement techniques. *Southeast Europe Journal of Soft Computing*, 8(1), 42–48.
2. Narasimhan, S. G., & Nayar, S. K. (2000, June). Chromatic framework for vision in bad weather. In *Proceedings IEEE Conference on Computer Vision and Pattern Recognition. CVPR 2000 (Cat. No. PR00662)* (Vol. 1, pp. 598–605). IEEE.
3. Roy, S. D., & Bhowmik, M. K. (2022). AWDMC-Net: Classification of Adversarial Weather Degraded Multiclass scenes using a Convolution Neural Network. *Computer Vision and Image Understanding*, 222, 103498.
4. Pal, T., Bhowmik, M. K., Bhattacharjee, D., & Ghosh, A. K. (2016, November). Visibility enhancement techniques for fog degraded images: A comparative analysis with performance evaluation. In *2016 IEEE region 10 conference (TENCON)* (pp. 2583–2588). IEEE.

5. Roy, S. D., & Bhowmik, M. K. (2017, December). A survey on visibility enhancement techniques in degraded atmospheric outdoor scenes. In *2017 IEEE Region 10 Humanitarian Technology Conference (R10-HTC)* (pp. 349–352). IEEE.

6. McCartney, E. J. (1976). *Optics of the atmosphere: Scattering by molecules and particles*. John Wiley & Sons: New York.

7. Pal, N. S., Lal, S., & Shinghal, K. (2018). A robust visibility restoration framework for rainy weather degraded images. *TEM Journal*, 7(4), 859–868.

8. Garg, K., & Nayar, S. K. (2004, June). Detection and removal of rain from videos. In *Proceedings of the 2004 IEEE Computer Society Conference on Computer Vision and Pattern Recognition, 2004. CVPR 2004* (Vol. 1, pp. I–I). IEEE.

9. Seya, Y., Shinoda, H., & Nakaura, Y. (2015). Up-down asymmetry in vertical vection. *Vision Research*, 117, 16–24. Elsevier.

10. Tan, R. T. (2008, June). Visibility in bad weather from a single image. In *2008 IEEE Conference on Computer Vision and Pattern Recognition* (pp. 1–8). IEEE.

11. Ancuti, C. O., & Ancuti, C. (2013). Single image dehazing by multi-scale fusion. *IEEE Transactions on Image Processing*, 22(8), 3271–3282.

12. Tripathi, A. K., & Mukhopadhyay, S. (2012, March). Single image fog removal using bilateral filter. In *2012 IEEE International Conference on Signal Processing, Computing and Control* (pp. 1–6). IEEE.

13. Narasimhan, S. G., & Nayar, S. K. (2003). Contrast restoration of weather degraded images. *IEEE Transactions on Pattern Analysis and Machine Intelligence*, 25(6), 713–724.

14. Schechner, Y. Y., Narasimhan, S. G., & Nayar, S. K. (2003). Polarization-based vision through haze. *Applied Optics*, 42(3), 511–525.

15. Narasimhan, S. G., & Nayar, S. K. (2001, December). Removing weather effects from monochrome images. In *Proceedings of the 2001 IEEE Computer Society Conference on Computer Vision and Pattern Recognition. CVPR 2001* (Vol. 2, pp. II–II). IEEE.

16. Tripathi, A. K., & Mukhopadhyay, S. (2012). Removal of fog from images: A review. *IETE Technical Review*, 29(2), 148–156.

17. Narasimhan, S. G., & Nayar, S. K. (2002). Vision and the atmosphere. *International Journal of Computer Vision*, 48(3), 233.

18. Schechner, Y. Y., Narasimhan, S. G., & Nayar, S. K. (2001, December). Instant dehazing of images using polarization. In *Proceedings of the 2001 IEEE Computer Society Conference on Computer Vision and Pattern Recognition. CVPR 2001* (Vol. 1, pp. I–I). IEEE.

19. Shwartz, S., Namer, E., & Schechner, Y. Y. (2006, June). Blind haze separation. In *2006 IEEE Computer Society Conference on Computer Vision and Pattern Recognition (CVPR'06)* (Vol. 2, pp. 1984–1991). IEEE.

20. Narasimhan, S. G., & Nayar, S. K. (2003, October). Interactive (de) weathering of an image using physical models. In *IEEE Workshop on color and photometric Methods in computer Vision* (Vol. 6, No. 6.4, p. 1). France.

21. Hautière, N., Tarel, J. P., & Aubert, D. (2007, June). Towards fog-free in-vehicle vision systems through contrast restoration. In *2007 IEEE Conference on Computer Vision and Pattern Recognition* (pp. 1–8). IEEE.

22. Kopf, J., Neubert, B., Chen, B., Cohen, M., Cohen-Or, D., Deussen, O., … Lischinski, D. (2008). Deep photo: Model-based photograph enhancement and viewing. *ACM Transactions on Graphics (TOG)*, 27(5), 1–10.

23. Hitam, M. S., Awalludin, E. A., Yussof, W. N. J. H. W., & Bachok, Z. (2013, January). Mixture contrast limited adaptive histogram equalization for underwater image enhancement. In *2013 International Conference on Computer Applications Technology (ICCAT)* (pp. 1–5). IEEE.

24. Khan, H., Xiao, B., Li, W., & Muhammad, N. (2022). Recent advancement in haze removal approaches. *Multimedia Systems*, 1–24.
25. Tripathi, A. K., & Mukhopadhyay, S. (2012). Single image fog removal using anisotropic diffusion. *IET Image Processing*, 6(7), 966–975.
26. Wang, W., Yuan, X., Wu, X., & Liu, Y. (2017). Fast image dehazing method based on linear transformation. *IEEE Transactions on Multimedia*, 19(6), 1142–1155.
27. Yuan, H., Liu, C., Guo, Z., & Sun, Z. (2017). A region-wised medium transmission based image dehazing method. *IEEE Access*, 5, 1735–1742.
28. Ling, Z., Fan, G., Gong, J., Wang, Y., & Lu, X. (2017). Perception oriented transmission estimation for high quality image dehazing. *Neurocomputing*, 224, 82–95.
29. Babari, R., Hautière, N., Dumont, É., Paparoditis, N., & Misener, J. (2012). Visibility monitoring using conventional roadside cameras–Emerging applications. *Transportation Research Part C: Emerging Technologies*, 22, 17–28.
30. Machot, F. A., Mosa, A. H., Fasih, A., Schwarzlmüller, C., Ali, M., & Kyamakya, K. (2012). A novel real-time emotion detection system for advanced driver assistance systems. *Autonomous Systems: Developments and Trends*, 391(1), 267–276. Springer.
31. He, K., Sun, J., & Tang, X. (2010). Single image haze removal using dark channel prior. *IEEE Transactions on Pattern Analysis and Machine Intelligence*, 33(12), 2341–2353.
32. Yeh, C. H., Kang, L. W., Lin, C. Y., & Lin, C. Y. (2012, August). Efficient image/video dehazing through haze density analysis based on pixel-based dark channel prior. In *2012 International Conference on Information Security and Intelligent Control* (pp. 238–241). IEEE.
33. Xu, Z., Liu, X., & Chen, X. (2009, December). Fog removal from video sequences using contrast limited adaptive histogram equalization. In *2009 International Conference on Computational Intelligence and Software Engineering* (pp. 1–4). IEEE.
34. Cai, B., Xu, X., Jia, K., Qing, C., & Tao, D. (2016). Dehazenet: An end-to-end system for single image haze removal. *IEEE Transactions on Image Processing*, 25(11), 5187–5198.
35. Ren, W., Liu, S., Zhang, H., Pan, J., Cao, X., & Yang, M. H. (2016). Single image dehazing via multi-scale convolutional neural networks. In *Computer Vision–ECCV 2016: 14th European Conference*, Amsterdam, The Netherlands, October 11–14, 2016, Proceedings, Part II 14 (pp. 154–169). Springer International Publishing.
36. Ren, W., Ma, L., Zhang, J., Pan, J., Cao, X., Liu, W., & Yang, M. H. (2018). Gated fusion network for single image dehazing. In *Proceedings of the IEEE Conference on Computer Vision and Pattern Recognition* (pp. 3253–3261).
37. Yang, D., & Sun, J. (2021). A model-driven deep dehazing approach by learning deep priors. *IEEE Access*, 9, 108542–108556.
38. Guo, T., & Monga, V. (2020, May). Reinforced depth-aware deep learning for single image dehazing. In *ICASSP 2020-2020 IEEE International Conference on Acoustics, Speech and Signal Processing (ICASSP)* (pp. 8891–8895). IEEE.
39. Wang, T., Zhao, L., Huang, P., Zhang, X., & Xu, J. (2021). Haze concentration adaptive network for image dehazing. *Neurocomputing*, 439, 75–85.
40. Singh, D., Garg, D., & Singh Pannu, H. (2017). Efficient landsat image fusion using fuzzy and stationary discrete wavelet transform. *The Imaging Science Journal*, 65(2), 108–114.
41. Yoon, S. M. (2016). Visibility enhancement of fog-degraded image using adaptive total variation minimisation. *The Imaging Science Journal*, 64(2), 82–86.
42. Singh, D., & Kumar, V. (2018). Comprehensive survey on haze removal techniques. *Multimedia Tools and Applications*, 77, 9595–9620.

43. Xie, C. H., Qiao, W. W., Liu, Z., & Ying, W. H. (2017). Single image dehazing using kernel regression model and dark channel prior. *Signal, Image and Video Processing*, 11, 705–712.

44. Singh, D., & Kumar, V. (2019). A comprehensive review of computational dehazing techniques. *Archives of Computational Methods in Engineering*, 26, 1395–1413.

45. Liu, Q., Zhang, H., Lin, M., & Wu, Y. (2011, July). Research on image dehazing algorithms based on physical model. In *2011 International Conference on Multimedia Technology* (pp. 467–470). IEEE.

46. Mittal, A., Moorthy, A. K., & Bovik, A. C. (2011, November). Blind/referenceless image spatial quality evaluator. In *2011 Conference Record of the Forty Fifth Asilomar Conference on Signals, Systems and Computers (ASILOMAR)* (pp. 723–727). IEEE.

47. Mittal, A., Moorthy, A. K., & Bovik, A. C. (2012). No-reference image quality assessment in the spatial domain. *IEEE Transactions on Image Processing*, 21(12), 4695–4708.

48. Mittal, A., Soundararajan, R., & Bovik, A. C. (2012). Making a "completely blind" image quality analyzer. *IEEE Signal Processing Letters*, 20(3), 209–212.

49. Venkatanath, N., Praneeth, D., Bh, M. C., Channappayya, S. S., & Medasani, S. S. (2015, February). Blind image quality evaluation using perception based features. In *2015 Twenty First National Conference on Communications (NCC)* (pp. 1–6). IEEE.

7 Object Detection in Degraded Vision

7.1 BACKGROUND MODELING–BASED APPROACHES FOR OBJECT DETECTION

Object detection plays a pivotal role in the field of computer vision, encompassing various methods and strategies, as illustrated in Figure 7.1. One of the most commonly used approaches for moving object detection is background modeling, which involves constructing a model of the static background scene and detecting moving objects as deviations from this model [1]. Background modeling–based approaches for object detection are used especially frequently for detection of moving objects in particular scenarios. Consequently, background modeling–based approaches are particularly useful in scenarios where the camera is stationary or the background scene is relatively static. These approaches typically involve three main steps: (a) background modeling, (b) foreground segmentation, and (c) postprocessing. In the background modeling step, a model of the static background scene is constructed using a sequence of images or video frames. The model can be a simple average or a more complex representation, such as a mixture of Gaussians or a deep neural network. In the foreground segmentation step, moving objects are detected as deviations from the background model. This is typically done by thresholding the difference between the current frame and the background model or by using more sophisticated techniques such as adaptive thresholding or edge detection. Finally, in the postprocessing step, the detected moving objects are filtered to remove noise and false positives.

One of the main challenges in background modeling–based approaches is dealing with changes in illumination or dynamic backgrounds, which can cause the background model to become inaccurate. To address this challenge, researchers have developed various techniques, such as adaptive background modeling [2–6], which update the background model over time to adapt to changes in the scene, and deep learning–based approaches, which can learn to model complex backgrounds and illumination changes. Overall, background modeling–based approaches are a powerful and widely used technique for moving object detection in computer vision. Figure 7.2 illustrates the background modeling–based object detection methods. However, they do have limitations, particularly in dynamic scenes or when there are significant changes in illumination. Future research in this area will focus on developing more robust and adaptive background modeling techniques, as well as integrating other sensing modalities such as LiDAR or radar [67, 68] for more accurate moving object detection in challenging scenarios.

DOI: 10.1201/9781003432036-7

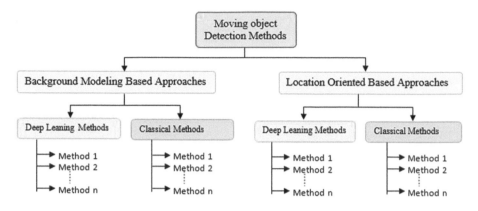

FIGURE 7.1   Taxonomy of object detection in computer vision tasks.

7.1.1   CLASSICAL METHODS BASED ON BACKGROUND MODELING FOR OBJECT DETECTION

Classical methods for moving object detection are still widely used and provide a solid foundation for more recent approaches. This chapter will provide an overview of classical methods for moving object detection, their strengths, and their limitations.

7.1.1.1   Background Subtraction

One of the earliest approaches to moving object detection is background subtraction; the backbone architecture of background subtraction is illustrated in Figure 7.3. This method assumes that the background of a scene remains relatively static, and any changes in the image can be attributed to the presence of moving objects (for further details, please refer to [69–71]). The algorithm involves subtracting a reference background image from each frame of the video stream and thresholding the resulting difference image to identify pixels that have changed. However, background subtraction methods can be sensitive to changes in illumination and shadows, which can lead to false detections. Some examples of background subtraction methods for moving object detection are Gaussian mixture model (GMM) [72], illumination-sensitive background modeling (ISBM) [73], pixel-based adaptive segmentation (PBAS) [74], visual background extractor (VIBE) [75], multiple temporal difference (MTD) [76], and extended center–symmetric local binary pattern (XCS-LBP) [77].

An example of a background modeling–based object detection approach is Akin-based Local Whitening Boolean Pattern (ALWBP), which has shown promising results in object detection [150]. The ALWBP algorithm begins by dividing an input image into overlapping blocks or regions as shown in Figure 7.4. For each block, the LBP operator computes the binary pattern based on the pixel intensities of its surrounding neighbors. However, unlike traditional LBP, ALWBP includes an additional step of local whitening. The local whitening operation is performed by calculating the mean value and standard deviation of the pixel intensities within each block. These statistical measures are used to normalize the pixel values in the block, making them more robust to illumination variations and enhancing local contrast. By effectively whitening the local regions, ALWBP increases the discriminative

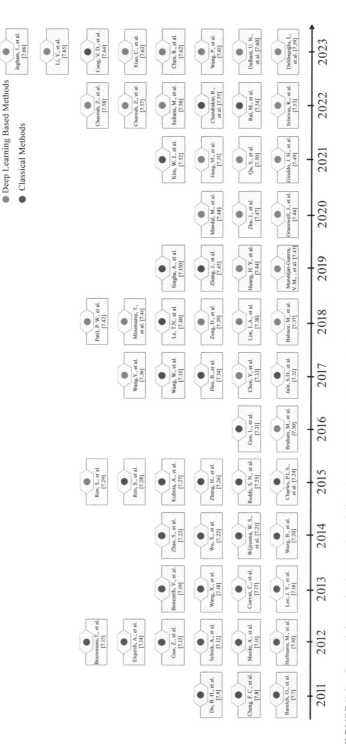

FIGURE 7.2 State-of-the-art background modeling–based object detection methods.

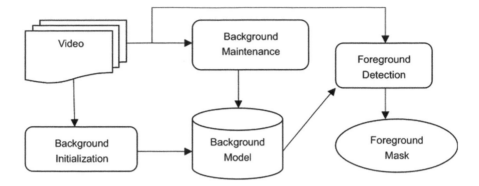

FIGURE 7.3   Stages of background subtraction method for object detection.

power of the pattern representation. After local whitening, a thresholding operation is applied to convert the whitened values into binary patterns. The thresholding is done by comparing each pixel intensity with the mean value of the block. If the intensity is greater than or equal to the mean, it is assigned a value of 1; otherwise, it is assigned a value of 0. This step creates the binary ALWBP pattern for each block. The final representation of the ALWBP is obtained by concatenating the binary patterns from all the blocks or regions within the image. This compact representation captures the local structural information while maintaining discrimination power against illumination variations.

The equation for the ALWBP pattern can be written as:

$$ALWBP_{(x,y)} = \Sigma\left[b = 0 \text{ to } B-1\right]2{^\wedge}b * s\left(i\left(x+x_b, y+y_b\right)-\mu\right) \qquad (7.1)$$

where $ALWBP_{(x, y)}$ denotes the ALWBP pattern at the coordinate (x, y) in the image, B represents the number of blocks or regions in the image, x_b and y_b represent the horizontal and vertical offsets of the block, $s(x)$ is the thresholding function that assigns a binary value based on whether or not x is greater than or equal to the mean μ, and $i_{(x, y)}$ represents the pixel intensity at the coordinate (x, y).

7.1.1.2   Frame Differencing

Another classical method for moving object detection is frame differencing. Figure 7.5 illustrates the basic steps for moving object detection using frame differencing, which involves subtracting consecutive frames from the video stream. This method is particularly useful for detecting fast-moving objects but can suffer from high false positives due to noise and lighting changes.

7.1.2   Deep Learning Methods Based on Background Modeling for Object Detection

In recent years, classical methods for object detection have been combined with deep learning approaches to improve their accuracy and robustness. For example,

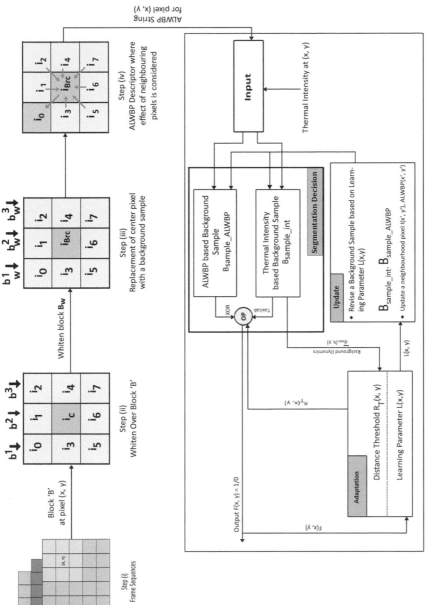

FIGURE 7.4 ALWBP architecture.

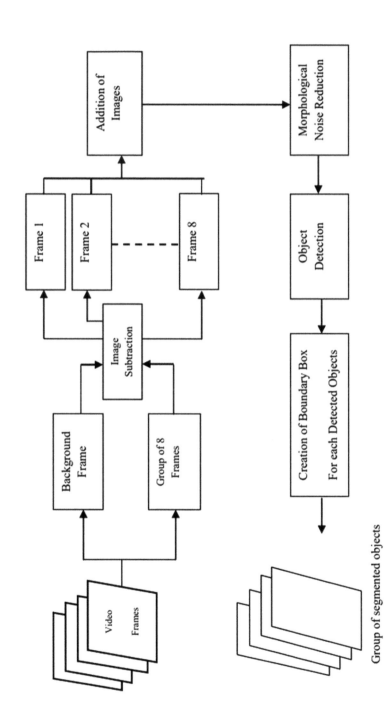

FIGURE 7.5   Steps for moving object detection using frame differencing.

background subtraction algorithms can be combined with convolutional neural networks (CNNs) to improve their performance in challenging lighting conditions. Classical methods for moving object detection provide a solid foundation for more recent approaches and are still widely used in computer vision applications. While these methods have their strengths and limitations, they can be combined with deep learning techniques to improve their accuracy and robustness. Consequently, traditional methods for moving object detection often rely on hand-crafted features and heuristics, which can be time-consuming and challenging to optimize. However, recent advancements in deep learning techniques have enabled the development of efficient and accurate methods for moving object detection. In this chapter, we will discuss some of the popular deep learning–based methods for moving object detection. Deep learning is an advanced version of machine learning that utilizes artificial neural networks to solve complex problems. It involves training a neural network with a large amount of data to learn the underlying patterns and features of the data. CNNs are the most commonly used deep learning architecture for image and video analysis. They are designed to automatically learn the spatial and temporal features of the data by applying convolutional filters over the input images. The basic idea behind deep learning–based background modeling is to train a CNN on a large dataset of static scenes and then use the learned model to detect moving objects in new video sequences.

i.   **Deep learning–based background modeling**: One popular approach to deep learning–based background modeling is to use a CNN to learn a feature representation of the scene, and then use this representation to segment the image into foreground and background pixels. This approach has been used in several recent works, such as [81]. The authors proposed a method that uses a scene-specific CNN to learn a feature representation of the background and then applies a simple thresholding operation to segment the image into foreground and background pixels.

ii. **Foreground mask prediction**: Another popular method is to use a CNN to directly predict the foreground mask from the input image. This approach has been used in several recent works; in [82] the authors proposed a method that uses a fully convolutional network (FCN) to predict the foreground mask from the input image and then applies object detection and tracking algorithms to the foreground mask to detect and track moving objects.

In summary, deep learning–based methods have shown promising results for background modeling and moving object detection in video sequences. These methods use CNNs to learn a representation of the scene that is robust to environmental factors and can be used to distinguish between foreground and background pixels. There are several recent works that have proposed different approaches to deep learning–based background modeling, and the field is still evolving rapidly.

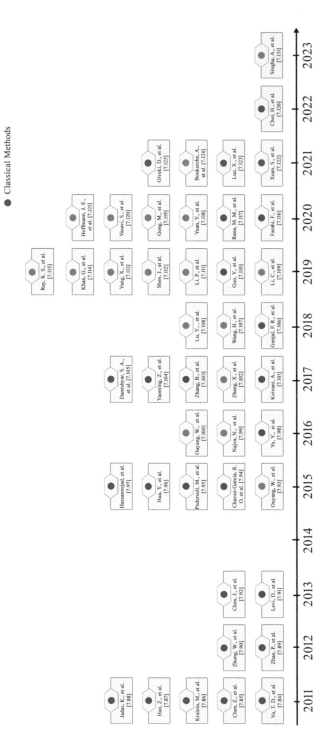

FIGURE 7.6 State-of-the-art location-oriented object detection methods.

7.2 LOCATION-ORIENTED OR BOUNDING BOX–BASED APPROACHES TO OBJECT DETECTION

Moving object detection is a fundamental task in various computer vision applications, such as surveillance, traffic monitoring, and autonomous driving. One of the critical factors in moving object detection is location information, which can help distinguish objects from the background and track their movements. Location-oriented-based approaches utilize location information in various ways to improve the accuracy and efficiency of moving object detection. In this section, we will discuss some of the popular location-oriented-based approaches for moving object detection. In Figure 7.6 we have illustrated all the location-oriented object detection methods designed by the research community.

7.2.1 CLASSICAL METHODS BASED ON LOCATION-ORIENTED OR BOUNDING BOX–BASED APPROACHES TO OBJECT DETECTION

Location information can be obtained from various sources, such as GPS, sensors, and cameras. In moving object detection, the location of the object in the previous frames can be used to predict its location in the current frame. Location-oriented-based approaches utilize this prediction to improve the accuracy and efficiency of moving object detection. Examples of classical methods based on location-oriented approaches for moving object detection are:

7.2.1.1 Kalman Filter

In Kalman filters, the future state of a system is predicted based on measurements taken previously. By using Kalman filters, moving objects can be detected by predicting their position in the next frame based on their previous locations. The basic Kalman filter equations [83] for moving object detection are as follows:

State prediction:

$$x(k) = A^* x(k-1) \qquad (7.2)$$

where $x(k)$ is the predicted state at time k, which consists of the position and velocity of the object. A is the state transition matrix, which describes how the state evolves over time.

Error covariance prediction:

$$P(k) = A^* P(k-1)^* A\_transpose + Q \qquad (7.3)$$

where $P(k)$ is the predicted error covariance at time k, which describes the uncertainty in the predicted state and Q is the process noise covariance matrix, which models the uncertainty in the state transition.

Measurement of update:

$$K(k) = P(k) * H\_transpose^* \left(H^* P(k) * H\_transpose + R\right)^{(-1)} \qquad (7.4)$$

where $K(k)$ is the Kalman gain at time k, which determines the amount of weight given to the measurement in updating the state estimate, H is the observation matrix, which maps the state to the measurement space, and R is the measurement noise covariance matrix, which models the uncertainty in the measurement.

Update state:

$$x(k) = x(k) + K(k)^* \left(z(k) - H^* x(k)\right) \qquad (7.5)$$

where $z(k)$ represents the measurement at time k, which is the observed position of the object.

Error covariance update:

$$P(k) = \left(I - K(k)^* H\right)^* P(k) \qquad (7.6)$$

where I is the identity matrix.

Kalman filters are used to detect moving objects based on position and velocity, while measurements are the observed positions. The Kalman filter estimates the true position and velocity of the object over time while taking into account the uncertainties in the measurement and the state transition. Video surveillance, object tracking, and motion analysis can be done using the Kalman filter by tracking the object's position and velocity.

7.2.1.2   Particle Filter

Particle filter is a Bayesian filtering method [127] that detects objects and tracks them across a variety of scenarios. It is a non-parametric approach that represents the state of an object as a set of particles, which are sampled from a prior distribution and updated using measurements and motion models. Particle filter is an approach to representing possible system states using a set of particles. In moving object detection, the particle filter can be used to estimate the location and motion of the object based on its location in the previous frames. The particle filter can handle nonlinear and non-Gaussian models and is robust to occlusion and noise. By propagating the particles through the state space, particle filter can estimate the posterior distribution of the object state, which includes the position, velocity, size, orientation, and other attributes. Particle filtering involves the following steps [128]:

- **Initialization**: Generate a set of particles from a prior distribution, which represents the initial state of the object.

- **Prediction**: Propagate the particles through the state space using a motion model, which predicts the new state of the object based on its previous state and external factors such as noise and dynamics.
- **Measurement update**: Compute the likelihood of each particle based on the observation of the object in the current frame. The likelihood function can be based on various features such as color, texture, shape, and motion.
- **Resampling**: Select a subset of particles with higher likelihood and resample them to generate a new set of particles with higher probability of representing the true state of the object. This step helps avoid particle degeneracy and maintain the diversity of the particle distribution.
- **State estimation**: Compute the estimated state of the object based on the weighted average or maximum likelihood of the particles.

Particle filter can be used for object detection by treating the object as a set of particles that represent its state in the image. The state of the object can include its position, size, shape, color, texture, and other attributes that are relevant to the detection task. The particles can be generated using various prior distributions, such as uniform, Gaussian, or mixture models, depending on the properties of the object and the scene. The motion model of the particle filter can be based on the dynamics of the object, such as its linear or nonlinear motion, or on the motion of the camera, such as its rotation and translation. The measurement model of the particle filter can be based on the appearance of the object, such as its color histogram, texture features, or deep neural network representations. There are various distance metrics that can be used to compute the likelihood function, such as Euclidean [129], Mahalanobis [130], or cosine distance, depending on the feature space and the similarity measure. The resampling step of the particle filter can be performed using various techniques, such as stratified resampling or residual resampling. These techniques aim to maintain the diversity of the particle distribution while selecting the particles with higher likelihood. There are various methods for estimating the state of a system, such as weighted average, maximum likelihood, or Bayesian inference, depending on the properties of the particle distribution and the task requirements.

7.2.1.3 Optical Flow

Optical flow [131–133] is another classical method that can be used to detect moving objects by calculating the motion vectors of pixels between consecutive frames. This method is particularly useful for detecting the direction and speed of moving objects but needs help with complex motion patterns. It is a computer vision technique that estimates the motion of objects in an image sequence. In moving object detection, optical flow can be used to predict the location of the object in the current frame based on its location in the previous frames. Optical flow is fast and can handle small displacements, so it can be used in real time [134]. The overall block diagram of optical flow is shown in Figure 7.7.

The basic equation for optical flow is well established in the computer vision literature and has been extensively used for moving object detection and tracking.

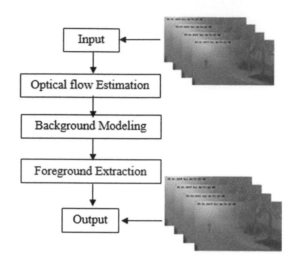

FIGURE 7.7 Overview of the object detection using optical flow method.

In [134] authors have introduced the basic optical flow equation and presented a method for solving it using an iterative approach:

$$i_x^* u + i_y^* v + i_t = 0 \qquad (7.7)$$

where i_x and i_y are the spatial gradients of the image intensity in the x and y directions, respectively; i_t is the temporal gradient of the image intensity (i.e., the difference between images at t and $t - 1$); and u and v are the horizontal and vertical components of the optical flow, respectively.

Location-oriented-based approaches for moving object detection utilize location information in various ways to improve the accuracy and efficiency of the detection. A wide range of computer vision applications use these approaches, and their effectiveness depends on the specific scenario and the type of location information available. Future research in this field may focus on developing more robust and efficient location-oriented-based approaches to detect moving objects in complex scenarios.

7.2.2 Deep Learning Methods Based on Location-Oriented or Bounding Box–Based Approaches for Object Detection

Object detection is challenging due to various factors, including complex scenes, varying illumination conditions, object appearance, and motion. Traditional methods for moving object detection rely on handcrafted features and are sensitive to changes in the environment. Conversely, deep learning methods offer a promising alternative for moving object detection, with remarkable performance in recent years. In this section, we will explore the advances in location-oriented deep learning–based methods for moving object detection. Here, we provide an overview of state-of-the-art deep learning–based moving object detection methods.

    (a)   (b)   (c)   (d)

FIGURE 7.8 (a) Input image. (b) Extraction of bottom-up region proposals (in different aspect ratio it may be horizontal, vertical, and square), (c) computes features for every region proposal by using CNN, and then (d) classifies each proposed region.

7.2.2.1 Region-Based Convolutional Neural Network (R-CNN)

The R-CNN framework is one of the earliest and most popular methods for detecting objects. R-CNN was introduced in 2014 by Ross Girshick et al. [135]. R-CNN consists of several stages (shown in Figure 7.8) that work together to detect objects in an image. The basic idea is to first propose regions in the inputted image that might contain objects and then classify those regions using a CNN. The key stages of R-CNN are as follows:

- **Region proposal**: At this stage, object regions are proposed using a selective search algorithm [136] as mentioned in Chapter 8. Selective search groups pixels in an image based on their similarity and spatial proximity to generate a set of candidate object regions. It generates a set of proposed regions $R = \{r1, r2, ..., rn\}$ for an input image I.
- **Feature extraction**: The proposed regions are then warped to a fixed size and, after being warped, fed into a CNN to extract a feature vector $x \in Rd$, such as VGG16 [137] or ResNet [138], to extract features. The CNN is typically trained on a large dataset such as ImageNet for object recognition.
- **Classification**: The features extracted from each region are fed into a set of fully connected (FC) layers that are trained to classify the proposed region into one of the object categories. The output of this stage is a set of class probabilities for each proposed region. The feature vector x is fed into a set of FC layers to compute class probabilities for each object category. An example of this would be a softmax function:

$$P(c \mid x) = \frac{e^{\left(w_c^T x + b_c\right)}}{\Sigma_k e^{\left(w_k^T x + b_k\right)}} \tag{7.8}$$

where w_c is weight, b_c are the biases for class c, T represents transpose operations, and Σ_k denotes the sum over all possible classes. $e^{\left(w_c^T x + b_c\right)}$, represents the unnormalized probability or score for the target class c. The exponentiation ensures that the score is positive, and the dot product between the input x and the weight vector w_c captures the relevance of the input features to the target class. $\Sigma_k e^{\left(w_k^T x + b_k\right)}$ represents the sum of unnormalized probabilities or scores for all classes. This term serves as a normalization factor, ensuring that the probabilities for all classes add up to 1.

- **Localization**: Finally, the regions that are classified as containing an object are refined using a bounding box regression algorithm [139]. At this stage, coordinates of the predicted region are adjusted to better align with the actual object location. The proposed region is adjusted using a bounding box regression algorithm to better align with the actual object location. This can be represented as:

$$t^* = \arg_{\min} \Delta t \, L\left(t, \Delta t\right) \tag{7.9}$$

where t^* is the refined bounding box, Δt is the adjustment to the bounding box, and L is the loss function used to optimize the bounding box regression. Upon publication, R-CNN achieves the best results in several object detection benchmarks. However, it has several limitations, including its slow inference time due to the need to run the CNN separately for each proposed region. These limitations were addressed in subsequent versions of R-CNN, including F-RCNN and Faster R-CNN.

7.2.2.2 Fast Region-Based Convolutional Neural Network (Fast R-CNN)

R-CNN is computationally expensive and slow, as it requires running the CNN separately for each region proposal. To address this issue, the Fast R-CNN architecture was proposed in 2015, which performs both region proposal and classification in a single forward pass of the CNN. The basic pipeline of Fast R-CNN [139] is the same as that of R-CNN and involves the proposal of regions, extraction of features, classification, and regression of bounding boxes. However, rather than computing features separately for each proposed region, Fast R-CNN computes features for the entire image and then extracts region features using a region of interest (RoI) pooling layer. An arbitrary-sized region can be mapped to a fixed-sized feature map using the RoI pooling layer; for classification and bounding box regression, it can be fed into fully connected layers. The Fast R-CNN architecture is shown in Figure 7.9.

- **Region proposal**: To generate a set of proposed regions $R = \{r1, r2, ..., rn\}$ for an input image I, Fast R-CNN uses a region proposal method such as selective search.

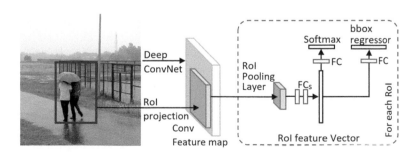

FIGURE 7.9   Fast R-CNN architecture.

- **Feature extraction**: The entire image *I* is passed through a pretrained CNN, such as VGG16 [138] or ResNet [140], to extract a feature map $F \in Rd \times W \times H$, where *d* is the number of feature channels and *W* and *H* are the spatial dimensions of the feature map.
- **RoI pooling**: Each proposed region *ri* is mapped to a fixed-sized feature map using RoI pooling. RoI pooling divides the region into a grid of subregions and applies max pooling within each subregion to obtain a fixed-sized feature map of size $K \times K$. The resulting feature map is denoted as $pi \in Rd \times K \times K$.
- **Classification**: The feature map *pi* is passed through a set of *FC* layers to compute class probabilities for each object category by using a softmax function:

$$P(c \mid pi) = \frac{e^{\left(w_c^T \, pi + b_c\right)}}{\Sigma_k e^{\left(w_k^T \, pi + b_k\right)}}$$ (7.10)

where w_c is weights, b_c are the biases for class *c*, *T* represents the transpose operations, and Σ_k denotes the sum over all possible classes.
- **Localization**: The proposed region is adjusted using a bounding box regression algorithm to better align with the actual object location. This can be represented as:

$$t^* = \arg_{\min} \Delta t \, L\left(t, \Delta t\right)$$ (7.11)

where t^* is the refined bounding box, Δt is the adjustment to the bounding box, and *L* is the loss function used to optimize the bounding box regression.

Compared with R-CNN, Fast R-CNN provides faster inference due to the use of RoI pooling, which allows multiple region proposals to be processed in parallel using a single forward pass through the CNN.

7.2.2.3   Faster Region-Based Convolutional Neural Network (Faster R-CNN)

Faster R-CNN is another object detection framework, proposed by Shaoqing Ren et al. [141] and shown in Figure 7.10. It introduces the region proposal network (RPN) in order to address the issue of manual region proposal on top of Fast R-CNN. The RPN generates region proposals by learning to predict presence of objects scores and bounding box offsets at each location in a feature map. Here, we will discuss the key concepts and equations of Faster R-CNN. It consists of two main components: the RPN and the Fast R-CNN detector. The RPN generates region proposals, which are then refined by the Fast R-CNN detector for classification and bounding box regression. The advantage of Faster R-CNN over previous methods is that it learns to generate region proposals directly from the input image, eliminating the need for separate region proposal methods such as selective search.

The key stages of Faster R-CNN are:

- **Feature extraction**: A traditional CNN extracts a fcature map based on the entire input image in Faster R-CNN.

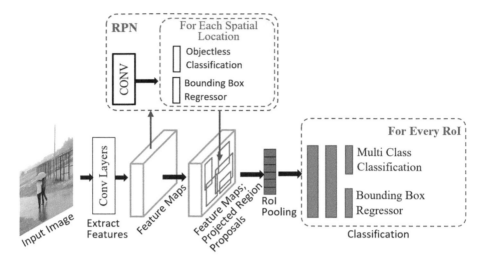

FIGURE 7.10   The backbone architecture of Faster R-CNN.

- **Region proposal network (RPN)**: As an input to the RPN, the feature map F is used to generate region proposals. The RPN consists of two sibling, fully convolutional networks: a classification network that predicts the presence of object scores for each proposal, and a regression network that predicts bounding box offsets for each proposal. The presence of object score represents the probability of the proposal containing an object, while the bounding box offset is used to refine the proposal to better align with the object.
- **RoI pooling and classification**: Each proposed region is mapped to a fixed-sized feature map using RoI pooling, as in Fast R-CNN. A set of fully connected layers is then used to classify the resulting feature map. Fast R-CNN can also represent classification using the softmax function.
- **Bounding box regression**: The proposed region is adjusted using a bounding box regression algorithm to better align with the actual object location, as in Fast R-CNN. The key difference is that the RPN predicts the initial proposal, and the Fast R-CNN detector refines it further. A combination of classification and regression losses is used to train the RPN and Fast R-CNN detectors. The total loss can be written as:

$$L = L_{cls} + \lambda L_{reg} \tag{7.12}$$

where L_{cls} is the classification loss, L_{reg} is the regression loss, and λ is a balancing parameter. The classification loss is defined as a binary cross-entropy loss for the presence of objects score:

$$L_{cls}(p,t) = -\left(t \log p + (1-t)\log(1-p)\right) \tag{7.13}$$

where p is the predicted objectness score, t is the ground truth objectness label (1 for positive, 0 for negative), and log denotes the natural logarithm. Here, the regression loss is defined as a smooth $L1$ loss for the bounding box offset:

$$L_{reg}\left(t,t^*\right) = \Sigma\, i \in \left\{x,y,w,h\right\} \text{smooth } L1\left(ti - ti^*\right) \qquad (7.14)$$

where t is predicted bounding box offset, t^* is the ground truth box offset, and smooth $L1$ is a smoothed $L1$ loss function.

The key advantage of Faster R-CNN over previous methods is its end-to-end training of both the RPN and the Fast R-CNN detector, which allows for better integration between the two components and improved performance on object detection benchmarks.

7.2.2.4 Mask RCNN

Mask R-CNN is an extension of Faster R-CNN that adds a branch for predicting object masks in addition to the existing branch for bounding box recognition. It was introduced by Kaiming He et al. [142]. Mask R-CNN builds on Faster R-CNN and shares the same basic architecture. It consists of three main components: the backbone network, the region proposal network (RPN), and the mask head as shown in Figure 7.11.

The basics of Mask R-CNN are similar to those of Faster R-CNN:

- **Feature extraction**: The entire image I is fed into a pretrained CNN to extract a feature map $F \in Rd \times W \times H$.
- **Region Proposal Network (RPN)**: The RPN takes the feature map F as input and generates a set of region proposals. The RPN consists of two sibling, fully convolutional networks: a classification network that predicts presence of objects scores for each proposal, and a regression network that predicts bounding box offsets for each proposal.

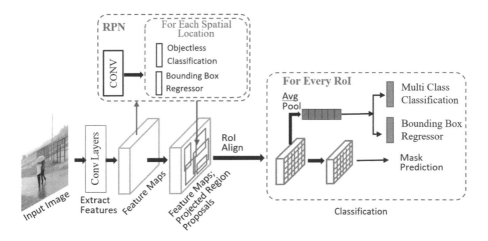

FIGURE 7.11 Mask R-CNN architecture.

- **RoI pooling and classification**: Each proposed region is mapped to a fixed-sized feature map using RoI pooling, as in Faster R-CNN. This feature map is then fed into a set of FC layers for classification and bounding box regression.
- **Mask Head**: The mask head takes the proposed region and the feature map as input and generates a binary mask for each object shown in Figure 7.11. It consists of a small, fully convolutional network that takes the feature map as input and outputs a binary mask with the same size as the RoI. The mask is generated by applying a sigmoid activation function to the output of the final convolutional layer.
- The total loss function is shown in Equation 7.15, which is used to train Mask R-CNN is a combination of classification, regression, and segmentation losses:

$$L = L_{cls} + \lambda L_{reg} + \gamma L_{mask} \qquad (7.15)$$

where L_{cls} and L_{reg} are the classification loss and regression loss, L_{mask} is the mask loss, and λ and γ are balancing parameters. The classification and regression losses are the same as those used in Faster R-CNN. The mask loss is a pixel-wise binary cross-entropy loss, defined as:

$$L_{mask} = -1/N_{mask} \sum i \in M \log(pi) + (1 - mi)\log(1 - pi) \qquad (7.16)$$

where N_{mask} is the number of mask pixels, M is the set of mask pixels, pi is the predicted probability of the ith pixel belonging to the object, and mi is the ground truth label of the ith pixel.

7.2.2.5 Single-Shot MultiBox Detector (SSD)

SSD is a popular deep learning–based object detection method that is widely used in computer vision applications [137]. It involves using a single CNN for both object detection and localization. SSD uses anchor boxes to detect objects at different scales and aspect ratios. It also uses a non-maximum suppression (NMS) algorithm to remove duplicate detections. It uses anchor boxes, which are predefined boxes with various sizes and aspect ratios placed around the image at various points. SSD is efficient and can achieve high real-time performance on GPU hardware. The SSD model uses a single neural network to predict the class and location of multiple objects in an image. The SSD architecture is composed of a base network followed by multiple detection layers. The base network can be any pretrained deep convolutional neural network, such as VGG [138], Inception [143], or ResNet [140]. The detection layers are responsible for detecting objects of different sizes and aspect ratios in the input image. Each detection layer consists of a convolutional layer that outputs a fixed number of feature maps. Every feature map is then fed to a set of convolutional filters that predict the class labels and the bounding boxes of the objects in that feature map. The SSD architecture is illustrated in Figure 7.12.

The predictions from all the detection layers are concatenated to generate the final set of predictions for the input image. The SSD architecture has several advantages,

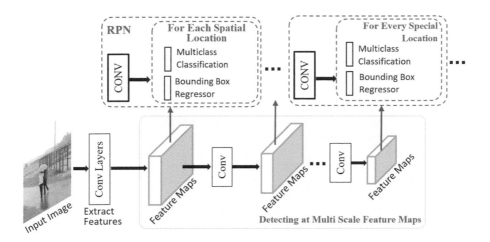

FIGURE 7.12 SSD architecture.

including low computational cost, high detection accuracy, and the ability to handle objects of different sizes and aspect ratios. The training process of SSD involves optimizing two objectives, the classification loss and the localization loss. The classification loss is calculated by comparing predicted class probabilities with true class labels. The localization loss is measured based on the predicted bounding boxes compared to the ground truth bounding boxes. The total loss function is the weighted sum of the classification loss and the localization loss. The weights are used to balance the two objectives and prevent one from dominating the other during the training process. Total loss of SSD can be calculated as follows:

$$L(x,c,l,g) = \left(L_{conf}(x,c) + \alpha L_{loc}(x,l,g)\right) \tag{7.17}$$

where x is the input image, c is the predicted class labels, N is the total number of default boxes, p is the predicted class probabilities, l is the predicted bounding box coordinates, and g is the ground truth bounding box coordinates. $L_{conf}(x, c)$: The classification loss, which measures how well the predicted class labels match the ground truth labels for each object. This term is often computed using a cross-entropy loss function. $L_{loc}(x, l, g)$: The localization loss, which measures how well the predicted bounding box locations match the ground truth locations for each object. This term is often computed using a smooth L_1 loss function. The α parameter is a hyper-parameter that controls the trade-off between the classification and localization losses. A larger value of α places more emphasis on the localization loss, while a smaller value of α places more emphasis on the classification loss. Based on the predicted bounding boxes and the ground truth bounding boxes, SSD is evaluated based on the mean average precision (mAP) and intersection over union (IoU). The mAP measures the average precision across different levels of recall. By measuring the overlap between the predicted bounding boxes and the ground truth bounding boxes, the IoU measures the accuracy of the prediction as shown in Figure 7.13.

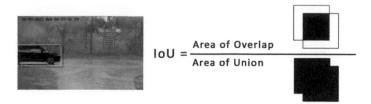

FIGURE 7.13   Intersection over Union.

The mAP for SSD can be computed as follows:

$$\text{mAP} = 1/K \sum i = 1^K AP(i) \tag{7.18}$$

where K is the number of object classes being detected and $AP(i)$ is the average precision (AP) for the ith class. The AP for a given class i is computed by first calculating the precision-recall curve for that class. This is done by varying a confidence threshold that determines which predicted bounding boxes are considered as positive detections. Then, the area under the precision-recall curve is calculated to obtain the AP. The final mAP score is the average of the AP scores across all object classes being detected. The mAP score ranges from 0 to 1, with higher values indicating better object detection performance.

7.2.2.6 You Only Look Once (YOLO)

YOLO is a real-time object detection system introduced in 2016 by Joseph Redmon et al. [144]; the architecture is shown in Figure 7.14. It is a single-stage detector that takes an entire image as input and directly predicts bounding boxes and class probabilities for each object presence in the image. The YOLO algorithm consists of a CNN that predicts the bounding boxes and class probabilities for each object in an image. The CNN is trained end-to-end on a large dataset of labeled images. It also uses anchor boxes to detect objects at different scales and aspect ratios. It is efficient and can achieve real-time performance on CPU hardware. The YOLO architecture consists of two main components: a convolutional neural network and a postprocessing step for detecting objects.

- **Convolutional Neural Network**: To extract features from the input image, YOLO uses a CNN (deep neural network). YOLO uses a modified version of the GoogLeNet architecture, which is composed of 24 conv layers and 2 FC_{layers}.
- **Postprocessing Step**: The postprocessing step in YOLO consists of two stages: anchor box assignment and non-maximum suppression.
  - i.   **Anchor Box Assignment**: YOLO divides the input image into a grid of cells and assigns anchor boxes to each cell. Each anchor box is responsible for predicting the bounding box of a single object. YOLO predicts four coordinates for each anchor box, representing the x and y coordinates of the center of the box, the width, and the height of the box.

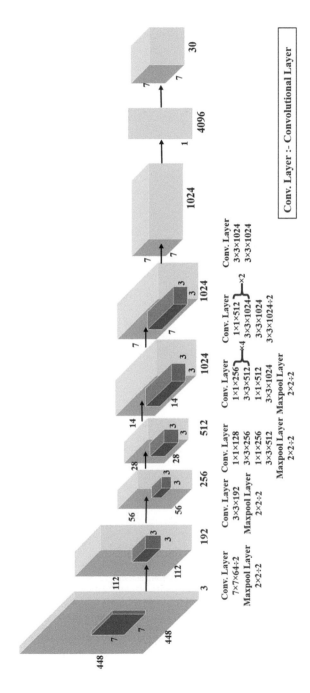

FIGURE 7.14 The overall architecture of YOLO [144].

ii. **Non-Maximum Suppression**: After predicting the bounding boxes, YOLO applies non-maximum suppression to remove redundant detections. Non-maximum suppression compares the predicted bounding boxes based on their overlap and selects only the most confident one for each object.

The YOLO architecture predicts both the class probabilities and the bounding box coordinates for each anchor box. The class probabilities are represented as a vector of size C, where C is the number of object classes. The bounding box coordinates are represented as a vector of size 4, which contains the x and y coordinates of the center of the box and the width and height of the box. The final output of the YOLO architecture is a tensor of size $(S \times S \times (B \times 5 + C))$, where S is the size of the grid, B is the number of anchor boxes per grid cell, and 5 is the number of predicted values per anchor box (4 for bounding box coordinates and 1 for presence of objects score). The YOLO loss function is defined as a sum of four components: presence of objects loss, localization loss, confidence loss, and class loss. The presence of objects loss penalizes the network for predicting a false positive or a false negative, the localization loss penalizes the network for predicting inaccurate bounding boxes, the confidence loss penalizes the network for predicting a low confidence score for the correct bounding box, and the class loss penalizes the network for predicting the wrong class probabilities. The YOLO loss function is defined as follows:

$$
\begin{aligned}
\text{YOLO}_{\text{loss}} = {} & \lambda_{coord} \sum_{i=0}^{S^2} \sum_{j=0}^{B} 1_{ij}^{obj} \left[\left(x_i - \hat{x}_i \right)^2 + \left(y_i - \hat{y}_i \right)^2 \right] \\
& + \lambda_{coord} \sum_{i=0}^{S^2} \sum_{j=0}^{B} 1_{ij}^{obj} \left[\left(\sqrt{w_i} - \sqrt{\hat{w}_i} \right)^2 + \left(\sqrt{h_i} - \sqrt{\hat{h}_i} \right)^2 \right] \\
& + \sum_{i=0}^{S^2} \sum_{j=0}^{B} 1_{ij}^{obj} \left(C_i - \hat{C}_i \right)^2 + \lambda_{noobj} \sum_{i=0}^{S^2} \sum_{j=0}^{B} 1_{ij}^{obj} \left(C_i - \hat{C}_i \right)^2 \\
& + \sum_{i=0}^{S^2} 1_{ij}^{obj} \sum_{c \in classes} \left(p_i(c) - \hat{p}_i(c) \right)^2
\end{aligned}
\tag{7.19}
$$

where 1_{ij}^{obj} denotes if object presence in cell i and 1_{ij}^{obj} denotes that the jth bounding box predictor in cell i is "responsible" for that prediction.

7.2.2.7 Adaptive Weighted Residual Dilated Network (AWRDNet)

The proposed model combines restoration and detection capabilities into a single network architecture shown in Figure 7.15. It employs a multi-stream structure, where each stream specializes in handling a particular aspect of the problem. One

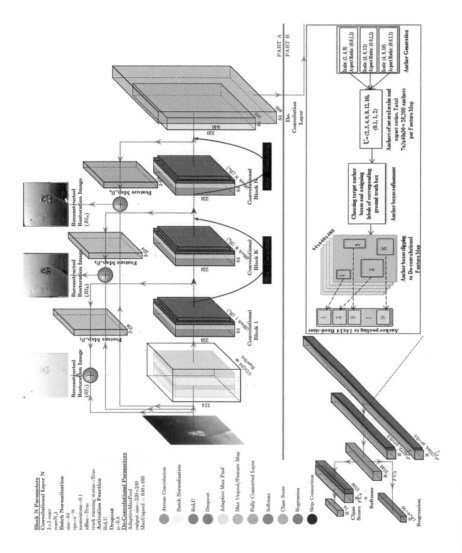

FIGURE 7.15 AWRDNet architecture.

stream focuses on restoring images affected by adverse weather conditions, while another stream concentrates on object detection. The restoration stream of Deeper AWRDNet [151] employs a combination of convolutional neural networks (CNNs) and recurrent neural networks (RNNs) to restore image details and enhance visibility. The detection stream utilizes state-of-the-art object detection frameworks, to accurately identify objects within the restored images. By incorporating object-specific information and leveraging advanced feature extraction techniques, the model achieves precise and robust object detection results. The model effectively handles challenges posed by rain, fog, snow, and other adverse weather conditions, providing reliable object detection even in low-light environments. By improving the accuracy of object detection in adverse weather and low-light conditions, Deeper AWRDNet contributes to enhancing the safety and efficiency of various computer vision tasks in challenging environments.

AWRDNet is a deep learning architecture designed for image super-resolution tasks. It utilizes residual learning, dilated convolutions, and adaptive weighting to enhance the quality of low-resolution images. The basic equations of AWRDNet can be described as follows:

- **Residual Block Equation**: AWRDNet consists of multiple residual blocks, which are the main building blocks of the network. Each residual block takes an input feature map, applies a series of convolutional operations, and adds the residual connection to the output. The equation for a generic residual block can be represented as:

$$F_n = F_{n-1} + \left(W_n * F_{n-1} \right) \tag{7.20}$$

  where F_n is the output feature map of the nth residual block, F_{n-1} is the input feature map of the nth residual block, W_n represents the learnable convolutional weights specific to the nth residual block, and $*$ denotes the convolution operation.

- **Dilated Convolution Equation**: Dilated convolutions are used in AWRDNet to expand the receptive field of the network without increasing the number of parameters. The dilation rate controls the spacing between the kernel elements. The equation for dilated convolution can be written as:

$$O = \left(W * \left(i \otimes d \right) \right) \tag{7.21}$$

  where O represents the output feature map, i is the input feature map, W denotes the learnable convolutional weights, $\otimes$ represents the dilated convolution operation, and d is the dilation rate.

- **Adaptive Weighting Equation**: AWRDNet incorporates adaptive weighting to selectively emphasize or suppress certain features based on their importance. Adaptive weights are learned during the training process. The equation for adaptive weighting can be expressed as:

$$O = W * F \qquad (7.22)$$

where O denotes the output feature map, F is the input feature map, and W represents the adaptive weighting coefficients.

- **Upsampling Equation**: In image super-resolution tasks, AWRDNet is often used to upscale low-resolution images. The upsampling operation increases the spatial resolution of the input. The equation for upsampling can be represented as:

$$O = \left(F \right) \qquad (7.23)$$

where O represents the output high-resolution image and F is the low-resolution input image.

Table 7.1 presents the fundamental key characteristics of the deep learning–based object detection methods.

7.3 PERFORMANCE EVALUATION MEASURES FOR OBJECT DETECTION

The experimental results reveal important insights into the strengths and weaknesses of each method. While deep learning–based methods demonstrate high accuracy, they often require significant computational resources. On the other hand, traditional approaches such as background subtraction show faster processing but may struggle with dynamic backgrounds. Performance evaluation metrics play a crucial role in assessing the effectiveness and efficiency of various systems, algorithms, and models. These metrics provide quantitative measures that enable researchers, practitioners, and decision-makers to compare different approaches, analyze their strengths and weaknesses, and make informed decisions. This chapter presents an overview of commonly used performance evaluation metrics, their definitions, and their applications in different domains. Furthermore, it discusses their strengths, limitations, and considerations for their appropriate usage. Some well-known performance measure matrices are Accuracy, Precision, Recall, and F1-Score. To calculate the above-mentioned evaluation matrices in segmentation tasks, we need to compare the predicted segmentation masks with the ground truth masks [145] as shown in Figure 7.16.

Here's a step-by-step guide on how to calculate these evaluation metrics:

- **Step 1**: Prepare the ground truth and predicted segmentation masks:
  i. Obtain or create the ground truth masks for each image in your dataset.
  ii. Generate the predicted segmentation masks using your segmentation model.

TABLE 7.1

Key Characteristic of Deep Learning–Based Object Detection Methods

Approach	Model	Published in	Learning Type	Detection Modules			Training, Inference Speed	Localization Accuracy	Detection, Segmentation
				Backbone Network (Feature Extractor)	Region Proposal/ Default Box Generation	Classification and Regression for Localization			
Two Stage Detector: **Basic Principle**: They use a two-step approach (one for generation of region proposal and another for classification and localization of the proposals) for object detection.	RCNN [135]	CVPR-2014	Supervised	AlexNet	Selective Search Algorithm	SVM Classifier and BB_Regressor	Slower, Slower	High	Yes, No
	Fast R-CNN [139]	ICCV-2015	Supervised	VGG-16	Selective Search Algorithm	FCN and BB_Regressor	Faster, Slower	High	Yes, No
	Faster R-CNN [141]	NIPS-2015	Supervised	VGG-16	Region Proposal Network (RPN)	FCN and BB_Regressor	Faster, Faster	High	Yes, No
General Steps: • **Stage I**: They generate a set of region proposals that likely contain objects using hypothesis region proposal networks/ algorithms. • **Stage II**: These region proposals are refined (regressed) and classified using a CNN-based classifier.	Mask R-CNN [142]	ICCV-2017	Supervised	ResNet-50, ResNet-101	Region Proposal Network (RPN)	FCN and BB_Regressor	Slower, Slower	High	Yes, Yes

Single Stage Detector:

Basic Principle: They directly predict default bounding boxes (pre-defined anchor boxes) and class labels for objects in a single pass over the input image.

General Steps:

- These detectors use CNNs to extract features from the input image.
- Then perform classification and regression tasks simultaneously on each anchor box (of different scales) to predict the object class and refine the box coordinates.

SSD [137]	ECCV-2016	Supervised	VGG-16	Multi-Scale Grid based Default Bounding Box Generation	FCN and BB_Regressor	Fast, Fast	Moderate to High	Yes, No
YOLO [144]	CVPR-2016	Supervised	GoogLeNet (Modified)	Grid based Default Bounding Box Generation	FCN and BB_Regressor	Very Fast, Very Fast	Moderate to High	Yes, No
AWRDNet [151]	NCA, 2023	Supervised	VGG-16	Default Box Generation	FCN and BB_Regressor	Faster, Faster	High	Yes, No

SVM, Support Vector Machine; *FCN*, Fully Connected Network; *BB_Regressor*, Bound Box Regression Method; *CVPR-2014*, In Proceedings of Computer Vision and Pattern Recognition-2014; *ICCV-2015*, In Proceedings of International Conference on Computer Vision-2015; *NIPS-2015*, In Proceedings of Neural Information Processing Systems-2015; *ICCV-2017*, In Proceedings of International Conference on Computer Vision-2017; *ECCV-2016*, In Proceedings of European Conference on Computer Vision-2016; *CVPR-2016*, In Proceedings of Computer Vision and Pattern Recognition-2016; *NCA, 2023*, Neural Computing and Applications, Springer, 2023.

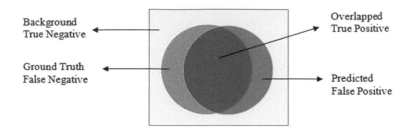

FIGURE 7.16 Performance evaluation metrics for background modelling based object detection methods.

- **Step 2**: Calculate true positives (TP), false positives (FP), and false negatives (FN) for each class:
  i. For each class in your segmentation task, compare the corresponding pixels in the ground truth mask and the predicted mask.
  ii. If the pixel is correctly predicted as a positive (belonging to the class), it is a true positive (TP).
  iii. If the pixel is predicted as positive but actually belongs to a different class or background, it is a false positive (FP).
  iv. If the pixel belongs to the class but is not predicted as positive, it is a false negative (FN).
- **Step 3**: Calculate the evaluation matrices values by using given equations.
  i. **Accuracy**:
     The accuracy measures the overall correctness of your segmentation model. Calculate the number of pixels that are correctly predicted as positive (TP) divided by the total number of pixels:

$$\text{Accuracy} = \frac{(TP + TN)}{(TP + FP + FN + TN)} \tag{7.24}$$

     Accuracy measures the percentage of correctly classified instances compared to the total number of instances. When there is an imbalance in the dataset, it can be misleading, but it gives a general overview of the system's performance.
  ii. **Recall**:
     The recall is the percentage of positive pixels that your model correctly identifies. Calculate the number of pixels that are correctly predicted as positive (TP) divided by the total number of actual positive pixels:

$$\text{Recall} = \frac{(TP)}{(TP + FN)} \tag{7.25}$$

iii. Precision:

A precision measurement measures how many pixels are actually positive out of those predicted to be positive. Calculate the number of pixels that are correctly predicted as positive (TP) divided by the total number of predicted positive pixels:

$$\text{Precision} = \frac{(\text{TP})}{(\text{TP} + \text{FP})} \tag{7.26}$$

iv. F1 score:

This score provides a balanced measure of precision and recall by using the harmonic mean of precision and recall. Calculate the F1 score using the following formula:

$$\text{F1 Score} = 2 * \left(\frac{(\text{Precision} * \text{Recall})}{(\text{Precision} + \text{Recall})} \right) \tag{7.27}$$

It is important to note that the metrics described above assume a binary classification for each class. If you have more than two classes, you can calculate these metrics for each class independently or calculate the average metrics across all classes depending on your requirements. Additionally, keep in mind that there are other evaluation metrics specific to segmentation tasks, such as IoU or Dice coefficient, which are commonly used alongside accuracy, recall, and F1 score to provide a more comprehensive evaluation of the segmentation performance. Here is a step-by-step guide on how to calculate these evaluation metrics for bounding box–based object detection methods:

- **Step 1**: Prepare the ground truth and predicted boxes as shown in Figure 7.17:
  i. Obtain or create the ground truth boxes for each object instance in your dataset.
  ii. Generate the predicted bounding boxes using your object detection model.

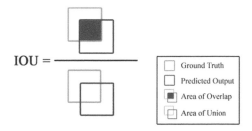

FIGURE 7.17 Performance evaluation metrics for location-oriented-based object detection methods.

- **Step 2**: Determine the IoU between the ground truth boxes and predicted bounding boxes:
    i. Calculate the IoU between each predicted box and its corresponding ground truth box.
    ii. IoU is defined as the ratio of the intersection area to the union area of the two bounding boxes.
- **Step 3**: Set a threshold for considering a predicted bounding box as a true positive:
    Define a threshold value (e.g., 0.5) for IoU above which a predicted bounding box is considered a true positive, indicating a successful detection.
    i. **Average precision (AP)**: Average precision is a value that represents the average precision across all precision values in a precision-recall curve. According to Equation 7.28, the AP is calculated [146]. A loop is used to go through all precisions/recalls and calculate the difference between the current and next recall, then multiply it by the current precision. Therefore, the AP is the weighted sum of precisions at each threshold, where recall increases are weighted by the precision.

$$AP = \sum_{k=0}^{k=n-1} \left[recalls(k) - recalls(k+1) \right] * precisions(k) \qquad (7.28)$$

    where k is number of thresholds.

    ii. **Mean Average Precision (mAP)**: The mean average precision (mAP) is often used to measure the performance of models for retrieving documents and detecting objects [147]. The mean average precision (mAP) can be calculate by:

$$mAP = \frac{1}{n} \sum_{k=1}^{k=n} AP_k \qquad (7.29)$$

7.4 PERFORMANCE COMPARISON OF PUBLISHED RESULTS OF STATE-OF-THE-ART METHODS FOR OBJECT DETECTION

Performance of these state-of-the-art methods heavily depends on the specific dataset and evaluation metrics used. Different datasets have distinct characteristics, such as object size, occlusion, and clutter, which can affect the performance of moving object detection algorithms. Therefore, it is crucial to select appropriate methods and fine-tune them according to the specific requirements of the application. We have tabulated all the state-of-the-art moving object detection methods in this section by various evaluation matrices used by the research community. Table 7.2 illustrated output of all the background modeling–based methodologies, and Table 7.3 contains the results of state of the art location–oriented object detection methodologies.

TABLE 7.2
Results of Background Modelling–Based Methods for Object Detection

Dataset	Publication	Detection Results in Percentage (%)					
		Accuracy	Recall	Precision	F1	mAP	IOU
PETS2001	[7]	98	-	-	-	-	-
NP	[8]	-	81.42	88.66	84.34	-	-
NP	[9]	-	-	-	86.75	-	-
[148]	[10]	-	78.40	81.60	75.32	-	-
	[11]	-	82.66	91.43	86.46	-	-
	[12]	-	91.93	93.13	92.51	-	-
PETS2009	[17]	-	82	87	84	-	-
CD.NET 2012	[20]	-	71.03	71.65	66.06	-	-
	[24]	-	82.82	85.76	82.60	-	-
	[31]	-	79.91	81.88	76.71	-	-
Online	[26]	-	71.03	-	66.06	-	-
PASCAL VOC 2007	[28]	-	-	-	-	73.20	-
CD.NET 2014	[30]	-	-	-	90.46	-	-
	[33]	-	-	-	82.92	-	-
	[36]	-	-	-	95	-	-
	[37]	-	75.45	83.32	75.48	-	-
	[38]	-	-	-	97.70	-	-
	[39]	-	-	-	98.14	-	-
	[42]	-	-	-	91.40	-	-
	[46]	-	54.49	64.36	57.60	-	-
	[48]	-	-	-	-	79.7	-
	[49]	-	-	-	75.93	-	-
	[50]	-	93.62	91.44	92.43	-	-
	[64]	-	-	-	84	-	-
DAVIS	[32]	-	-	-	-	-	71.51
YouTube-Objects dataset	[32]	-	-	-	-	-	68.43
Segtrack-v2	[32]	-	-	-	-	-	61.40
	[35]	-	-	-	-	-	81.6
LASIESTA	[33]	-	-	-	87.61	-	-
	[42]	-	-	-	87.17	-	-
PTIS	[42]	-	-	-	82.41	-	-
NP	[45]	-	85.0	78.9	81.82	-	-
MDR105	[47]	-	86	96	91	91	-
UCSD	[49]	-	-	-	67.27	-	-
MOT 20	[53]	98	85	94	-	-	-
NP	[57]	-	-	-	-	46.72	-
VIVID	[59]	-	-	-	35.40	-	-
Online Sources	[60]	-	-	67.50	-	-	-
Own Designed	[62]	-	-	-	92	-	-
NP	[63]	98	-	-	-	-	-

TABLE 7.3

Results of Location-Oriented Methods for Object Detection

Dataset	Publication	Detection Results in Percentage (%)					
		Accuracy	Recall	Precision	F1	mAP	IOU
ILSVRC2014	[93]	-	-	-	-	50.7	-
PASCAL VOC-2007	[93]	-	-	-	-	64.1	-
Daimler	[94]	97.1	-	-	-	-	-
PASCAL VOC 2009	[95]	-	-	-	-	28.11	-
VOT2014	[96]	73.3	-	-	-	-	-
VIVID	[101]	90					
NP	[103]	-	85.34	92.09	-	-	-
CUHK	[107]	-	-	-	-	67.42	-
XJTU	[107]	-	-	-	-	75.95	-
AVSS	[107]	-	-	-	-	88.52	-
NP	[108]	-	-	-	-	11.4	-
UADETRAC	[109]	-	-	-	-	40.45	-
SkySat	[110]	71	-	-	-	-	-
KITTI	[111]	-	-	-	-	59.13	-
COCO	[113]	92.97	-	-	-	-	-
VOT2016	[118]	49	-	-	-	-	-
NP	[119]	-	-	-	-	87	-
COWC	[120]	96.26	75.37	92.41	0.83	-	-
[149]	[122]	-	-	99.84	-	-	-
CD.Net 2014	[125]	-	-	-	82.15	-	-

HOMEWORK PROBLEMS

1 What are the common types of degradation that can affect object detection accuracy?

2 How can illumination changes affect object detection performance, and what are some methods to handle it?

3 What are the challenges in detecting objects in low-light conditions, and what are some solutions to address them?

4 How can motion blur affect object detection accuracy, and what are some approaches to handle it?

5 What is the impact of occlusion on object detection performance, and what are some techniques to handle it?

6 How can deep learning models be adapted to perform better in degraded conditions, such as low resolution or noisy images?

7 What is transfer learning, and how can it be applied to object detection in degraded conditions?

8 How can data augmentation techniques help improve object detection performance in degraded conditions?

9 What are some evaluation metrics used to assess object detection performance in degraded conditions, and how do they differ from standard metrics used in ideal conditions?

REFERENCES

1. Yang, Y., Zhang, Q., Wang, P., Hu, X., & Wu, N. (2017). Moving object detection for dynamic background scenes based on spatiotemporal model. *Advances in Multimedia*, 2017.
2. Kalli, S., Suresh, T., Prasanth, A., Muthumanickam, T., & Mohanram, K. (2021). An effective motion object detection using adaptive background modeling mechanism in video surveillance system. *Journal of Intelligent & Fuzzy Systems*, 41(1), 1777–1789.
3. Angelo, K. M. (2018, February). A novel approach on object detection and tracking using adaptive background subtraction method. In *2018 Second International Conference on Computing Methodologies and Communication (ICCMC)* (pp. 1055–1059). IEEE.
4. Savaş, M. F., Demirel, H., & Erkal, B. (2018). Moving object detection using an adaptive background subtraction method based on block-based structure in dynamic scene. *Optik*, 168, 605–618.
5. Yamamoto, A., & Iwai, Y. (2010). Real-time object detection with adaptive background model and margined sign correlation. In *Computer Vision–ACCV 2009: 9th Asian Conference on Computer Vision, Xi'an*, September 23–27, 2009, Revised Selected Papers, Part III 9 (pp. 65–74). Springer Berlin Heidelberg.
6. Yoshimura, H., Iwai, Y., & Yachida, M. (2006, August). Object detection with adaptive background model and margined sign cross correlation. In *18th International Conference on Pattern Recognition (ICPR'06)* (Vol. 3, pp. 19–23). IEEE.
7. Barnich, O., & Droogenbroeck, M.V. (2011). ViBe: A universal background subtraction algorithm for video sequences. *IEEE Transactions on Image Processing*, 20(6), 1709–1724.
8. Cheng, F. C., Huang, S. C., & Ruan, S. J. (2011). Illumination-sensitive background modeling approach for accurate moving object detection. *IEEE Transactions on Broadcasting*, 57(4), 794–801.
9. Do, B. H., & Huang, S. C. (2011, July). Dynamic background modeling based on radial basis function neural networks for moving object detection. In *2011 IEEE International Conference on Multimedia and Expo* (pp. 1–4). IEEE.
10. Hofmann, M., Tiefenbacher, P., & Rigoll, G. (2012). Background segmentation with feedback: The pixel-based adaptive segmenter, in *Proc. 2012 IEEE Computer Society Conference on Computer Vision and Pattern Recognition Workshops (CVPRW 2012)*, pp. 38–43.
11. Morde, A., Ma, X., & Guler, S. (2012). Learning a background model for change detection, in *Proc. 2012 IEEE Computer Society Conference on Computer Vision and Pattern Recognition Workshops (CVPRW 2012)*, pp. 15–20.
12. Schick, A., Bauml, M., & Stiefelhagen, R. (2012). Improving foreground segmentations with probabilistic superpixel markov random fields, in *Proc. 2012 IEEE Computer Society Conference on Computer Vision and Pattern Recognition Workshops (CVPRW 2012)*, pp. 27–31.
13. Guo, Z., Zou, B., & Zhao, X. (2012). Efficient adaptive background modeling using kernel density estimation for foreground object detection. *Signal Processing*, 92(7), 1655–1664.

14. Elqursh, A., Ali, A., & Khalaf, M. (2012). A new background subtraction algorithm based on multi-scale adaptive local binary patterns. *Journal of Real-Time Image Processing*, 7(4), 299–312.

15. Bouwmans, T., El Baf, F., Vachon, B., & El Moataz, A. (2012). Background modeling using mixture of Gaussians for foreground detection—a survey. *Recent Patents on Computer Science*, 5(1), 1–1.

16. Lee, J. Y., Kim, J., & Grauman, K. (2013). Key-segments for video object segmentation. In *Proceedings of the IEEE Conference on Computer Vision and Pattern Recognition* (pp. 1990–1997).

17. Cuevas, C., & García, N. (2013). Improved background modeling for real-time spatio-temporal non-parametric moving object detection strategies. *Image and Vision Computing*, 31(9), 616–630.

18. Wang, X., & Xu, Y. (2013). Improving multi-modal background modeling using belief functions. *Pattern Recognition Letters*, 34(5), 543–550.

19. Benezeth, Y., Jodoin, P. M., Emile, B., Laurent, H., & Rosenberger, C. (2013). Review and evaluation of commonly-implemented background subtraction algorithms. In *Proceedings of the 9th International Conference on Computer Vision Theory and Applications (VISAPP)* (Vol. 1, pp. 409–416).

20. Wang, B., & Dudek, P. (2014). A fast self-tuning background subtraction algorithm, in *Proc. IEEE Conference on Computer Vision and Pattern Recognition Workshops(CVPRW 2014)*, pp. 395–398.

21. Wijesoma, W. S., Makris, D., & Ellis, T. (2014). Adaptive background modeling for change detection in crowded scenes. *Image and Vision Computing*, 32(10), 856–868.

22. Wu, X., Chen, J., Liu, H., & Chen, K. (2014). An improved adaptive background modeling algorithm based on OpenCV. *Journal of Software Engineering and Applications*, 7(10), 843–850.

23. Zhao, S., Gong, X., & Wang, Z. (2014). Incremental probabilistic principal component analysis for adaptive background modeling. *Neurocomputing*, 129, 1–10.

24. Charles, P.L.S., Bilodeau, G.A., & Bergevin, R. (2015). Subsense: A universal change detection method with local adaptive sensitivity. *IEEE Transactions on Image Processing*, 24(1), 359–373.

25. Reddy, S. N., & Biswas, P. K. (2015). A survey on background modeling and subtraction techniques for outdoor and indoor videos. *Journal of Visual Communication and Image Representation*, 32, 245–262.

26. Zhang, H., Liu, J., Yang, Y., Li, Z., & Yang, J. (2015). Gaussian mixture model and adaptive learning for robust background subtraction. *Neurocomputing*, 166, 101–111

27. Kubota, A., & Kudo, M. (2015). Spatial-temporal-based background modeling for video surveillance in real-world applications. *Journal of Real-Time Image Processing*, 10(3), 587–597.

28. Ren, S., He, K., Girshick, R., & Sun, J. (2015). Faster r-cnn: Towards real-time object detection with region proposal networks. *Advances in Neural Information Processing Systems*, 28.

29. Snyder, D., Garcia-Romero, D., & Povey, D. (2015, December). Time delay deep neural network-based universal background models for speaker recognition. In *2015 IEEE Workshop on Automatic Speech Recognition and Understanding (ASRU)* (pp. 92–97). IEEE.

30. Braham, M., & Droogenbroeck, M.V. (2016). Deep background subtraction with scene-specific convolutional neural networks, in *Proceedings of 2016 International Conference on Systems, Signals and Image Processing (IWSSIP)*, pp. 1–4, IEEE.

31. Guo, L., Xu, D., & Qiang, Z. (2016). Background subtraction using local svd binary pattern, in *Proc. IEEE Conference on Computer Vision and Pattern Recognition Workshops (CVPRW 2016)*, pp. 86–94.

32. Jain, S.D., Xiong, B., & Grauman, K. (2017). Fusionseg: Learning to combine motion and appearance for fully automatic segmentation of generic objects in videos, in *Proc. IEEE Conference on Computer Vision and Pattern Recognition (CVPR 2017)*, pp. 2117–2126.

33. Chen, Y., Wang, J., Zhu, B., Tang, M., & Lu, H. (2017). Pixel-wise deep sequence learning for moving object detection. *IEEE Transactions on Circuits and Systems for Video Technology*.

34. Heo, B., Yun, K., & Choi, J.Y. (2017). Appearance and motion based deep learning architecture for moving object detection in moving camera, in *Proc. 2017 IEEE International Conference on Image Processing (ICIP)*, pp. 1827–1831.

35. Wang, W., Shen, J., Yang, R., & Porikl, F. (2017). A Unified Spatiotemporal Prior based on Geodesic Distance for Video Object Segmentation. *IEEE Transactions on Pattern Analysis and Machine Intelligence*.

36. Wang, Y., Luo, Z., & Jodoin, P.M. (2017). Interactive deep learning method for segmenting moving objects. *Pattern Recognition Letters*, 96, 66–75.

37. Babaee, M., Dinh, D.T., & Rigoll, G. (2018). A deep convolutional neural network for video sequence background subtraction. *Pattern Recognition*, 76, 635–649.

38. Lim, L.A., & Keles, H.Y. (2018). Foreground segmentation using a triplet convolutional neural network for multiscale feature encoding, in *Proceedings of Conference on Computer Vision and Pattern Recognition (CVPR 2018)*, pp. 1–14.

39. Zeng, D., & Zhu, M. (2018). Background subtraction using multiscale fully convolutional network. *IEEE Access*, 6, 16010–16021.

40. Minematsu, T., Shimada, A., Uchiyama, H., & Taniguchi, R. I. (2018). Analytics of deep neural network-based background subtraction. *Journal of Imaging*, 4(6), 78.

41. Le, T.N., & Sugimoto, A. (2018). Video salient object detection using spatiotemporal deep features. *IEEE Transactions on Image Processing*, 27(10), 5002–5015.

42. Patil, P. W., & Murala, S. (2018). MSFgNet: A novel compact end-to-end deep network for moving object detection. *IEEE Transactions on Intelligent Transportation Systems*, 20(11), 4066–4077.

43. Mondéjar-Guerra, V. M., Rouco, J., Novo, J., & Ortega, M. (2019, September). An end-to-end deep learning approach for simultaneous background modeling and subtraction. In *BMVC* (p. 266).

44. Huang, H. Y., Lin, C. Y., Lin, W. Y., Lee, C. C., & Chang, C. Y. (2019, May). Deep learning based moving object detection for video surveillance. In *2019 IEEE International Conference on Consumer Electronics-Taiwan (ICCE-TW)* (pp. 1–2). IEEE.

45. Zhang, J., Jia, X., & Hu, J. (2019). Error bounded foreground and background modeling for moving object detection in satellite videos. *IEEE Transactions on Geoscience and Remote Sensing*, 58(4), 2659–2669.

46. Gracewell, J., & John, M. (2020). Dynamic background modeling using deep learning autoencoder network. *Multimedia Tools and Applications*, 79, 4639–4659.

47. Zhu, J., Wang, Z., Wang, S., & Chen, S. (2020). Moving object detection based on background compensation and deep learning. *Symmetry*, 12(12), 1965.

48. Mandal, M., Kumar, L. K., & Saran, M. S. (2020). MotionRec: A unified deep framework for moving object recognition. In *Proceedings of the IEEE/CVF Winter Conference on Applications of Computer Vision* (pp. 2734–2743).

49. Giraldo, J. H., Javed, S., Werghi, N., & Bouwmans, T. (2021). Graph CNN for moving object detection in complex environments from unseen videos. In *Proceedings of the IEEE/CVF International Conference on Computer Vision* (pp. 225–233).

50. Qu, S., Zhang, H., Wu, W., Xu, W., & Li, Y. (2021). Symmetric pyramid attention convolutional neural network for moving object detection. *Signal, Image and Video Processing*, 15(8), 1747–1755.

51. Jiang, M., Shimasaki, K., Hu, S., Senoo, T., & Ishii, I. (2021). A 500-fps pan-tilt tracking system with deep-learning-based object detection. *IEEE Robotics and Automation Letters*, 6(2), 691–698.

52. Kim, W. J., Hwang, S., Lee, J., Woo, S., & Lee, S. (2021). Aibm: Accurate and instant background modeling for moving object detection. *IEEE Transactions on Intelligent Transportation Systems*, 23(7), 9021–9036.

53. Srinivas, K., Singh, L., Chavva, S. R., Dappuri, B., Chandrasekaran, S., & Qamar, S. (2022). Multi-modal cyber security based object detection by classification using deep learning and background suppression techniques. *Computers and Electrical Engineering*, 103, 108333.

54. Rai, M., Sharma, R., Satapathy, S. C., Yadav, D. K., Maity, T., & Yadav, R. K. (2022). An improved statistical approach for moving object detection in thermal video frames. *Multimedia Tools and Applications*, 1–23.

55. Chandrakar, R., Raja, R., Miri, R., Sinha, U., Kushwaha, A. K. S., & Raja, H. (2022). Enhanced the moving object detection and object tracking for traffic surveillance using RBF-FDLNN and CBF algorithm. *Expert Systems with Applications*, 191, 116306.

56. Sultana, M., Mahmood, A., & Jung, S. K. (2022). Unsupervised moving object segmentation using background subtraction and optimal adversarial noise sample search. *Pattern Recognition*, 129, 108719.

57. Charouh, Z., Ezzouhri, A., Ghogho, M., & Guennoun, Z. (2022). A resource-efficient CNN-based method for moving vehicle detection. *Sensors*, 22(3), 1193.

58. Li, Y. (2022). Moving object detection for unseen videos via truncated weighted robust principal component analysis and salience convolution neural network. *Multimedia Tools and Applications*, 81(23), 32779–32790.

59. Delibaşoğlu, İ. (2023). Moving object detection method with motion regions tracking in background subtraction. *Signal, Image and Video Processing*, 1–9.

60. Dulhare, U. N., & Ali, M. H. (2023). Underwater human detection using faster R-CNN with data augmentation. *Materials Today: Proceedings*, 80, 1940–1945.

61. Wang, P., Wu, J., Fang, A., Zhu, Z., Wang, C., & Ren, S. (2023). Fusion representation learning for foreground moving object detection. *Digital Signal Processing*, 104046.

62. Chen, R., Ferreira, V. G., & Li, X. (2023). Detecting Moving Vehicles from Satellite-Based Videos by Tracklet Feature Classification. *Remote Sensing*, 15(1), 34.

63. Xiao, C., Liu, T., Ying, X., Wang, Y., Li, M., Liu, L., ... Chen, Z. (2023). Incorporating Deep Background Prior Into Model-Based Method for Unsupervised Moving Vehicle Detection in Satellite Videos. *IEEE Transactions on Geoscience and Remote Sensing*, 61, 1–14.

64. Cong, V. D. (2023). Extraction and classification of moving objects in robot applications using GMM-based background subtraction and SVMs. *Journal of the Brazilian Society of Mechanical Sciences and Engineering*, 45(6), 317.

65. Li, Y. (2023). Detection of Moving Object using SuperPixel Fusion Network. ACM Transactions on Multimedia Computing, Communications and Applications.

66. Jegham, I., Alouani, I., Khalifa, A. B., & Mahjoub, M. A. (2023). Deep learning-based hard spatial attention for driver in-vehicle action monitoring. *Expert Systems with Applications*, 219, 119629.

67. Liu, Z., Cai, Y., Wang, H., & Chen, L. (2021). Surrounding Objects Detection and Tracking for Autonomous Driving Using LiDAR and Radar Fusion. *Chinese Journal of Mechanical Engineering*, 34, 1–12.

68. Farag, W. (2021). Lidar and radar fusion for real-time road-objects detection and tracking. *Intelligent Decision Technologies*, 15(2), 291–304.

69. Kalsotra, R., & Arora, S. (2022). Background subtraction for moving object detection: explorations of recent developments and challenges. *The Visual Computer*, 38(12), 4151–4178.

70. Shaikh, S. H., Saeed, K., Chaki, N., Shaikh, S. H., Saeed, K., & Chaki, N. (2014). *Moving object detection using background subtraction* (pp. 15–23). Springer International Publishing.

71. Xu, Y., Ji, H., & Zhang, W. (2020). Coarse-to-fine sample-based background subtraction for moving object detection. *Optik*, 207, 164195.

72. Stauffer, C., & Grimson, W.E.L., 1999, June. Adaptive background mixture models for real-time tracking. In cvpr (p. 2246). IEEE.

73. Cheng, F.C., Huang, S. C., & Ruan, S.J., 2011. Illumination-sensitive background modeling approach for accurate moving object detection. *IEEE Transactions on Broadcasting*, 57(4), 794–801.

74. Hofmann, M., Tiefenbacher, P., & Rigoll, G., 2012, June. Background segmentation with feedback: The pixel-based adaptive segmenter. In *Computer Vision and Pattern Recognition Workshops (CVPRW), 2012 IEEE Computer Society Conference on* (pp. 38–43). IEEE.

75. Barnich, O., & Van Droogenbroeck, M., 2011. ViBe: A universal background subtraction algorithm for video sequences. *IEEE Transactions on Image Processing*, 20(6), 1709–1724.

76. Ha, J.-E., & Lee, W.-H. (2010). Foreground objects detection using multiple difference images. *Optical Engineering*, 49(4), 047201.

77. Silva, C., Bouwmans, T., & Frélicot, C. (2015, March). An extended center-symmetric local binary pattern for background modeling and subtraction in videos. In *International Joint Conference on Computer Vision, Imaging and Computer Graphics Theory and Applications, VISAPP* 2015.

78. Pathak, A. R., Pandey, M., & Rautaray, S. (2018). Application of deep learning for object detection. *Procedia Computer Science*, 132, 1706–1717.

79. Zhou, X., Yang, C., & Yu, W. (2012). Moving object detection by detecting contiguous outliers in the low-rank representation. *IEEE Transactions on Pattern Analysis and Machine Intelligence*, 35(3), 597–610.

80. Elhabian, S. Y., El-Sayed, K. M., & Ahmed, S. H. (2008). Moving object detection in spatial domain using background removal techniques-state-of-art. *Recent Patents on Computer Science*, 1(1), 32–54.

81. Braham, M., & Van Droogenbroeck, M. (2016, May). Deep background subtraction with scene-specific convolutional neural networks. In *2016 International Conference on Systems, Signals and Image Processing (IWSSIP)* (pp. 1–4). IEEE.

82. Song, K. et al. (2018). Foreground-Aware Object Detection and Tracking from Videos with Deep Learning, in *Proceedings of the European Conference on Computer Vision (ECCV)*.

83. Patel, H. A., & Thakore, D. G. (2013). Moving object tracking using kalman filter. *International Journal of Computer Science and Mobile Computing*, 2(4), 326–332.

84. Vu, T. D., Burlet, J., & Aycard, O. (2011). Grid-based localization and local mapping with moving object detection and tracking. *Information Fusion*, 12(1), 58–69.

85. Chen, Z., Cao, J., Tang, Y., & Tang, L. (2011, December). Tracking of moving object based on optical flow detection. In *Proceedings of 2011 International Conference on Computer Science and Network Technology* (Vol. 2, pp. 1096–1099). IEEE.

86. Krainin, M., Henry, P., Ren, X., & Fox, D. (2011). Manipulator and object tracking for in-hand 3D object modeling. *The International Journal of Robotics Research*, 30(11), 1311–1327.

87. Han, Z., Jiao, J., Zhang, B., Ye, Q., & Liu, J. (2011). Visual object tracking via sample-based Adaptive Sparse Representation (AdaSR). *Pattern Recognition*, 44(9), 2170–2183.

88. Jadav, K., Lokhandwala, M., & Gharge, A. (2011, May). Vision based moving object detection and tracking. In *National Conference on Recent Trends in Engineering & Technology* (pp. 13–14).

89. Zhao, P., Zhu, H., Li, H., & Shibata, T. (2012). A directional-edge-based real-time object tracking system employing multiple candidate-location generation. *IEEE Transactions on Circuits and Systems for Video Technology*, 23(3), 503–517.

90. Zhong, W., Lu, H., & Yang, M. H. (2012, June). Robust object tracking via sparsity-based collaborative model. In *2012 IEEE Conference on Computer vision and pattern recognition* (pp. 1838–1845). IEEE.

91. Levi, D., Silberstein, S., & Bar-Hillel, A. (2013). Fast multiple-part based object detection using kd-ferns. In *Proceedings of the IEEE Conference on Computer Vision and Pattern Recognition* (pp. 947–954).

92. Chen, J., Zhen, Y., & Yang, D. (2013). Fast moving object tracking algorithm based on hybrid quantum PSO. target, 2, 0.

93. Ouyang, W., Wang, X., Zeng, X., Qiu, S., Luo, P., Tian, Y., & Tang, X. (2015). Deepid-net: Deformable deep convolutional neural networks for object detection. In *Proceedings of the IEEE Conference on Computer Vision and Pattern Recognition* (pp. 2403–2412).

94. Chavez-Garcia, R. O., & Aycard, O. (2015). Multiple sensor fusion and classification for moving object detection and tracking. *IEEE Transactions on Intelligent Transportation Systems*, 17(2), 525–534.

95. Pedersoli, M., Vedaldi, A., Gonzalez, J., & Roca, X. (2015). A coarse-to-fine approach for fast deformable object detection. *Pattern Recognition*, 48(5), 1844–1853.

96. Hua, Y., Alahari, K., & Schmid, C. (2015). Online object tracking with proposal selection. In *Proceedings of the IEEE International Conference on Computer Vision* (pp. 3092–3100).

97. Hassannejad, H., Medici, P., Cardarelli, E., & Cerri, P. (2015). Detection of moving objects in roundabouts based on a monocular system. *Expert Systems with Applications*, 42(9), 4167–4176.

98. Ye, Y., Fu, L., & Li, B. (2016, November). Object detection and tracking using multi-layer laser for autonomous urban driving. In *2016 IEEE 19th International Conference on Intelligent Transportation Systems (ITSC)* (pp. 259–264). IEEE.

99. Najva, N., & Bijoy, K. E. (2016). SIFT and tensor based object detection and classification in videos using deep neural networks. *Procedia Computer Science*, 93, 351–358.

100. Ouyang, W., Zeng, X., Wang, X., Qiu, S., Luo, P., Tian, Y., & Tang, X. (2016). DeepID-Net: Object detection with deformable part based convolutional neural networks. *IEEE Transactions on Pattern Analysis and Machine Intelligence*, 39(7), 1320–1334.

101. Keivani, A., Tapamo, J. R., & Ghayoor, F. (2017, September). Motion-based moving object detection and tracking using automatic K-means. In *2017 IEEE AFRICON* (pp. 32–37). IEEE.

102. Zhang, X., & Xiang, J. (2017, November). Moving object detection in video satellite image based on deep learning. In *LIDAR Imaging Detection and Target Recognition 2017* (Vol. 10605, pp. 1149–1156). SPIE.

103. Zhang, B., Jiao, D., Pei, H., Gu, Y., & Liu, Y. (2017). Infrared moving object detection based on local saliency and sparse representation. *Infrared Physics & Technology*, 86, 187–193.

104. Yaoming, Z., Chengdong, W., Yunzhou, Z., & Sheng, F. (2017, May). Realization of moving object detection and tracking algorithm based on frame difference method and particle filter algorithm. In *2017 29th Chinese Control And Decision Conference (CCDC)* (pp. 161–166). IEEE.

105. Daneshyar, S. A., & Nahvi, M. (2017). Moving objects tracking based on improved particle filter algorithm by elimination of unimportant particles. *Optik*, 138, 455–469.

106. Gunjal, P. R., Gunjal, B. R., Shinde, H. A., Vanam, S. M., & Aher, S. S. (2018, February). Moving object tracking using kalman filter. In *2018 International Conference On Advances in Communication and Computing Technology (ICACCT)* (pp. 544–547). IEEE.

107. Wang, H., Wang, P., & Qian, X. (2018). MPNET: An end-to-end deep neural network for object detection in surveillance video. *IEEE Access*, 6, 30296–30308.

108. Lu, Y., Chen, Y., Zhao, D., & Li, H. (2018, November). Hybrid deep learning based moving object detection via motion prediction. In *2018 Chinese Automation Congress (CAC)* (pp. 1442–1447). IEEE.

109. Li, C., Dobler, G., Feng, X., & Wang, Y. (2019). Tracknet: Simultaneous object detection and tracking and its application in traffic video analysis. arXivpreprint arXiv:1902.01466.

110. Guo, Y., Yang, D., & Chen, Z. (2019). Object tracking on satellite videos: A correlation filter-based tracking method with trajectory correction by Kalman filter. *IEEE Journal of Selected Topics in Applied Earth Observations and Remote Sensing*, 12(9), 3538–3551.

111. Li, P., Chen, X., & Shen, S. (2019). Stereo r-cnn based 3d object detection for autonomous driving. In *Proceedings of the IEEE/CVF Conference on Computer Vision and Pattern Recognition* (pp. 7644–7652).

112. Shen, J., Tang, X., Dong, X., & Shao, L. (2019). Visual object tracking by hierarchical attention siamese network. *IEEE Transactions on Cybernetics*, 50(7), 3068–3080.

113. Yang, X., Wu, T., Zhang, L., Yang, D., Wang, N., Song, B., & Gao, X. (2019). CNN with spatio-temporal information for fast suspicious object detection and recognition in THz security images. *Signal Processing*, 160, 202–214.

114. Khan, G., Tariq, Z., Khan, M. U. G., Mazzeo, P. L., Ramakrishnan, S., & Spagnolo, P. (2019). Multi-person tracking based on faster R-CNN and deep appearance features. In *Visual Object Tracking with Deep Neural Networks* (pp. 1–23). London, UK: IntechOpen.

115. Ray, K. S., & Chakraborty, S. (2019). Object detection by spatio-temporal analysis and tracking of the detected objects in a video with variable background. *Journal of Visual Communication and Image Representation*, 58, 662–674.

116. Farahi, F., & Yazdi, H. S. (2020). Probabilistic Kalman filter for moving object tracking. *Signal Processing: Image Communication*, 82, 115751.

117. Rana, M. M., Halim, N., Rahamna, M. M., & Abdelhadi, A. (2020, February). Position and velocity estimations of 2D-moving object using Kalman filter: Literature review. In *2020 22nd International Conference on Advanced Communication Technology (ICACT)* (pp. 541–544). IEEE.

118. Yuan, Y., Chu, J., Leng, L., Miao, J., & Kim, B. G. (2020). A scale-adaptive object-tracking algorithm with occlusion detection. *EURASIP Journal on Image and Video Processing*, 2020, 1–15.

119. Gong, M., & Shu, Y. (2020). Real-time detection and motion recognition of human moving objects based on deep learning and multi-scale feature fusion in video. *IEEE Access*, 8, 25811–25822.

120. Vasavi, S., Priyadarshini, N. K., & Harshavaradhan, K. (2020). Invariant feature-based darknet architecture for moving object classification. *IEEE Sensors Journal*, 21(10), 11417–11426.

121. Hoffmann, J. E., Tosso, H. G., Santos, M. M. D., Justo, J. F., Malik, A. W., & Rahman, A. U. (2020). Real-time adaptive object detection and tracking for autonomous vehicles. *IEEE Transactions on Intelligent Vehicles*, 6(3), 450–459.

122. Xuan, S., Li, S., Zhao, Z., Zhou, Z., Zhang, W., Tan, H., … Gu, Y. (2021). Rotation adaptive correlation filter for moving object tracking in satellite videos. *Neurocomputing*, 438, 94–106.

123. Luo, X., Wang, Y., Cai, B., & Li, Z. (2021). Moving object detection in traffic surveillance video: new MOD-AT method based on adaptive threshold. *ISPRS International Journal of Geo-Information*, 10(11), 742.

124. Boukerche, A., & Hou, Z. (2021). Object detection using deep learning methods in traffic scenarios. *ACM Computing Surveys (CSUR)*, 54(2), 1–35.

125. Giveki, D. (2021). Robust moving object detection based on fusing Atanassov's Intuitionistic 3D Fuzzy Histon Roughness Index and texture features. *International Journal of Approximate Reasoning*, 135, 1–20.

126. Choi, H., Kang, B., & Kim, D. (2022). Moving object tracking based on sparse optical flow with moving window and target estimator. *Sensors*, 22(8), 2878.

127. Kumar, T. S., & Sivanandam, S. N. (2012, July). Object detection and tracking in video using particle filter. In *2012 Third International Conference on Computing, Communication and Networking Technologies (ICCCNT'12)* (pp. 1–10). IEEE.

128. Ying, H., Qiu, X., Song, J., & Ren, X. (2010, October). Particle filtering object tracking based on texture and color. In *2010 International Symposium on Intelligence Information Processing and Trusted Computing* (pp. 626–630). IEEE.

129. Smith, K. J. (2011). *Precalculus: A functional approach to graphing and problem solving*. Jones & Bartlett Publishers.

130. McLachlan, G. J. (1999). Mahalanobis distance. *Resonance*, 4(6), 20–26.

131. Fan, L., Zhang, T., & Du, W. (2021). Optical-flow-based framework to boost video object detection performance with object enhancement. *Expert Systems with Applications*, 170, 114544.

132. Huang, J., Zou, W., Zhu, J., & Zhu, Z. (2018). Optical flow based real-time moving object detection in unconstrained scenes. arXiv preprint arXiv:1807.04890.

133. Aslani, S., & Mahdavi-Nasab, H. (2013). Optical flow based moving object detection and tracking for traffic surveillance. *International Journal of Electrical, Computer, Energetic, Electronic and Communication Engineering*, 7(9), 1252–1256.

134. Horn, B. K. (1981). BG Schunck Determining optical flow. *Artificial Intelligence*, 17 (1–3), 185–203

135. Girshick, R., et al. (2014). Rich feature hierarchies for accurate object detection and semantic segmentation, in *Proceedings of the IEEE Conference on Computer Vision and Pattern Recognition*.

136. Uijlings, J. R. R., et al. (2013). Selective search for object recognition. *International Journal of Computer Vision* 104(2), 154–171.

137. Liu, W., Anguelov, D., Erhan, D., Szegedy, C., Reed, S., Fu, C. Y., & Berg, A. C. (2016). Ssd: Single shot multibox detector. In *Computer Vision–ECCV 2016: 14th European Conference*, Amsterdam, The Netherlands, October 11–14, 2016, Proceedings, Part I 14 (pp. 21–37). Springer International Publishing.

138. Simonyan, K., & Zisserman, A. (2014). Very deep convolutional networks for large-scale image recognition. arXiv preprint arXiv:1409.1556.

139. Girshick, Ross. Fast R-CNN., in *Proceedings of the IEEE International Conference on Computer Vision*. 2015.

140. He, K., Zhang, X., Ren, S., & Sun, J. (2016). Deep residual learning for image recognition. In *Proceedings of the IEEE Conference on Computer Vision and Pattern Recognition* (pp. 770–778).

141. Ren, S., He, K., Girshick, R., & Sun, J. (2015). Faster r-cnn: Towards real-time object detection with region proposal networks. *Advances in Neural Information Processing Systems*, 28.

142. He, K., Gkioxari, G., Dollár, P., & Girshick, R. (2017). Mask r-cnn. In *Proceedings of the IEEE International Conference on Computer Vision* (pp. 2961–2969).

143. Szegedy, C., Liu, W., Jia, Y., Sermanet, P., Reed, S., Anguelov, D., … Rabinovich, A. (2015). Going deeper with convolutions. In *Proceedings of the IEEE Conference on Computer Vision and Pattern Recognition* (pp. 1–9).

144. Redmon, J., Divvala, S., Girshick, R., & Farhadi, A. (2016). You only look once: Unified, real-time object detection. In *Proceedings of the IEEE Conference on Computer Vision and Pattern Recognition* (pp. 779–788).

145. Performance Evaluaion Matices. [Online]. Available: https://towardsdatascience.com/performance-metrics-confusion-matrix-precision-recall-and-f1-score-a8fe076a2262

146. Mean Average Precision (mAP). [Online]. Available: https://blog.paperspace.com/mean-average-precision/

147. Mean Average Precision (mAP). [Online]. Available: https://towardsdatascience.com/map-mean-average-precision-might-confuse-you-5956f1bfa9e2

148. Jodoin, P.-M., Porikli, F., Konrad, J., & Ishwar, P. Change Detection Challenge, 2012. [Online]. Available: http://www.changedetection.net

149. Xia, G.-S., Bai, X., Ding, J., Zhu, Z., Belongie, S., Luo, J., Datcu, M., Pelillo, M., & Zhang, L. (2018). Dota: A large-scale dataset for object detection in aerial images, in: *The IEEE Conference on Computer Vision and Pattern Recognition (CVPR)*.

150. Singha, A., & Bhowmik, M. K. (2019). Salient features for moving object detection in adverse weather conditions during night time. *IEEE Transactions on Circuits and Systems for Video Technology*, 30(10), 3317–3331.

151. Singha, A., & Bhowmik, M. K. (2023). Novel deeper AWRDNet: Adverse weather-affected night scene restorator cum detector net for accurate object detection. *Neural Computing and Applications*, 35(17), 12729–12750.

8 Hands-on Practical for Object Detection Approaches in Degraded Vision

8.1 DEEP LEARNING ALGORITHMS

In this chapter, rather than elaborating on the machine learning approaches [1–3], various well-known deep learning–based object classification and detection algorithms most frequently adopted by the researchers are presented. Convolutional Neural Networks (CNNs) are the main pillars for deep learning–based algorithms. This section provides fundamentals of CNNs along with a detailed description of the state-of-the-art CNN models used for classification and detection of objects from various scenes.

8.1.1 CONVOLUTION NEURAL NETWORK FOR BINARY/MULTI-CLASS CLASSIFICATION PROBLEM

CNNs are used to extract features from the images and to learn the visual contexts that will be used to classify the images using the learned features. The feature extractions from an image are done via a set of filters that extract information. Different sets of filters are available (edge, horizontal, vertical, etc.) that help identify the type of image classification [4]. The CNN model follows a two-step process, i.e., feature extraction and classifications as shown in Figure 8.1. The process of locating and extracting significant features from input images is referred to as feature extraction. It consists of some of the following layers:

- **Input Layer**: The input layer consists of input of the entire block of CNN architecture. In neural networks, it generally represents the mathematical operations of matrices of all pixel values of corresponding images. In this layer, first, inputs used to standardize the data need to be normalized. In the example that follows we are taking -1 as the blank pixels (which is not containing any significant information) and 1 for the pixels where the pixels contain raw information of 'X', which is provided as an image in Figure 8.2.
- **Convolutional Layers**: Extraction of features from the input data is the main goal of convolutional layers. These layers apply with a set of filters (also known as kernels) to the input and perform convolution operations [5]. The resultant operation of the convolutional layer generates a set of feature maps. Suppose I_f^{n-1} as an input feature map (i.e., output feature map from

 DOI: 10.1201/9781003432036-8

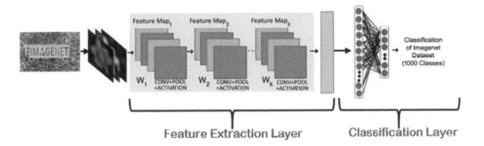

FIGURE 8.1   Basic building blocks of CNN architecture.

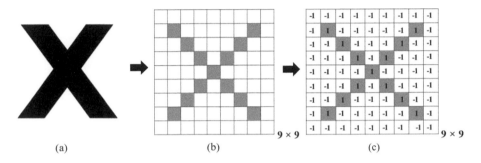

FIGURE 8.2   (a) Real image of 'X'; (b) Represents 'X' in the form of a matrix; (c) Assigned pixel values to separate ground and background pixels (i.e., background: -1 and foreground: 1)

the n−1 layer) and C_k^n as the convolutional kernel at the nth layer. Then for a kth output feature map at n^{th} layer, the rth receptive field inputted from the n−1 layer is convolved with the kth kernel of the nth layer. The process is repeated in each convolution layer of the considered architecture, as shown in Equation 8.1:

$$I_{f_k}^{n-1} = \sum_{r=1}^{m} I_{f_r}^{n-1} * C_{kr}^{n} \tag{8.1}$$

Considering the above-mentioned example, the convolution operation is explained. Let's take a 9×9 image, where each pixel's value is either −1 or 1, and a 3×3 kernel for implementing convolution. To obtain the convolved feature matrices, slide the filter over the image and compute the dot product as shown in Figure 8.3(a)–(d). Depending upon this convolution operation, the size of the output feature maps (S_{FM}) after each convolution layers is calculated by Equation 8.2:

$$S_{FM} = \frac{n - f + 2p}{s} + 1 \tag{8.2}$$

Here, n is the feature map size, f is the filter size, p is the number of padding, and s is the number of strides. Suppose, as shown in Figure 8.3(a), the size of the input image is 9×9 (i.e., $n = 9$) with filter/kernel size 3×3 (i.e., $f = 3$). Also let us assume that no padding is carried out (i.e., $p = 0$) and the convolution operation is performed with stride value of 1 (i.e., $s = 1$). Using Equation (8.2), S_{FM} will be 7 and therefore the size of the output feature map after the convolution operation will be 7×7 as shown in Figure 8.3(d).

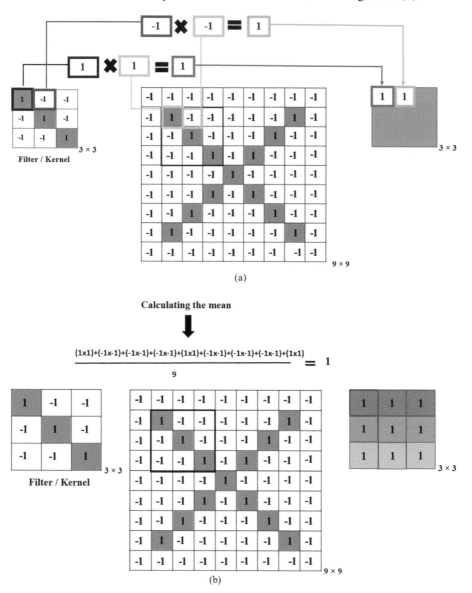

FIGURE 8.3 (a) Taking a 3×3 filter for the image of 'X' and performs pixel-wise multiplication with input image; (b) Performing the mean operation.

(Continued)

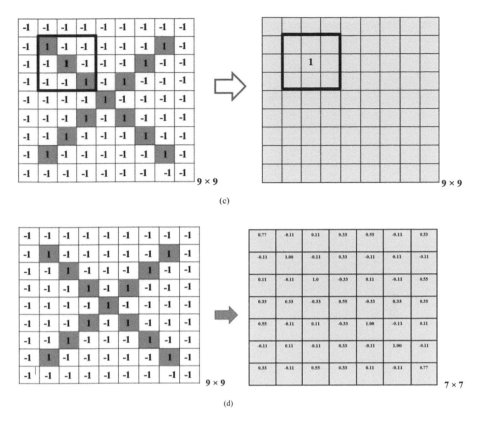

FIGURE 8.3 (CONTINUED) (c) Assigning the mean value in the center of the convolved area; (d) Final feature map extracted after performing convolution operation over the input image.

x	f(x)=x	F(x)
-3	f(-3)=0	0
-5	f(-5)=0	0
3	f(3)=3	3

$$f(x) = \begin{cases} 0 \text{ if } x < 0 \\ x \text{ if } x \geq 0 \end{cases}$$

FIGURE 8.4 Working principle of ReLU activation function.

- **Activation Layer**: Due to activation functions, the network enables nonlinearity. Rectified linear unit (ReLU) is a commonly used activation function in CNNs, which enables a set of negative values as zero while maintaining positive values as it is as shown in Figure 8.4. In the given example presented below, we have removed negative values of the feature maps as shown in Figure 8.5.

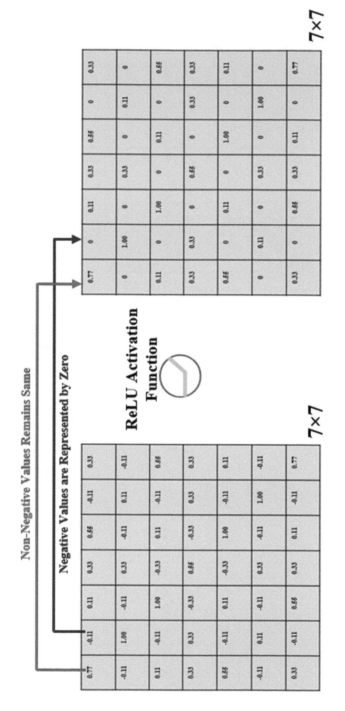

FIGURE 8.5 Feature map with implementing ReLU activation function.

- **Pooling Layer**: The pooling layer is used in CNN to reduce unwanted features. By using this layer, large-scale feature maps reduce into small sizes. Max (maximum) pooling, min (minimum) poling, and average pooling are the three common types of pooling [4]. As compared to convolution operations, the pooling layer also uses a filter and a stride applied to the feature maps to be reduced. In the demonstration, we use max pooling with a size of 2 × 2 filter size of stride 2 as shown in Figure 8.6.
- **Flattened Layer and Fully Connected Layer**: The fully connected layer is responsible for flattening the feature maps with size two-dimensional (2D) matrices to one-dimensional (1D) vectors (i.e., in flattened layer). We have converted the 2D feature map into a vector for 'X' as shown in Figure 8.7. As shown in the aforementioned step, we have applied a similar thing to find the feature vector for 'O' as shown in Figure 8.8(b).

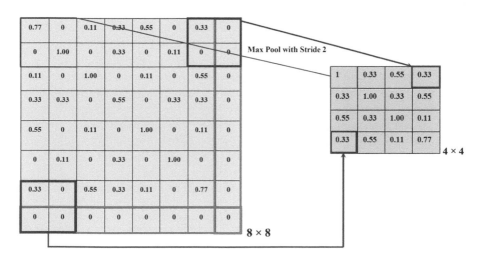

FIGURE 8.6   Performing max pooling operation with 2 × 2 filter size of stride 2.

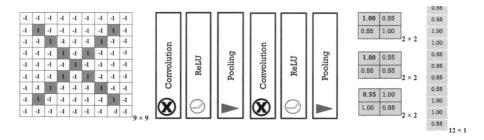

FIGURE 8.7   Flattening the 2D matrix into a 1D vector for further classification.

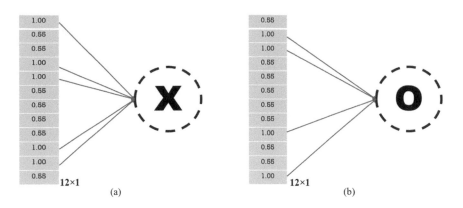

FIGURE 8.8 (a) Feature vector of pattern (i.e., Alphabet) 'X'; (b) Feature vector of pattern (i.e., Alphabet) 'O'.

- **Output Layer/Classification Layer**: For classification purposes in this layer, the softmax function has been used. The function stores the locations of feature maps that contain the highest values. In Figure 8.8, we can see there are five positions containing the highest values (i.e., 1) in the feature vector of 'X' and four positions containing the highest values in feature vectors of 'O'. This layer is the last layer of the training process of CNN architecture. After training the CNN Network as mentioned above, now we will test our trained model. To test our model, we have taken an image and fed it into the same CNN architecture and found the feature vector of the imputed image. Now, the final classification layer will match the feature maps with the trained features map as shown in Figure 8.9. The input image is 51% matched with feature vector 'O' and 91% matched with feature vector 'X', which means the imputed test image is 'X'.

8.1.2 DEEP LEARNING ARCHITECTURES USED FOR BINARY/MULTI-CLASS CLASSIFICATION

In this subsection, some well-known deep learning–based models commonly used as classification algorithms are described. Some of the key characteristics of these described CNN models are summarized in Table 8.1.

8.1.2.1 Visual Geometry Group-16 (VGG-16)

VGG-16 is considered to be the best computer vision–based CNN model to date. It is mostly used in the application of image-based classification tasks [5]. VGG-16 architecture consists of 13 convolutional layers, 5 max pooling layers, and 3 dense layers, which totals 21 layers with 16 weighted layers or learnable parameters as shown in Figure 8.10. The mathematical operations discussed in the preceding section are generally performed in every step of this architecture to get the output vectors.

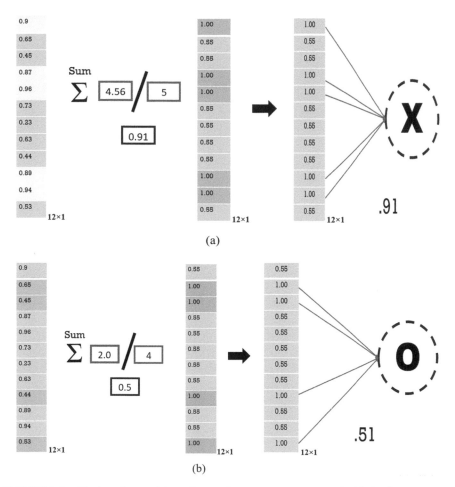

FIGURE 8.9   Testing phases: (a) test image feature vector compared with the feature vector of 'X'; (b) test image feature vector compared with the feature vector of 'O'.

Steps for implementing the VGG-16 are as follows:

The VGG-16 architecture tends to use convolution layers with 3×3 filter with a stride 1 throughout. For the dimensionality reduction, max pooling layer is used with a filter of 2×2 of stride 2.

- **Step 1**: The network requires a 224×224 input image with three RGB channels. This image is passed through a convolution layer having 64 numbers of filters with filter size of 3×3 each and through the RELU (or sometimes written ReLU) activation function that is performed two times, getting an output of $224 \times 224 \times 64$.
- **Step 2**: From the current output of $224 \times 224 \times 64$, it is further passed through the max pooling layer with current filter size of 2×2 with stride 2 to get an output of $112 \times 112 \times 64$.

TABLE 8.1

Differentiate the Key Characteristics of Various Deep Learning–Based Classification Models

Classification Networks	Input Size	Total Layer	Convolutional Layers / Pooling Layer/ Activation Layer	Filter size	Activation Function	Skip Connection	Pooling (Filter size, stride)	No. of Fully Connected Layer	No. of Dropout/ Dropout rate	No. of Neurons	Total Learnable Parameters	Advantage	Disadvantage
VGG-16 [5]	224× 224×3	16	13/5/14	(3×3)	ReLU (13), SoftMax (1)	Not Available	Max-Pooling (2×2, 2)	3	0	4096,4096, 1000	134,268, 738	• Simplicity and uniformity • Good performance • Suitable for transfer learning	• Computational complexity • Limited memory resources
VGG-19 [6]	224× 224×3	19	16/5/19	(3×3)	ReLU (18), SoftMax (1)	Not Available	Max-Pooling (2×2, 2)	3	3/0.5	4096,4096, 1000	14,714, 688	• Enhanced representational power • Learning complexity and hierarchical representations of images • Suitable for transfer learning	• Computationally expensive • Memory-intensive
ResNet-50 [7]	224× 224×3	50	49/2/17	(7×7) (3×3) (1×1)	ReLU (16), SoftMax (1)	Available	Max-Pooling (3×3, 2), Average Pooling (1×1,1)	1	0	1000	234,355, 586	• Vanishing Gradient problem solved • Leading to higher accuracy with state-of-the-art methods • Suitable for transfer learning	• Residual connections increase the computational complexity of the network. • Less memory requirement for resource constrained environment.

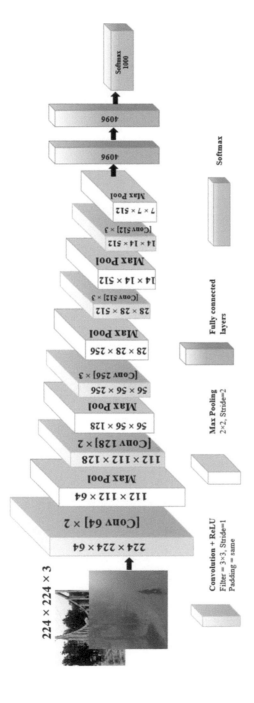

FIGURE 8.10 Backbone architecture of VGG-16.

- **Step 3**: Again, repeating above step 1 for additional two times, i.e., convolutions over the input image of 112 × 112 × 64 with 128 filters and filter size of 3 × 3 each, to get the output of 112 × 112 × 128.
- **Step 4**: With the current dimension of 112 × 112 × 128, it is further passed to the max pooling layer for dimension reduction to get an output of 56 × 56 × 128.
- **Step 5**: In the current step, we perform convolutional operations three times with 256 filters and filter size of 3 × 3 each to get an image of 56 × 56 × 256.
- **Step 6**: The image is further passed to the max pooling layer to get an output of 28 × 28 × 256.
- **Step 7**: Similar to step 5, three times convolution operations are performed with 512 filters over the image with filter size of 3 × 3 each to get an output of 28 × 28 × 512.
- **Step 8**: With the max pooling operation, the dimension is reduced to 14 × 14 × 512.
- **Step 9**: Again, three times convolution operations are performed on the 14 × 14 × 512 with 512 filters with filter size of 3 × 3 each to get an output of 14 × 14 × 512.
- **Step 10**: Once again max pooling is performed to get a dimension of 7 × 7 × 512.
- **Step 11**: Next we flatten the output image of 7 × 7 × 512 of two stacks of 4,096 channels with an image classification of 1,000 channels (one of each class) with the softmax layer.

8.1.2.2   Visual Geometry Group-19 (VGG-19)

This is another standard deep learning–based architecture with multiple layers. In VGG-19 an additional number of layers is added compared to the VGG-16 network. VGG-19 consists of 19 convolution layers, such layers being added for the breakpoint of object recognition and classification [5]. The architecture uses ReLU as the activation function and convolution layers with a kernel size of 3 × 3 and a stride of 1. Max pooling is applied with stride 2's (2 × 2) for the reduction in dimensionality, after the three fully connected layers. Two of the fully connected layers include size 4,096, and the last layer serves as a classification for the softmax as shown in Figure 8.11.

Steps for implementing the VGG-19 are:

- **Step 1**: The architecture takes a fixed input size of 224 × 224 RGB images of shape (224, 224, 3).
- **Step 2**: The input image is passed through the convolution layers of conv1_1, conv1_2, followed by a ReLU activation giving an output of 224 × 224 × 64 followed by a max pooling applied for reducing spatial dimensions, producing a feature maps of size 112 × 112 × 64.
- **Step 3**: With the dimension of 112 × 112 × 64, the image is passed through the second stack of convolution layers of conv2_1,conv2_2 with a ReLU activation applied to convolved feature maps generating 112 × 112 × 128, followed by a 2 × 2 filter max pooling operation that reduces the dimension to 56 × 56 × 128

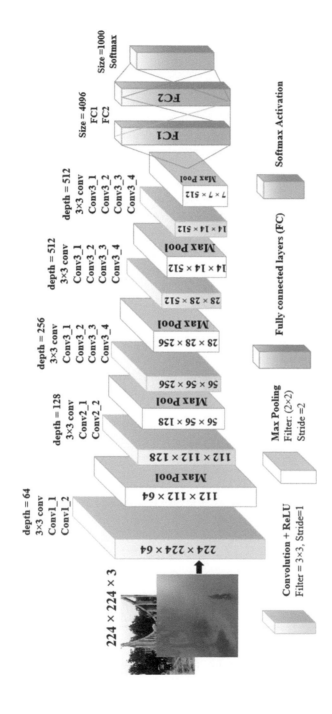

FIGURE 8.11 Backbone architecture of VGG-19 [6].

- **Step 4**: The input of $56 \times 56 \times 128$ is used for the third stack of convolution layers of conv3_1,conv3_2,conv3_3,con4_4 followed by a ReLU activation generating $56 \times 56 \times 256$ feature maps, within a dimension reduction of $28 \times 28 \times 256$ with a 2×2 filter.
- **Step 5**: The $56 \times 56 \times 256$ image is passed through the fourth stack of convolution layers of conv4_1,conv4_2,conv4_3,con4_4 followed by activation function ReLU generating a $28 \times 28 \times 512$ feature maps within max pooling for the reduction to $14 \times 14 \times 512$.
- **Step 6**: Once again $28 \times 28 \times 512$ is passed through the input stack of the fifth convolution layer of conv5_1,conv5_2,conv5_3,conv5_4,conv5_5 followed by ReLU activation generating $14 \times 14 \times 512$ and finally with the max pooling of 2×2 window reducing the dimension to $7 \times 7 \times 512$.
- **Step 7**: Flattening enables conversion into a vector from the feature maps from the most recent pooling layers. The layer has 4,096 neurons that are completely connected. A second layer (F2) has the number of neurons equal to the number of classes passed through the first fully connected layer (F1).
- **Step 8**: The following fully connected layer's output is subjected to softmax activation, which at first is taken into consideration for further class prediction over the input image.

8.1.2.3   Residual Network-50 (ResNet-50)

ResNet is also known as classical neural network used as a backbone in many computer vision tasks. ResNet introduces the concept called skip-connection, which connects activations (i.e., the activated feature map) of a layer to further layers (i.e., the next feature map) by skipping some layers (as needed) in between [7]. This forms a residual block as shown in Figure 8.12. ResNets are made by stacking these residual blocks together. The advantage of adding skip-connection is that if the network performance is reduced due to any subsequent layers, then those layers can be skipped by adding certain skip connections (as shown in Figure 8.12).

Residual Block: The overall residual block is discussed below:

- It takes input data (x) and passes it via a set of convolution layers that give an output (F(x)).
- Then the initial input (x) is added to the immediate output F(x) as shown in Figure 8.12.
- The additional result (i.e., F(x)+x) is passed through the activation function. Most of the time ReLU activation function is used for nonlinearity.

Steps for implementing the ResNet-50 are mentioned below:
The following components are part of the 50-layer ResNet-50 architecture:

- **Input Preprocessing**: Resize your input images to a fixed size (usually 224×224 pixels) and normalize the pixel values.
- **Convolutional Layers**: The first layer is a 7×7 convolutional layer with 64 filters, stride 2, and padding 3. Following the convolution operation, apply batch normalization and ReLU activation function. Follow it with a 3×3 max pooling layer with stride 2.

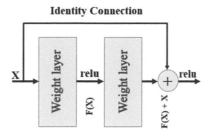

FIGURE 8.12   A single residual block.

- **Residual Blocks**: ResNet-50 consists of several residual blocks. Each residual block has three convolutional layers, and the input is added to the output of the block through a skip connection. There are four types of residual blocks in ResNet-50: Type A (residual block 1 to 3), Type B (residual block 4 to 7), Type C (residual block 8 to 13), and type D (residual block 14 to 16) (as shown in Figure 8.13).
  - **Residual Block Type A**: It starts with a 1×1 convolutional layer with 32 filters, followed by a 3×3 convolutional layer with 32 filters, and ends with a 1×1 convolutional layer with 128 filters. The first and last layers have a 1×1 kernel, and the middle layer has a 3×3 kernel. After each convolution operation, apply batch normalization and ReLU activation function.
  - **Residual Block Type B**: It starts with a 1×1 convolutional layer with 64 filters and stride 2 (only for the first residual block of type B), followed by a 3×3 convolutional layer with 64 filters, and ends with a 1×1 convolutional layer with 256 filters. After each convolution operation, apply batch normalization and ReLU activation function.
  - **Residual Block Type C**: It starts with a 1×1 convolutional layer with 128 filters and stride 2 (only for the first residual block of type C), followed by a 3×3 convolutional layer with 128 filters, and ends with a 1×1 convolutional layer with 512 filters. After each convolution operation, apply batch normalization and ReLU activation function.
  - **Residual Block Type D**: It starts with a 1×1 convolutional layer with 256 filters and stride 2 (only for the first residual block of type D), followed by a 3×3 convolutional layer with 256 filters, and ends with a 1×1 convolutional layer with 1,024 filters. After each convolution operation, apply batch normalization and ReLU activation function.
- **Global Average Pooling**: After the last residual block, apply global average pooling to reduce the spatial dimensions to 1×1 while retaining the channel dimensions.
- **Fully Connected Layer**: Add a fully connected layer with 1,000 units (assuming you have 1,000 classes for classification). Apply softmax activation to obtain class probabilities.

The result is a deep convolutional network with 50 layers $(1 + 9 + 12 + 18 + 9 + 1)$ once everything has been added together as shown in Figure 8.13.

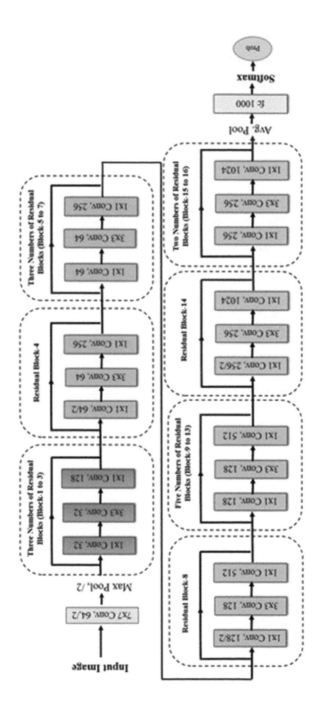

FIGURE 8.13   ResNet-50 architecture.

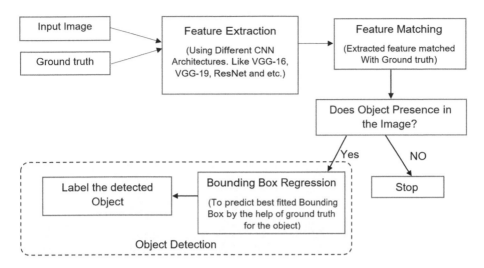

FIGURE 8.14 Basic block diagram of classification and localization for object detection methods.

8.1.3 DEEP LEARNING ARCHITECTURES USED FOR OBJECT DETECTION

The general block diagram of the deep learning–based object detection algorithms is shown in Figure 8.14.

8.1.3.1 Region-Based Convolutional Neural Network (R-CNN)

Region-based CNN includes three components: region proposal, feature extractor, and classifier network. The fundamental idea behind the R-CNN series are region proposals. The region proposals are considered mainly the bounding boxes, and the labeling of their class of an image. It employs a selective search algorithm to propose bounding boxes that cover the object presence in an image [8]:

$$S\left(r_i,r_j\right)=S_{color}\left(r_i,r_j\right)+S_{texture}\left(r_i,r_j\right)+S_{size}\left(r_i,r_j\right)+S_{fill}\left(r_i,r_j\right) \qquad (8.3)$$

where r_i and r_j are two regions of an image and $S(r_i, r_j)$ represents the overall similarity between two regions. $S_{color}(r_i, r_j)$ is color similarity of the two regions calculated by $S_{color}\left(r_i,r_j\right)=\sum_{k=1}^{n}\min\left(c_i^k,c_j^k\right)$, where c_i^k is the histogram for k^{th} grey value in a color descriptor. $S_{texture}(r_i, r_j)$ represents the texture similarity between two regions, $S_{texture}\left(r_i,r_j\right)\sum_{k=1}^{n}\min\left(t_i^k,t_j^k\right)$, where, t_i^k is the histogram for k^{th} grey value in texture descriptor. $S_{size}(r_i, r_j)$ represents size similarity between two regions, $S_{size}\left(r_i,r_j\right)=1-\dfrac{size\left(r_i\right)+size\left(r_j\right)}{size\left(im\right)}$, where $size(im)$ is the image size in pixels. $S_{fill}(r_i, r_j)$ is used to find the shape compatibility measures, meaning how well the two regions fit into each other. If r_i fits into r_j, merge them to discard the repeated regions, and if the regions do not touch each other, they did not merge. It can be defined as

$$S_{fill}\left(r_i, r_j\right) = 1 - \frac{size\left(B_{ij}\right) - size\left(r_i\right) - size\left(r_j\right)}{size\left(im\right)}, \text{ where } B_{ij} \; x \text{ is the bounding box of } r_i$$

and r_j.

Steps for implementing the region-based convolutional neural network (R-CNN):

- **Step 1**: First, it takes an input image with more than one object presence inside it. Then the selective search algorithm generates ~2,000 region proposals (bounding boxes) as shown in Figure 8.15. Then each region proposal will be fed into a CNN to extract the features. Selective search algorithm consists of the following steps:
  - **Image Segmentation**: The initial step is to segment the input image into smaller regions using a selective search algorithm based on color, texture, and other low-level image features. This step generates a set of image segments or regions, each representing a distinct region within the image.
  - **Region Similarity**: The next step involves measuring the similarity between different regions based on various criteria such as color similarity, texture similarity, and size similarity. Similar regions are grouped together to form larger regions while dissimilar regions remain separate.
  - **Region Merging**: The similar regions are successively merged based on their similarity scores, forming a hierarchy of regions. This process is performed using a hierarchical clustering algorithm, where the most similar regions are merged first, and the merging continues until all regions are merged into a single region.
  - **Region Selection**: The region hierarchy generated in the previous step contains regions at different scales and levels of granularity. In this step, a set of object proposals is obtained by selecting regions at multiple scales and levels of the hierarchy. The aim is to capture potential objects of various sizes and aspect ratios.
  - **Object Proposal Refinement**: The final step involves refining the object proposals to improve their quality and accuracy. Various strategies can be applied, such as eliminating proposals that are too small or too large,

FIGURE 8.15   Selective search algorithm applied to the input image for region proposals.

Proposed Regions

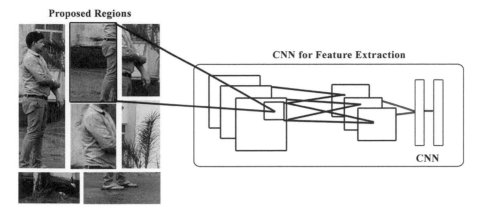

FIGURE 8.16   Region's proposals warped and passed to the CNN network.

removing low-confidence proposals based on a confidence score, and
reducing the number of redundant proposals.

- **Step 2**: After that, each region is fed into a CNN to extract the features as
  shown in Figure 8.16.
- **Step 3: Bounding Box Regression**: After extracting the features for individual region proposals, R-CNN employs a bounding box regression step
  to refine the initially proposed bounding box coordinates. This regression
  process aims to adjust the coordinate locations of the bounding box to
  more accurately align with the object's boundaries. The regression is typically achieved through another network branch that anticipated the relative
  adjustments for the coordinates of the bounding box.
- **Step 4: Non-Maximum Suppression (NMS)**: Removing redundant and
  overlapping bounding boxes, R-CNN applies a technique called non-maximum suppression (NMS). NMS compares the predicted bounding boxes
  based on their confidence scores and suppresses the boxes that overlap significantly, using Equation (8.4). This step ensures that only the most confident and non-overlapping bounding boxes are retained for further analysis.

$$S_i = \begin{cases} S_i, & \text{iou}(M,b_i) \geq N_t \\ S_i(1-\text{iou}(M,b_i)), & \text{iou}(M,b_i) \geq N_t \end{cases} \tag{8.4}$$

where S_i is score of region proposal for image I, b_i is the proposed bounding
box for i, M is the bounding box with maximum confidence score, and N_t is
the IOU threshold.

- **Step 5: Classification**: Once the refined bounding boxes are obtained,
  R-CNN performs object classification for each bounding box to determine
  the object category. The CNN features extracted earlier are used as classifier input (e.g., a fully connected layer or a support vector machine) trained
  to recognize various object classes. This step assigns a label to each proposed bounding box, indicating the detected object category as shown in
  Figure 8.17. For further details, see Section 7.2.2.1.

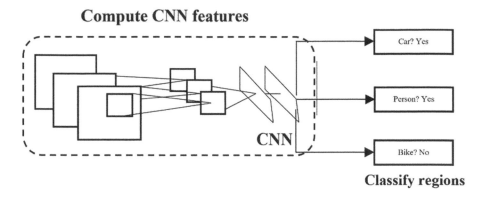

Classify regions

FIGURE 8.17   Classification output.

8.1.3.2   Fast Region-Based Convolutional Neural Network (Fast R-CNN)

A redesigned form of Fast R-CNN is employed to address the object detection issues. This network was designed to address several shortcomings of R-CNN. The proposed network has a new layer called the ROI pooling layer. The key difference between Fast R-CNN and R-CNN is that with Fast R-CNN the whole image is fed to the network directly whereas R-CNN just takes the region proposal parts [9].

   Steps for implementing the Fast R-CNN:

- **Step 1**: F-RCNN receives the whole image as an input and passes it through the sets of convolution layers to extract features from the given image. The network is also able to generate extraction of region proposals similar to R-CNN-based selective search approach as illustrated in Figure 8.18.
- **Step 2**: These feature maps are passed to the ROI pooling layer. The ROI pooling layer is accountable for aligning the region proposals with the fixed-size feature maps obtained from the CNN. Since the region proposals

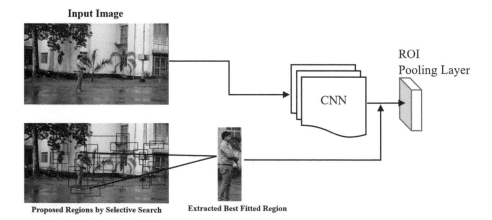

FIGURE 8.18   Extraction of features from region proposals and the corresponding image.

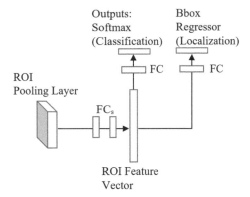

FIGURE 8.19   Detection results for each ROI.

can have different sizes and aspect ratios, they need to be resized to a consistent spatial resolution to be fed into fully connected layers for bounding box regression and classification. The layer of ROI pooling divides each proposed region into equal-sized spatial bins or cells. It then performs max pooling within each bin to obtain a fixed-sized output representation. The size of the output representation is typically set to a predetermined value, such as 7 × 7. This pooling operation allows the network to maintain spatial information while converting variable-sized regions into fixed-sized feature maps. In Fast R-CNN, the ROI pooling layer employs adaptive pooling, which dynamically adjusts the output size based on the size of the region proposal. This adaptive pooling mechanism ensures that the output feature maps have a consistent spatial resolution, regardless of the size or aspect ratio of the proposed region. It allows the network to handle regions of different sizes effectively.

- **Step 3**: After ROI pooling, the fixed-sized feature maps from each region proposal are transmitted through fully connected layers for bounding box and object classification regression. These layers learn to predict the object class and refine the coordinates of the proposed bounding boxes. For further details, see Section 7.2.2.2.

8.1.3.3   Faster Region-Based Convolutional Neural Network (Faster R-CNN)

In contrast to Fast R-CNN, Faster R-CNN is computationally faster. Faster R-CNN introduces the region proposal network (RPN) for the generation of bounding boxes or localization of objects along with their label to predict under which class the object falls, with a regression layer to make the coordinates of the object bounding box to be more precise [10].

Steps for implementing Faster R-CNN follow.

- **Step 1**: Takes an input image and passes it to the backbone network, basically CNN, to get feature maps as shown in Figure 8.20, similar to the Fast R-CNN step.

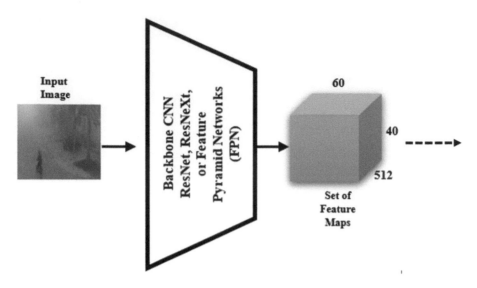

FIGURE 8.20   Features extracted backbone layers.

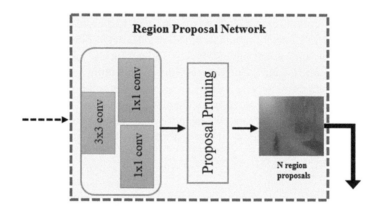

FIGURE 8.21   RPN network tends to generate N region proposals.

- **Step 2: Region Proposal Network (RPN)**: Implement the RPN component, which generates region proposals within the network. The RPN is typically a separate subnetwork that shares the convolutional layers with the backbone network. It proposes potential object regions and assigns objectness scores to these regions based on their likelihood of containing an object as shown in Figure 8.21.
- **Step 3: Anchor Generation**: In the RPN, anchors are predefined boxes of different scales and aspect ratios that are used to generate region proposals. Implement the anchor generation mechanism by selecting appropriate anchor scales and aspect ratios that are suited to the objects being detected. After generating anchor boxes across the image using predefined scales and aspect ratios, the next step is to filter the anchor boxes based on their quality.

This is typically done by discarding anchor boxes that have significant overlap with ground truth bounding boxes. Anchor boxes that have an intersection over union (IoU) overlap above a certain threshold (e.g., 0.7) with any ground truth box are considered positive anchors as shown in Figure 8.22.

- **Step 4: Object Classification and Bounding Box Regression**: The fixed-sized feature maps from the ROI pooling layer are utilized in object classification and bounding box regression. The region proposals are fed into fully connected layers, where object classification probabilities are computed for each proposal, indicating the presence of different object classes. Additionally, bounding box regression is performed to refine the coordinates of the proposals, improving their alignment with the actual objects (Figure 8.23). For more details, see Section 7.2.2.3.

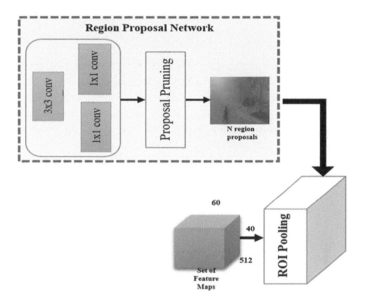

FIGURE 8.22   Region proposals passed through ROI pooling.

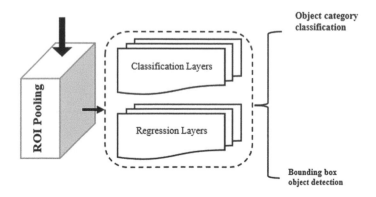

FIGURE 8.23   Final output with object classification and object detection.

8.1.3.4 Mask Region-Based Convolutional Neural Network (Mask R-CNN)

Object detection using Mask R-CNN is another state-of-the-art computer vision technique that combines the capabilities of object detection and instance segmentation. Mask R-CNN extends the Faster R-CNN framework by incorporating a pixel-level segmentation branch. It enables not only identifying and localizing objects within an image but also generating high-resolution instance masks for each object. By leveraging deep learning–based convolutional neural networks, Mask R-CNN can accurately detect and segment objects of various classes in complex scenes. This powerful technique finds applications in areas such as robots, autonomous vehicles, and medical imaging, where precise object detection and segmentation are crucial for understanding visual data [11].

- **Step 1**: Takes an input image and passes it to the backbone network as ResNet [12], ResNeXt [13], or Feature Pyramid Networks (FPN) to get a set of various feature maps as shown in Figure 8.24, similar to the Faster RCNN step.
- **Step 2: Region proposal network (RPN)**: RPN is a key component of the Mask R-CNN framework in terms of segmentation and object detection. It plays a vital role in generating regional proposals that are likely to contain objects of interest. RPN operates on a feature maps extracted from the backbone network (such as ResNet or ResNeXt) and generates a set of region proposals as shown in Figure 8.24. These proposals serve as potential bounding box candidates for objects in the image (Figure 8.25).
- **Step 3**: After the RPN generates region proposals as shown in Figure 8.26, the first step is to perform ROI Align. ROI Align addresses the misalignment problem that arises when mapping region proposals to the feature maps. Unlike the ROI pooling method in Fast R-CNN, ROI Align uses bilinear interpolation to sample feature points within each region proposal, enabling more precise localization and preserving spatial information.

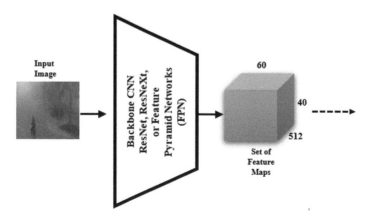

FIGURE 8.24 Feature extraction module.

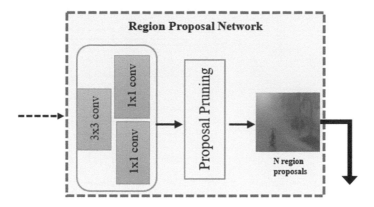

FIGURE 8.25   Region proposal network (RPN) module.

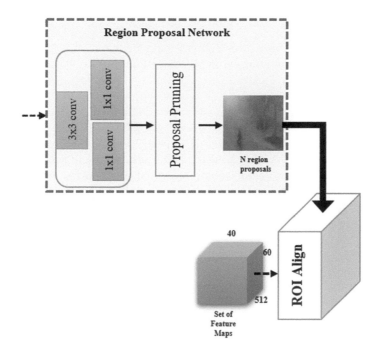

FIGURE 8.26   Region of interest (ROI) alignment module.

- **Step 4: Feature Extraction**: The ROI-aligned region proposals are passed through a feature extraction network, typically a convolutional neural network (CNN) backbone such as ResNet or ResNeXt. The feature extraction stage aims to extract high-level features that capture semantic information and discriminative characteristics of the proposed regions.
- **Step 5: Region Classification**: The extracted features from each region proposal are used for region classification. A classifier, often implemented

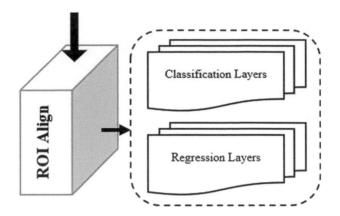

FIGURE 8.27 Two different heads of two layers.

as fully connected layers, is employed to predict the object class probabilities for each region proposal as shown in Figure 8.27. This step assigns a label to the individual proposed region, indicating the detected object category.

- **Step 6: Bounding Box Regression**: In addition to region classification, Mask R-CNN performs bounding box regression to refine the coordinates of the proposed bounding boxes as shown in Figure 8.27. Another set of fully connected layers is utilized to predict adjustments to the initially proposed bounding box coordinates, improving their alignment with the actual objects.
- **Step 7: Prediction of Mask**: Mask R-CNN goes beyond object detection by incorporating an instance segmentation branch. This step involves predicting a binary mask for each proposed region, which outlines the pixel-level boundaries of the object. A mask prediction network is typically employed, which takes the features extracted from each region proposal and generates a mask for the corresponding object instance.
- **Step 8**: After mask prediction, postprocessing techniques are applied to refine the results. This may involve filtering out low-confidence detections, performing non-maximum suppression (NMS) to remove redundant bounding boxes, and applying thresholding or other techniques to enhance the quality of the predicted masks. For more information, see Section 7.2.2.4.

8.1.3.5 Single-Shot Multibox Detector (SSD)

Single-Shot Multibox Detector, introduced by Wei Liu et al. in 2016 [14], is a deep learning–based method that is mostly used for the purpose of object detection in real-time applications. It is a popular object detection algorithm that combines object localization and classification in a single-shot manner. The main goal of the SSD algorithm is to perform detection by predicting the bounding box and the class labels of the objects in a single pass of a neural network, i.e., they directly predict default bounding boxes (predefined anchor boxes) and class labels for objects in a single pass over the input image. It generates multiple bounding boxes of different aspect ratios and scores if an instance of the object class is present in those boxes, preceded by a non-maximum suppression step performed to generate the final bounding boxes [15]. Steps for implementation of the single-shot multibox detector (SSD) are:

- **Step 1**: SSD takes an input image and divides it into a grid of evenly spaced cells as given in Figures 8.28 and 8.29.
- **Step 2: Feature Extraction**: The input image is processed by a feature extraction network, typically a pretrained CNN such as VGGNet or ResNet. The CNN extracts high-level features that capture various levels of spatial information and semantic content from the input image. These features are essential for accurately detecting objects of different scales and aspect ratios. The network for feature extraction produces a series of convolutional feature maps at different spatial resolutions. These feature maps represent the output of different convolutional layers in the CNN. Each feature map encodes specific spatial information and semantic features, with higher-level feature maps containing more abstract representations as in Figure 8.30.
- **Step 3: Base Network**: Utilizing a base CNN architecture, such as VGG-16 or ResNet, to process the input image and extract high-level features as shown in Figure 8.31.

FIGURE 8.28   N × N input image.

FIGURE 8.29   N × N input image with grid cells.

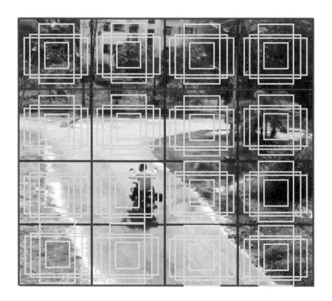

FIGURE 8.30   Multiple default boxes of different sizes and different aspect ratio.

- **Step 4: Multiscale Feature Maps**: To handle objects at different scales, SSD applies a set of additional convolutional layers, known as extra layers (as shown in a red box in Figure 8.31), on top of the feature maps. These extra layers produce additional feature maps at various scales because of different scaled feature maps shown in Figure 8.31. The multiscale feature

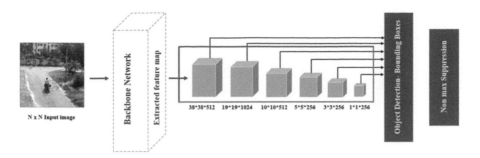

FIGURE 8.31   SSD architecture.

maps allow SSD to detect objects at different sizes and adaptively adjust the size of the default anchor boxes used for localization.

- **Step 5: Anchor Box Generation**: For each spatial position in the feature maps, SSD generates a collection of standard anchor boxes with various sizes and aspect ratios. These anchor boxes act as reference boxes at different locations, enabling the network to predict object bounding boxes. The number and sizes of anchor boxes per spatial position are predefined according to the features of the dataset and the desired object scales.
- **Step 6: Object Localization**: SSD predicts the offset values for each default anchor box (i.e., location-oriented information for default anchor boxes) to localize the objects within the image. These offset values, typically represented as offsets in terms of coordinates (e.g., x, y, width, and height), are learned during training. By applying the predicted offsets to the default anchor boxes, SSD obtains the final bounding box predictions for the detected objects as given in Figure 8.32.
- **Step 7: Object Classification**: In addition to localization, SSD performs object classification to determine the object class for each detected bounding box. For each default anchor box, SSD predicts class probabilities using a set of convolutional layers preceded by fully connected layers.

 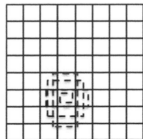 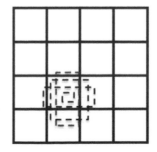

FIGURE 8.32   (a) Image and their corresponding ground truth; (b) feature map with a 8 × 8 dimension; (c) feature map with a 4 × 4 dimension.

FIGURE 8.33   Image with predicted boxes.

These layers learn to classify the objects into predefined groups based on the characteristics that were retrieved from the feature maps as shown in Figure 8.33.

- **Step 8: Non-Maximum Suppression (NMS)**: To remove unwanted and overlapping bounding box predictions, SSD employs non-maximum suppression (NMS). NMS identifies the most confident bounding box predictions for each object class and eliminates duplicate predictions that significantly overlap highly similarity matching boxes (i.e., IOU of the generated default boxes is greater than threshold value [usually 0.45]) as mentioned in Figure 8.34. This postprocessing step ensures that only the most accurate and distinct bounding boxes are retained.
- **Step 9: Object Detection Output**: The final output of SSD includes the detected bounding boxes and corresponding class labels. These results represent the objects detected in the input image, along with their respective categories and class levels, as shown in Figure 8.35.

8.1.3.6 You Only Look Once (YOLO)

YOLO is a single-phase network trained over the images and directly predicts what objects are present within the image. **This network tries to predict the probability of classes along with bounding box coordinates of the current input** [16]. The

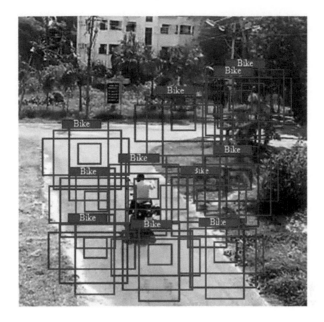

FIGURE 8.34   Image before non-maximal suppression.

FIGURE 8.35   Output image after non-max suppression.

algorithm uses single forward circulation, which indicates that a single algorithm run is used to perform prediction on the whole image through a neural network for object detection. The goal of the architecture is to predict the class probabilities synchronously with the bounding boxes. Steps for implementing YOLO are:

- **Step 1: The input image splits into S × S grid cells**. Each cell is responsible for the object being in the center of the grid cell, which may be the grid cell accountable for the current detection of that object. For each grid position, predict the classes with bounding boxes of objects that reside on the grid as given in Figure 8.36.
- **Step 2**: Each grid predicts B bounding boxes and its confidence scores. Confidence is calculated using Equation 8.5:

$$C_i = \Pr(object) * IOU_{pred}^{truth} \qquad (8.5)$$

where C_i is the confidence score for predicted bounding box and $Pr(object)$ is probability estimation that the object is present or not. If $Pr(object) = 0$, that means the background area contains the bounding box, and $Pr(object) = 1$ if the region where the object is located is included in the bounding box; IoU represents the intersection over union between the predicted box and the ground truth. In the absence of any objects on the cell, **zero is the confidence score**. Meanwhile, the presence of an object means there is a confidence score defined by IoU, which is a popular metric for calculating localization errors and localization accuracy between the predicted box and the ground truth. **Each bounding box consists of five predictions: x (x coordinate of center), y (y coordinate of center), w (width of bounding box), h (height of bounding box), and c (confidence).**

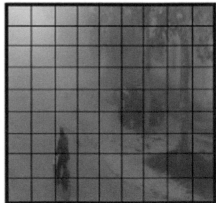

Input Image   **S x S grid over input image**

FIGURE 8.36   Input image divided into S × S grid.

The center of the field is related to the grid cell boundaries representing (x,y) coordinates. Width and height are anticipated for the entire image. Finally, the confidence prediction shows IoU between any ground truth boxes and the anticipated boxes. The combination of bounding boxes and confidence generation with class probability map is pictured in Figure 8.37.

- **Step 3**: Along with this each **grid cell, predict conditional class probabilities** (C), *Pr(Class$_i$ | Object)*. The condition depends on the grid cells containing any object. Regardless of number of boxes B, it only anticipates class probabilities of one set. The final prediction is based on multiplying probabilities of class along with the separate confidence with bounding box predictions as shown in Equation 8.6:

$$\Pr(class_i \mid object) * \Pr\left(object\right) * IOU_{truth}^{pred} = \Pr\left(class_i\right) * IOU_{pred}^{truth} \qquad (8.6)$$

where *Pr(class$_i$ | object)* is the probability of the object belongs to *class$_i$*, given as object presence; *Pr(object)* is probability the box contains the object; *IoU* represents the intersection over union between predicted box and ground truth; and *Pr(class$_i$)* is the probability the object belongs to *class$_i$*.

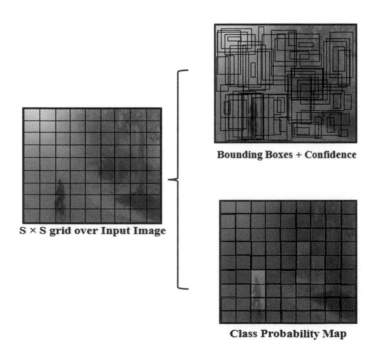

Bounding Boxes + Confidence

S × S grid over Input Image

Class Probability Map

FIGURE 8.37   Bounding boxes + confidence generation with class probability map.

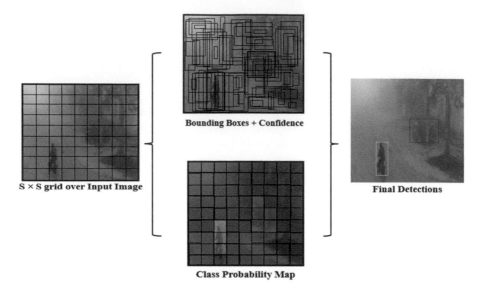

S × S grid over Input Image | Bounding Boxes + Confidence | Final Detections

Class Probability Map

FIGURE 8.38 Final predicted boxes with object detection.

Equation 8.4 gives the confidence score for each box based on class. These scores represent the likelihood that a certain class will appear in the box as well as how well the predicted box matches the actual object. Final predicted boxes for object detection using YOLO architecture are shown in Figure 8.38. YOLO-related detailed description with architecture is previously discussed in Chapter 7 (Section 7.2.2.6).

8.2 PRACTICAL APPROACHES AND APPLICATIONS

In this section, source codes of deep learning–based algorithms for classification and detection of objects in various scenes are presented. Each of these source codes is provided on the Python platform, and various prerequisites for execution of the source codes are provided in the following subsection.

8.2.1 INTRODUCTION TO PYTHON

Python is a highly interpreted programming language released in 1991 by Guido van Rossum [17]. This language is known for clear indentation, prior readability, versatility alongside many applications in fields of web development, data analysis, etc. It is also an open-source language, which means its source code is available for anyone to view, modify, and distribute freely. It is distinct from other languages, with immense libraries of modules that provide prewritten code for a wide variety of tasks, making it easier and faster to develop applications. Some of the popular libraries in Python include NumPy, Pandas, Matplotlib, TensorFlow, and PyTorch. This language also allows a community to support and document the code with choices for both learners and experienced programmers.

8.2.2 Installation of Python

Python can be installed on Windows and Unix operating systems; users can download it from the https://www.python.org/ or https://www.anaconda.com/download/ [18]. From the above link download the latest version of Python IDE and install it.

8.2.3 Source Codes of Deep Learning–Based Algorithms for Classification and Object Detection

8.2.3.1 Source Code of Basic CNN [19]

```python
import tensorflow as tf
from tensorflow.keras import layers

# Create a sequential model
model = tf.keras.Sequential()

# Add a convolutional Layer with 32 filters, a 3×3 kernel, and ReLU activation
model.add(layers. Conv2D(32, (3, 3), activation='relu', input_shape=(64, 64, 3)))

# Add a max pooling layer with 2×2 pool size
model.add(layers. MaxPooling2D((2, 2)))

# Add another convolutional layer with 64 filters, a 3×3 kernel, and ReLU activation
model.add(layers. Conv2D(64, (3, 3), activation='relu'))

# Add a max pooling layer with 2×2 pool size
model.add(layers. MaxPooling2D((2, 2)))
# Add a flatten Layer to convert the 2D output to a 1D feature vector
model.add(layers.Flatten())

# Add a dense Layer with 64 units and ReLU activation
model.add(layers. Dense (64, activation='relu'))

# Add an output layer with 10 units (assuming 10 classes) and softmax activation
model.add(layers. Dense (10, activation='softmax'))

# Compile the model
model.compile(optimizer='adam',
        loss='categorical_crossentropy',
        metrics=['accuracy'])

# Print the model summary
model.summary()
```

8.2.3.2   Source Code of VGG-16 [20]

```python
from keras.models import Sequential
from keras.layers import Conv2D, MaxPooling2D, Flatten, Dense

def VGG16():
    model = Sequential()

    # Block 1
    model.add(Conv2D (64, (3, 3), activation='relu', padding='same', input_
    shape=(224, 224, 3)))
    model.add(Conv2D(64, (3, 3), activation='relu', padding='same'))
    model.add(MaxPooling2D((2, 2), strides=(2, 2)))

    # Block 2
    model.add(Conv2D (128, (3, 3), activation='relu', padding='same'))
    model.add(Conv2D (128, (3, 3), activation='relu', padding='same'))
    model.add(MaxPooling2D ((2, 2), strides (2, 2)))

    # Block 3
    model.add(Conv2D (256, (3, 3), activation='relu', padding='same'))
    model.add(Conv2D (256, (3, 3), activation='relu', padding='same'))
    model.add(Conv2D (256, (3, 3), activation='relu', padding='same'))
    model.add(MaxPooling2D((2, 2), strides (2, 2)))

    # Block 4
    model.add(Conv2D(512, (3, 3), activation= 'relu', padding='same'))
    model.add(Conv2D(512, (3, 3), activation='relu', padding='same'))
    model.add(Conv2D(512, (3, 3), activation='relu', padding='same'))
    model.add(MaxPooling2D((2, 2), strides (2, 2)))
    # Block 5
    model.add(Conv2D(512, (3, 3), activation='relu', padding='same'))
    model.add(Conv2D(512, (3, 3), activation='relu', padding='same'))
    model.add(Conv2D(512, (3, 3), activation='relu', padding='same'))
    model.add(MaxPooling2D((2, 2), strides=(2, 2)))

    # Classification Layers
    model.add(Flatten())
    model.add(Dense (4096, activation='relu'))
    model.add(Dense (4096, activation='relu'))
    model.add(Dense (1000, activation='softmax')) # Assumes 1000 classes

    return model

# Create an instance of the VGG16 model
vgg16 model = VGG16()
```

8.2.3.3   Source Code of VGG-19 [21]

```
from keras.models import Sequential
from keras.layers import Conv2D, MaxPooling2D, Flatten, Dense

def VGG16():
    model = Sequential()

    # Block 1
    model.add(Conv2D (64, (3, 3), activation='relu', padding='same', input_
    shape=(224, 224, 3)))
    model.add(Conv2D(64, (3, 3), activation='relu', padding='same'))
    model.add(MaxPooling2D((2, 2), strides=(2, 2)))

    # Block 2
    model.add(Conv2D (128, (3, 3), activation='relu', padding='same'))
    model.add(Conv2D (128, (3, 3), activation='relu', padding='same'))
    model.add(MaxPooling2D ((2, 2), strides (2, 2)))

    # Block 3
    model.add(Conv2D (256, (3, 3), activation='relu', padding='same'))
    model.add(Conv2D (256, (3, 3), activation='relu', padding='same'))
    model.add(Conv2D (256, (3, 3), activation='relu', padding='same'))
    model.add(Conv2D (256, (3, 3), activation='relu', padding='same'))
    model.add(MaxPooling2D((2, 2), strides (2, 2)))

    # Block 4
    model.add(Conv2D(512, (3, 3), activation= 'relu', padding='same'))
    model.add(Conv2D(512, (3, 3), activation='relu', padding='same'))
    model.add(Conv2D(512, (3, 3), activation='relu', padding='same'))
    model.add(Conv2D(512, (3, 3), activation='relu', padding='same'))
    model.add(MaxPooling2D((2, 2), strides (2, 2)))

    # Block 5
    model.add(Conv2D(512, (3, 3), activation='relu', padding='same'))
    model.add(Conv2D(512, (3, 3), activation='relu', padding='same'))
    model.add(Conv2D(512, (3, 3), activation='relu', padding='same'))
    model.add(Conv2D(512, (3, 3), activation='relu', padding='same'))
    model.add(MaxPooling2D((2, 2), strides=(2, 2)))

    # Classification Layers
    model.add(Flatten())
    model.add(Dense (4096, activation='relu'))
    model.add(Dense (4096, activation='relu'))
    model.add(Dense (1000, activation='softmax')) # Assumes 1000 classes

    return model
```

```python
# Create an instance of the VGG19 model
vgg16 model = VGG19()
```

8.2.3.4 Source Code of ResNet-50 [22]

```python
import tensorflow as tf
from tensorflow. keras import layers

def identity_block (input_tensor, kernel_size, filters, stage, block):
    filters1, filters2, filters3 = filters

    conv_name_base = 'res' + str(stage) + block + '_branch'
    bn_name_base = 'bn' + str(stage) + block + '_branch'

    x = layers.Conv2D (filters1, (1, 1), name=conv_name_base + '2a') (input_tensor)
    x = layers. BatchNormalization (name=bn_name_base + '2a') (x)
    x = layers. Activation ('relu')(x)

    x = layers.Conv2D(filters2, kernel_size, padding='same', name=conv_name_
        base + '2b')(x)
    x= layers.BatchNormalization (name=bn_name_base + '2b') (x)
    x = layers.Activation('relu') (x)

    x = layers.Conv2D(filters3, (1, 1), name=conv_name_base + '2c')(x)
    x = layers.BatchNormalization (name=bn_name_base + '2c') (x)

    x = layers.add([x, input_tensor])
    x = layers.Activation ('relu') (x)
    return x
def conv_block(input_tensor, kernel_size, filters, stage, block, strides=(2, 2)):
    filters1, filters2, filters3 = filters

    conv_name_base = 'res' + str(stage) + block + '_branch'
    bn_name_base = 'bn' + str(stage) + block + '_branch'

    x =layers.Conv2D(filters1, (1, 1), strides strides, name=conv_name_base + '2a')
        (input_tensor)
    x = layers.BatchNormalization (name=bn_name_base + '2a') (x)
    x = layers.Activation('relu')(x)

    x = layers.Conv2D(filters2, kernel_size, padding='same', name=conv_name_
        base + '2b')(x)
    x = layers.BatchNormalization (name=bn_name_base + '2b') (x)
    x = layers.Activation('relu')(x)

    x = layers.Conv2D(filters3, (1, 1), name=conv_name_base + '2c') (x)
    x = layers.BatchNormalization (name=bn_name_base + '2c')(x)
```

```python
        shortcut = layers.Conv2D(filters3, (1, 1), strides=strides, name=conv_name_base
        + '1') (input_tensor)
        shortcut = layers. BatchNormalization (name=bn_name_base + '1') (shortcut)

        x = layers.add([x, shortcut])
        x = layers.Activation ('relu') (x)
        return x

def ResNet50(input_shape=(224, 224, 3), classes=1000):
        img_input layers. Input (shape=input_shape)

        x = layers.ZeroPadding2D(padding=(3, 3)) (img_input)
        x = layers.Conv2D(64, (7, 7), strides (2, 2), name='conv1')(x)
        x = layers. BatchNormalization (name='bn_conv1') (x)
        x = layers.Activation('relu')(x)
        x = layers.MaxPooling2D((3, 3), strides (2, 2))(x)

        x = conv_block(x, 3, [64, 64, 256], stage=2, block='a', strides=(1, 1))
        x = identity_block(x, 3, [64, 64, 256], stage=2, block='b')
        x = identity_block(x, 3, [64, 64, 256], stage=2, block='c')

        x = conv_block(x, 3, [128, 128, 512], stage=3, block='a')
        x = identity_block(x, 3, [128, 128, 512], stage=3, block='b')
        x = identity_block(x, 3, [128, 128, 512], stage=3, block='c')
        x = identity_block(x, 3, [128, 128, 512], stage=3, block='d')

        x = conv_block(x, 3, [256, 256, 1024], stage=4, block='a')
        x = identity_block(x, 3, [256, 256, 1024], stage=4, block='b')
        x = identity_block(x, 3, [256, 256, 1024], stage=4, block='c')
        x = identity_block(x, 3, [256, 256, 1024], stage=4, block='d')
        x = identity_block(x, 3, [256, 256, 1024], stage=4, block='e')
        x = identity_block(x, 3, [256, 256, 1024], stage=4, block='f')

        x = conv_block(x, 3, [512, 512, 2048], stage=5, block='a')
        x = identity_block(x, 3, [512, 512, 2048], stage=5, block='b')
        x = identity_block(x, 3, [512, 512, 2048], stage=5, block='c')

        x = layers.GlobalAveragePooling2D (name='avg_pool')(x)
        x = layers. Dense (classes, activation='softmax', name='fc' + str(classes))(x)

        model = tf.keras. Model (img_input, x, name='resnet50')
        return model

# Create ResNet-50 model
resnet50 = ResNet50()
```

```
# Print model summary
resnet50.summary()
```

8.2.3.5   Source Code of R-CNN [23]

```
import cv2
import numpy as np

# Function to perform selective search for region proposal
def selective_search(image):
    # Load the image
    cv2.setUseOptimized(True)
    cv2.setNumThreads (4)
    ss = cv2.ximgproc.segmentation.createSelectiveSearchSegmentation()

    # Set the input image
    ss.setBaseImage(image)

    # Switch to fast mode (optional)
    ss.switchToSelectiveSearchFast()

    # Perform selective search to generate regions
    regions = ss.process()

    return regions

# Load the input image
image = cv2.imread('input_image.jpg')

# Perform selective search for region proposal
regions = selective_search(image)

# Display the number of proposed regions
print (f"Total proposed regions: {len (regions)}")

# Visualize the proposed regions
for i, (x, y, w, h) in enumerate (regions):
    # Draw rectangle around the proposed region
    cv2.rectangle(image, (x, y), (x + w, y + h), (0, 255, 0), 2)

    # Display the region number
    cv2.putText(image, str(i + 1), (x, y - 10), cv2.FONT_HERSHEY_SIMPLEX,
        0.9, (0, 255, 0), 2)

# Display the image with proposed regions
cv2.imshow("Proposed Regions", image)
cv2.waitKey(0)
```

```
cv2.destroyAllWindows()

import numpy as np
import os
import cv2
import xml.etree.Element Tree as ET

# Define the class Labels
class_labels = ['person', 'car', 'cat', 'dog', ...] # Add your class labels here

# Function to load and preprocess the dataset
def load_dataset (dataset_dir):
    images = []
    annotations = []

    # Iterate over each image file and corresponding annotation file
    for filename in os.listdir (dataset_dir):
        if filename.endswith('.jpg'):
            # Load image
            img_path = os.path.join(dataset_dir, filename)
            image = cv2.imread(img_path)
            images.append(image)

            # Load annotation
            xml:filename = os.path.splitext (filename) [0] + '.xml'
            xml:path = os.path.join(dataset_dir, 'Annotations', xml:filename)
            annotation = parse_annotation(xml:path)
            annotations.append(annotation)
    # Preprocess the dataset
    images = np.array(images)
    annotations = np.array(annotations)

    # Normalize images (e.g., convert pixel values to [0, 1])
    images = images.astype (np.float32) / 255.0

    return images, annotations

def parse_annotation (xml:path):
    tree = ET.parse(xml:path)
    root = tree.getroot()

    boxes = []
    labels = []

    # Iterate over each object in the annotation
    for obj in root.findall('object'):
```

```python
        label = obj.find('name').text
        bbox = obj.find('bndbox')
        xmin = float(bbox.find('xmin').text)
        ymin = float(bbox.find('ymin').text)
        xmax = float(bbox.find('xmax').text)
        ymax = float(bbox.find('ymax').text)

        boxes.append([xmin, ymin, xmax, ymax])
        labels.append(class_labels.index(label))

    annotation = {
        'boxes': np.array (boxes, dtype=np.float32),
        'labels': np.array (labels, dtype=np.int32)
    }

    return annotation

# Example usage
dataset_dir = '/path/to/dataset'
images, annotations = load_dataset (dataset_dir)

# Split the dataset into training and validation sets
train_images = images[:800]
train_annotations = annotations[:800]
val_images = images [800:]
val_annotations = annotations [800:]

import tensorflow as tf

# Define the CNN feature extraction model
def cnn_feature_extractor (input_shape):
    base_model = tf.keras.applications. ResNet50 (include_top=False, weights=
    'imagenet', input_shape=input_shape)

    # Freeze the pre-trained weights
    base_model.trainable = False

    # Get the output layer from the pre-trained model
    output_layer = base_model.output

    # Add a global average pooling layer
    output_layer = tf.keras.layers. GlobalAverage Pooling2D() (output_layer)

    # Create the feature extraction model
    model = tf.keras. Model (inputs-base_model.input, outputs-output_layer)
```

```
    return model

# Set the input shape
input_shape = (224, 224, 3)

# Initialize the CNN feature extraction model
cnn_model = cnn_feature_extractor (input_shape)

# Load your dataset and preprocess the images

# Extract features from the images
features = cnn_model.predict(preprocessed_images)

import tensorflow as tf

# Define the RCNN model
def rcnn_model():
    input_layer = tf.keras.Input(shape=(224, 224, 3))

    # Region proposal network
    # ...

    # CNN feature extraction
    #...

    # Output Layer
    output = tf.keras.layers. Dense (num_classes, activation='softmax')
    (fc_layers_output)

    model = tf.keras. Model (inputs=input_layer, outputs=output)
    return model

# Initialize the RCNN model
model = rcnn_model()

# Compile the model
model.compile(optimizer='adam', loss='categorical_crossentropy', metrics=
['accuracy'])

# Train the model
model.fit(x_train, y_train, epochs=10, batch_size=32, validation_data= (x_val,
y_val))

# Evaluate the model
test_loss, test_acc = model.evaluate(x_test, y_test)
```

```python
# Make predictions
predictions = model.predict(x_test)
```

8.2.3.6 Source Code of Fast R-CNN [24]

```python
import tensorflow as tf

# Function to implement ROI Pooling Layer
def roi_pooling (feature_map, rois, pooled_height, pooled_width):
    # Calculate the height and width of each ROI bin
    bin_height = tf.cast (tf.divide (tf.shape (feature_map) [1], pooled_height),
    tf.float32)
    bin_width = tf.cast(tf.divide (tf.shape (feature_map) [2], pooled_width),
    tf.float32)

    # Generate grid cells for each ROI bin
    grid_cells = tf.meshgrid(tf.range(pooled height), tf.range(pooled width),
    indexing='ij')
    grid_cells = tf.stack(grid_cells, axis=-1)
    grid_cells = tf.cast(grid_cells, tf.float32)

    # Scale the grid cells by the bin size and add ROI coordinates
    pooled_rois = tf.expand_dims (rois, axis=1) # (num_rois, 1, 4)
    pooled_rois = tf.tile(pooled_rois, [1, pooled_height * pooled_width, 1]) #
    (num_rois, pooled_height * pooled_width, 4)
    pooled_rois = tf.reshape(pooled rois, [-1, 4]) # (num_rois pooled_height * pooled
    width, 4)

    grid_cells = tf.reshape(grid_cells, [1, -1, 2]) # (1, pooled_height *
    pooled_width, 2)
    grid_cells = grid_cells * tf.constant([bin_height, bin_width], dtype=tf.float32)
    grid_cells = grid_cells + tf.constant([0.5, 0.5], dtype=tf.float32)
    pooled rois += tf.reshape(grid_cells, [-1, 1, 2]) # (num_rois pooled_height *
    pooled_width, 4)
    # Clip the coordinates to match the feature map size
    pooled_rois = tf.clip_by_value(pooled rois, [0, 0, 0, 0], [tf.cast(tf.shape(feature_
    map)[1], tf.float32),

                                                   tf.cast(tf.shape
                                                   (feature_map) [2],
                                                   tf.float32),
                                                   tf.cast(tf.shape
                                                   (feature_map) [1],
                                                   tf.float32),
                                                   tf.cast(tf.shape
                                                   (feature_map) [2],
                                                   tf.float32)])
```

```
        # Perform ROI pooling
        pooled_rois = tf.cast(pooled rois, tf.int32)
        pooled features = tf.image.crop_and_resize(feature_map, pooled_rois,
        tf.range(tf.shape (pooled_rois)[0]), [pooled height, pooled_width])

        return pooled features

# Example usage
# Assuming you have a feature map of shape (batch_size, height, width,
num_channels)
feature_map = tf.random.normal((1, 32, 32, 256))
rois = tf.constant([[0, 10, 10, 20, 20], [0, 15, 15, 25, 25]], dtype=tf.float32) #
    [batch_index, x1, y1, x2, y2]
pooled_features = roi_pooling (feature_map, rois, pooled_height=7,
pooled_width=7)

import tensorflow as tf

# Define the Fast R-CNN model
def fast_rcnn_model(num_classes):
        input_layer = tf.keras. Input (shape=(None, None, 3))

        # Region of interest (ROI) pooling
        roi_pooling = RoIPooling() (input_layer)

        # CNN feature extraction
        cnn_features = CNNFeatureExtraction () (input_layer)

        # Concatenate RoI pooled features with CNN features
        concatenated_features = tf.keras.layers.concatenate([roi_pooling, cnn_features],
        axis=-1)
        # Fully connected Layers
        fc1 = tf.keras.layers. Dense (4096, activation='relu') (concatenated_features)
        fc2 = tf.keras.layers. Dense (4096, activation= 'relu') (fc1)

        # Output layer for class predictions
        class_output = tf.keras.layers. Dense (num_classes, activation='softmax',
        name='class_output') (fc2)

        # Output Layer for bounding box regression
        bbox_output = tf.keras.layers. Dense (num_classes * 4, activation='linear',
        name='bbox_output') (fc2)

        model = tf.keras. Model (inputs-input_layer, outputs=[class_output,
        bbox_output])
        return model
```

```
# Initialize the Fast R-CNN model
num_classes = 10 # Change it to the number of classes in your dataset
model = fast_rcnn_model(num_classes)

# Compile the model
model.compile(optimizer='adam', loss=['categorical_crossentropy', 'smooth_11'],
metrics={'class_output': 'accuracy'})

# Train the model
model.fit(x train, [y_class_train, y_bbox_train], epochs=10, batch_size=32,
validation_data=(x_val, [y_class_val, y_bbox_val]))

# Evaluate the model
val loss, val_class_loss, val_bbox_loss, val_class_acc model.evaluate(x_val,
[y_class_val, y_bbox_val])

# Make predictions
class_predictions, bbox_predictions = model.predict(x_test)
```

8.2.3.7 Source Code of Faster R-CNN [25]

```
import tensorflow as tf

# Define the RPN model
def rpn_model(anchor_num):
    input_layer = tf.keras.Input (shape=(None, None, 3))

    # CNN feature extraction
    cnn_features = CNNFeatureExtraction () (input_layer)

    # Convolutional layer for objectness scores
    objectness_scores = tf.keras.layers.Conv2D(anchor_num, (1, 1),
    activation='sigmoid', name='objectness_scores') (cnn_features)

    # Convolutional Layer for bounding box regression
    bbox_regression = tf.keras.layers. Conv2D (anchor_num* 4, (1, 1),
    activation='linear', name='bbox_regression') (cnn_features)

    model = tf.keras.Model(inputs=input_layer, outputs=[objectness_scores,
    bbox_regression])
    return model

# Initialize the RPN model
anchor_num = 9 # Number of anchors per spatial position
rpn = rpn_model(anchor_num)

# Compile the RPN model
```

```
rpn.compile(optimizer='adam', loss=['binary_crossentropy', 'smooth_l1'])

# Train the RPN model
rpn.fit(x train, [y_objectness train, y_bbox_train], epochs=10, batch_size=32, vali-
    dation_data=(x_val, [y_objectness_val, y_bbox_val]))

#Evaluate the RPN model
val loss, val objectness_loss, val_bbox_loss = rpn.evaluate(x_val, [y_objectness_val,
y_bbox_val])

import tensorflow as tf

# Define the Faster R-CNN model
def faster_rcnn_model(num_classes):
    # Backbone network (e.g., VGG16, ResNet, etc.)
    backbone = tf.keras.applications.VGG16 (weights='imagenet', include_top=
    False)

    # Region Proposal Network (RPN)
    rpn= RPN() # Implement your own RPN module

    # Region of Interest (ROI) pooling
    roi_pooling = RoIPooling (pool_size=(7, 7)) # Implement your own RoI pooling
    layer

    # Fully connected layers for classification and bounding box regression
    fc1 = tf.keras.layers. Dense (4096, activation='relu')
    fc2 = tf.keras.layers. Dense (4096, activation='relu')

    # Output layers for classification and bounding box regression
    class_output = tf.keras.layers. Dense (num_classes, activation='softmax',
    name='class_output')
    bbox_output = tf.keras.layers. Dense (num_classes * 4, activation='linear',
    name='bbox_output')

    # Define the input layer
    input_layer = tf.keras. Input (shape=(None, None, 3))

    # Forward pass through the backbone network
    backbone_features = backbone (input_layer)

    # Forward pass through the RPN
    rpn_features = rpn(backbone_features)

    # Forward pass through the RoI pooling
```

```
roi_pooled_features = roi_pooling ([backbone_features, rpn_features])

# Flatten the ROI pooled features
flattened_features = tf.keras.layers. Flatten() (roi_pooled_features)

# Forward pass through the fully connected Layers
fc1_output = fc1(flattened_features)
fc2_output = fc2(fc1_output)


# Output predictions for class and bounding box regression
class_predictions = class_output (fc2_output)
bbox_predictions = bbox_output (fc2_output)

# Create the model
model = tf.keras.Model(inputs=input_layer, outputs=[class_predictions,
bbox_predictions])

return model

# Initialize the Faster R-CNN model
num_classes = 10 # Change it to the number of classes in your dataset
model = faster_rcnn_model(num_classes)

# Compile the model
model.compile(optimizer='adam', loss=['categorical_crossentropy', 'smooth_11'],
metrics={'class_output': 'accuracy'})

# Train the model
model.fit(x_train, [y_class_train, y_bbox_train], epochs 10, batch_size=32,
validation_data=(x_val, [y_class_val, y_bbox_val]))

# Evaluate the model
val loss, val_class_loss, val_bbox_loss, val_class_acc model.evaluate(x_val,
[y_class_val, y_bbox_val])

# Make predictions
class predictions, bbox predictions = model.predict(x_test)
```

8.2.3.8   Source Code of Mask R-CNN [26]

```
import tensorflow as tf
import numpy as np

# Define the Mask R-CNN model
def mask_rcnn_model(num_classes):
    # Backbone network (e.g., ResNet50, ResNet101, etc.)
```

```
backbone = tf.keras.applications. ResNet50 (weights='imagenet',
include_top=False)

# Feature pyramid network (FPN)
fpn = tf.keras.applications.ResNet50 (weights=None, include_top=False)

# Region proposal network (RPN)
rpn = RPN() # Implement your own RPN module

# Region of interest (ROI) pooling
roi_pooling = RoIPooling (pool_size=(14, 14)) # Implement your own RoI
pooling layer

# Fully connected layers for classification, bounding box regression, and mask
prediction
fc1 = tf.keras.layers. Dense (1024, activation='relu')
fc2 = tf.keras.layers. Dense (1024, activation='relu')
class_output = tf.keras.layers. Dense (num_classes, activation='softmax',
    name='class_output')
bbox_output = tf.keras.layers. Dense (num_classes * 4, activation='linear',
name='bbox_output')
mask_output = tf.keras.layers.Conv2D(num_classes, (1, 1),
activation='sigmoid', name='mask_output')

# Define the input layer
input_layer = tf.keras. Input (shape=(None, None, 3))

# Forward pass through the backbone network
backbone_features = backbone (input_layer)

# Forward pass through the feature pyramid network (FPN)
fpn_features = fpn (backbone_features)

# Forward pass through the RPN
rpn_features = rpn (fpn_features)

# Forward pass through the ROI pooling
roi_pooled_features = roi_pooling ([fpn_features, rpn_features])

# Flatten the RoI pooled features
flattened_features = tf.keras.layers. Flatten() (roi_pooled_features)

# Forward pass through the fully connected layers
fc1_output = fc1(flattened_features)
fc2_output = fc2(fc1_output)
```

```
# Output predictions for class, bounding box regression, and mask
class_predictions = class_output (fc2_output)
bbox_predictions = bbox_output(fc2_output)
mask_predictions = mask_output (roi_pooled_features)

# Create the model
model = tf.keras. Model (inputs-input_layer, outputs=[class_predictions, bbox_
predictions, mask_predictions])

return model

# Initialize the Mask R-CNN model
num_classes = 10 # Change it to the number of classes in your dataset
model = mask_rcnn_model(num_classes)

# Compile the model
model.compile(optimizer='adam', loss=['categorical_crossentropy', 'smooth_11',
'binary_crossentropy'], metrics={'class_output': 'accuracy'})

# Train the model
model.fit(x train, [y_class_train, y_bbox_train, y_mask_train], epochs 10, batch_
size=2, validation_data=(x_val, [y_class_val, y_bbox_val, y_mask_val]))

# Evaluate the model
val loss, val_class_loss, val_bbox_loss, val_mask_loss, val_class_acc model.
evaluate(x_val, (y_class_val, y_bbox_val, y_mask_val])

# Make predictions
class predictions, bbox predictions, mask predictions model.predict(x_test)
```

8.2.3.9   Source Code of SSD [27]

```
import tensorflow as tf
from tensorflow.keras.applications import VGG16
from tensorflow.keras.models import Model
from tensorflow.keras.layers import Conv2D, Input, MaxPooling2D, Flatten, Dense

# Define the SSD model
def ssd_model(num_classes, num_priors):
    # Load the pre-trained VGG16 model without the fully connected Layers
    base_model = VGG16 (weights='imagenet', include_top=False, input_
    shape=(300, 300, 3))

    # Add additional convolutional layers
    conv6 = Conv2D (1024, kernel_size=(3, 3), padding='same', activation='relu')
    (base_model.output)
```

```
conv7 = Conv2D (1024, kernel_size=(1, 1), padding='same', activation='relu')
(conv6)

# Class prediction branch
class_predictions = Conv2D (num_priors * num_classes, kernel_size=(3, 3),
padding='same', activation ='softmax')  (conv7)

# Bounding box prediction branch
bbox_predictions = Conv2D (num_priors 4, kernel_size=(3, 3), padding='same',
activation='linear') (conv7)

# Create the SSD model
model = Model(inputs=base_model. input, outputs=[class_predictions,
bbox_predictions])

    return model

# Initialize the SSD model
num_classes = 10 # Change it to the number of classes in your dataset
num_priors = 4 # Change it based on the number of anchor boxes per feature map
location
model = ssd_model (num_classes, num_priors)

# Compile the model
model.compile(optimizer='adam', loss=['categorical_crossentropy', 'smooth_11'],
metrics={'class_output': 'accuracy'})

# Train the model
model.fit(x_train, [y_class_train, y_bbox_train], epochs-18, batch_size-32,
validation_data=(x_val, [y_class_val, y_bbox_val]))

# Evaluate the model
val_loss, val_class_loss, val_bbox_loss, val_class_acc = model.evaluate(x_val,
[y_class_val, y_bbox_val])

# Make predictions
class_predictions, bbox_predictions = model.predict(x_test)
```

8.2.3.10   Source Code of YOLO-V1 [28]

```
import tensorflow as tf
import numpy as np

# Define the YOLOv1 model
def yolo_v1_model(input_shape, num_classes):
    input_layer = tf.keras. Input (shape=input_shape)
```

```python
# Convolutional layers
x = tf.keras.layers. Conv2D (64, (7, 7), strides=(2, 2), padding='same',
activation='relu') (input_layer)
x = tf.keras.layers. MaxPooling2D (pool_size=(2, 2), strides (2, 2))(x)
x = tf.keras.layers. Conv2D (192, (3, 3), padding='same', activation='relu')(x)
x = tf.keras.layers.MaxPooling2D(pool_size=(2, 2), strides=(2, 2)) (x)
x = tf.keras.layers.Conv2D(128, (1, 1), padding='same', activation='relu')(x)
x = tf.keras.layers.Conv2D(256, (3, 3), padding='same', activation='relu')(x)
x = tf.keras.layers.Conv2D(256, (1, 1), padding='same', activation='relu')(x)
x = tf.keras.layers.Conv2D(512, (3, 3), padding='same', activation='relu')(x)
x = tf.keras.layers. MaxPooling2D (pool_size=(2, 2), strides (2, 2))(x)
x = tf.keras.layers.Conv2D(256, (1, 1), padding='same', activation='relu')(x)
x = tf.keras.layers.Conv2D(512, (3, 3), padding='same', activation='relu')(x)
x = tf.keras.layers.Conv2D(256, (1, 1), padding='same', activation='relu')(x)
x = tf.keras.layers.Conv2D(512, (3, 3), padding='same', activation= 'relu')(x)
x = tf.keras.layers.Conv2D(256, (1, 1), padding='same', activation= 'relu')(x)
x = tf.keras.layers.Conv2D(512, (3, 3), padding='same', activation='relu')(x)
x = tf.keras.layers. Conv2D(256, (1, 1), padding='same', activation='relu')(x)
x = tf.keras.layers. Conv2D(512, (3, 3), padding='same', activation='relu')(x)
x = tf.keras.layers.Conv2D (512, (1, 1), padding='same', activation='relu')(x)
x = tf.keras.layers.Conv2D (1024, (3, 3), padding='same', activation= 'relu') (x)
x = tf.keras.layers.MaxPooling2D(pool_size=(2, 2), strides=(2, 2)) (x)
x = tf.keras.layers.Conv2D(512, (1, 1), padding='same', activation= 'relu')(x)
x = tf.keras.layers.Conv2D (1024, (3, 3), padding='same', activation='relu')(x)
x = tf.keras.layers.Conv2D(512, (1, 1), padding='same', activation= 'relu')(x)
x = tf.keras.layers.Conv2D (1024, (3, 3), padding='same', activation='relu')(x)
x = tf.keras.layers. Conv2D (1024, (3, 3), padding='same', activation='relu')(x)
x = tf.keras.layers.Conv2D (1024, (3, 3), strides (2, 2), padding='same',
    activation='relu')(x)
# Flatten and fully connected layers
x = tf.keras.layers. Flatten() (x)
x = tf.keras.layers. Dense (4096, activation='relu')(x)
x = tf.keras.layers. Dense (7* 7 * (num_classes + 5), activation='relu')(x)

# Reshape the output
output_layer = tf.keras.layers. Reshape((7, 7, num_classes + 5))(x)

model = tf.keras.Model (inputs=input_layer, outputs-output_layer)

return model

# Initialize the YOLOv1 model
input_shape = (448, 448, 3) # Change it based on your input image size
num_classes = 20 # Change it to the number of classes in your dataset
model = yolo_v1_model(input_shape, num_classes)
```

```
# Compile the model
model.compile(optimizer='adam', loss='mean_squared_error')

# Train the model
model.fit(x_train, y_train, epochs=10, batch_size=16, validation_data=(x_val,
y_val))

# Evaluate the model
val_loss = model.evaluate(x_val, y_val)

# Make predictions
predictions = model.predict(x_test)
```

REFERENCES

1. Felzenszwalb, P. F., Girshick, R. B., McAllester, D., & Ramanan, D. (2009). Object detection with discriminatively trained part-based models. *IEEE Transactions on Pattern Analysis and Machine Intelligence*, 32(9), 1627–1645.
2. Petrović, N., Jovanov, L., Pižurica, A., & Philips, W. (2008). Object tracking using naive bayesian classifiers. In *Advanced Concepts for Intelligent Vision Systems: 10th International Conference, ACIVS 2008*, Juan-les-Pins, France, October 20-24, 2008. Proceedings 10 (pp. 775–784). Springer Berlin Heidelberg.
3. Muralidharan, R. (2014). Object recognition using K-nearest neighbor supported by eigen value generated from the features of an image. *International Journal of Innovative Research in Computer and Communication Engineering*, 2(8).
4. Beginners Guide to Convolutional Neural Network with Implementation in Python "analyticsvidhya". [Online] Available: https://www.analyticsvidhya.com/blog/2021/08/beginners-guide-to-convolutional-neural-network-with-implementation-in-python/
5. Simonyan, K., & Zisserman, A. (2014). Very deep convolutional networks for large-scale image recognition. arXiv preprint arXiv:1409.1556.
6. Zheng, Y., Yang, C., & Merkulov, A. (2018, May). Breast cancer screening using convolutional neural network and follow-up digital mammography. In *Computational Imaging III* (Vol. 10669, p. 1066905). SPIE.
7. He, K., Zhang, X., Ren, S., & Sun, J. (2016). Deep residual learning for image recognition. In *Proceedings of the IEEE Conference on Computer Vision and Pattern Recognition* (pp. 770–778).
8. Girshick, R., Donahue, J., Darrell, T., & Malik, J. (2014). Rich feature hierarchies for accurate object detection and semantic segmentation. In *Proceedings of the IEEE Conference on Computer Vision and Pattern Recognition* (pp. 580–587).
9. Girshick, R. (2015). Fast r-cnn. In *Proceedings of the IEEE International Conference on Computer Vision* (pp. 1440–1448).
10. Ren, S., He, K., Girshick, R., & Sun, J. (2015). Faster r-cnn: Towards real-time object detection with region proposal networks. *Advances in Neural Information Processing Systems*, 28.
11. He, K., Gkioxari, G., Dollár, P., & Girshick, R. (2017). Mask r-cnn. In *Proceedings of the IEEE International Conference on Computer Vision* (pp. 2961–2969).

12. Qamar Bhatti, A., Umer, M., Adil, S. H., Ebrahim, M., Nawaz, D., & Ahmed, F. (2018). Explicit content detection system: An approach towards a safe and ethical environment. *Applied Computational Intelligence and Soft Computing.*

13. Xie, S., Girshick, R., Dollár, P., Tu, Z., & He, K. (2017). Aggregated residual transformations for deep neural networks. In *Proceedings of the IEEE Conference on Computer Vision and Pattern Recognition* (pp. 1492–1500).

14. Liu, W., Anguelov, D., Erhan, D., Szegedy, C., Reed, S., Fu, C. Y., & Berg, A. C. (2016). Ssd: Single shot multibox detector. In *Computer Vision–ECCV 2016: 14th European Conference*, Amsterdam, The Netherlands, October 11–14, 2016, Proceedings, Part I 14 (pp. 21–37). Springer International Publishing.

15. Single Shot Detector (SSD) + Architecture of SSD "OpenGenus". [Online] Available: https://iq.opengenus.org/single-shot-detector/

16. Redmon, J., Divvala, S., Girshick, R., & Farhadi, A. (2016). You only look once: Unified, real-time object detection. In *Proceedings of the IEEE Conference on Computer Vision and Pattern Recognition* (pp. 779–788).

17. Python_(programming_language)-Wikipedia. [Online]. Available: https://en.wikipedia.org/wiki/Python_(programming_language)

18. Anaconda Distribution-Free Download. [Online]. Available: https://www.anaconda.com/download/

19. Convolutional Neural Network (CNN). [Online]. Available: https://github.com/tensorflow/docs/blob/master/site/en/tutorials/images/cnn.ipynb

20. VGG-16 pre-trained model. [Online]. Available: https://gist.github.com/baraldilorenzo/07d7802847aaad0a35d3

21. VGG-19 pre-trained model. [Online]. Available: https://github.com/fchollet/deep-learning-models/blob/master/vgg19.py

22. Tensorflow-Sequential model Resnet. [Online]. Available: https://www.tensorflow.org/guide/keras/sequential_model

23. RCNN. [Online]. Available: https://github.com/rbgirshick/rcnn

24. Fast-RCNN. [Online] Available: https://github.com/rbgirshick/fast-rcnn

25. Object detection. [Online]. Available: https://github.com/tensorflow/models/tree/master/research/object_detection

26. Mask-rcnn-tensorflow. [Online]. Available: https://github.com/aws-samples/mask-rcnn-tensorflow/tree/master/MaskRCNN/model

27. SSD_keras. [Online]. Available: https://github.com/pierluigiferrari/ssd_keras/

28. YOLO: Real-Time Object Detection. [Online] Available: https://pjreddie.com/darknet/yolo/

Index

Pages in *italics* refer to figures and pages in **bold** refer to tables.